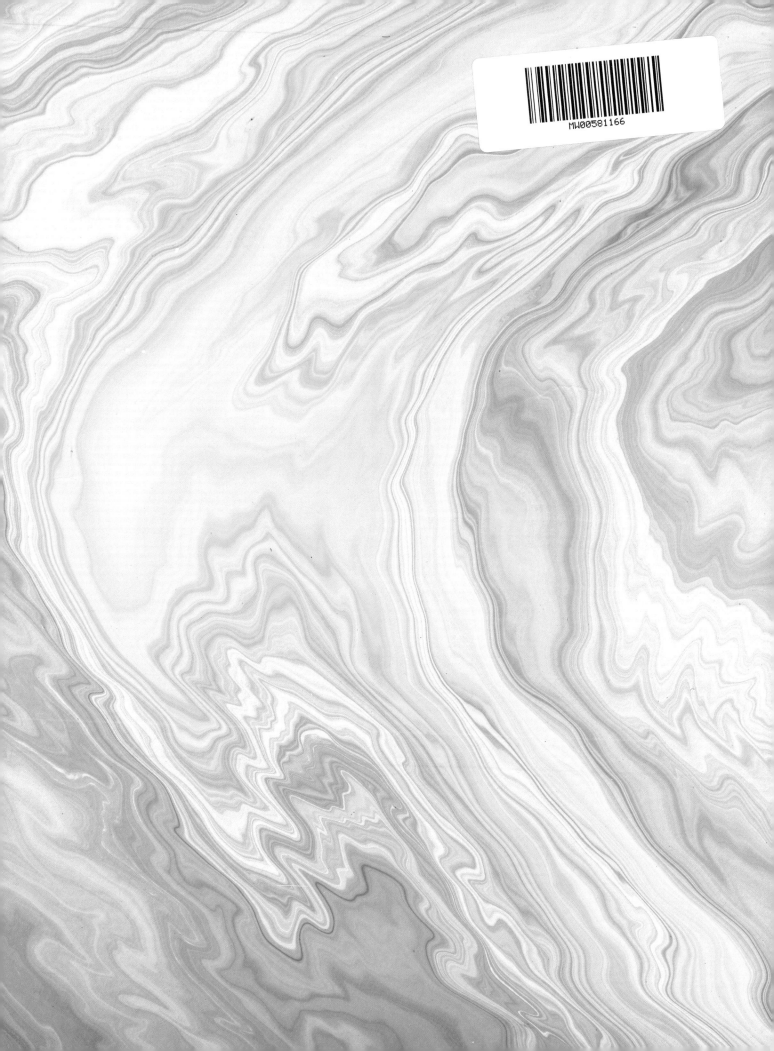

Jacket Front: Classic female Grecian Water Carrier, draped in citron colored toga, carrying gilt trimmed rose colored urn. Left arm extending over head to visually support an ormolu frame signed *Clark Cricklite*, supporting six cased Peach Blow domes, shading from lemon yellow to white, in six matching Clark Cricklite crystal lamp cups. This is the second of four sizes of Model 125 from the Royal Worcester Series, Midsummer Nights Dream. (Illustrated in Pears Christmas Annual 1898.) Statue base marked *Worcester Shot Enamels, Trade Mark "Cricklite"* and seven dots (1898). 41.5" x 19.5" w. $5000-7500

Library of Congress Cataloging-in-Publication Data

Ruf, Bob.
  Fairy lamps: elegance in candle lighting/Bob and Pat Ruf.
    p. cm.
  Includes index.
  ISBN 0-88740-975-X (hard)
  1. Fairy Lamps--Collectors and collecting--United States--
Catalogs. I. Ruf, Pat. II. Title.
  NK5440.F3R84   1996
  748.8--dc20   96-13538
                                                        CIP

Printed in China
ISBN: 0-88740-975-X

Published by Schiffer Publishing Ltd.
77 Lower Valley Road
Atglen, PA 19310
Phone: (610) 593-1777
Fax: (610) 593-2002
Please write for a free catalog.
This book may be purchased from the publisher.
Please include $2.95 for shipping.
Try your bookstore first.

We are interested in hearing from authors
with book ideas on related subjects.

———— To Mr. Douglas Gole,
our teacher and mentor. Like all superior teachers, he has encouraged us to seek even more knowledge. His quiet and unassuming demeanor hides a jovial and mirthful character. Above all, he is a true friend.

ACKNOWLEDGEMENTS

We wish to thank the following people who have contributed so much to the fulfillment of this book:

Doug and Nan Gole and Ralph and Sue Menning, for allowing us to disrupt their homes during photography sessions, and for their hospitality, their expertise, and their help with the price guide.

Fenton Art Glass Company, Frank, Bill and Tom Fenton, and Howard Seufer for their interest, and especially to Frank for allowing us to photograph the original Clarke sales literature from his files.

Ellen Gorelick and staff at the Tulare Historical Museum in Tulare, California, for allowing us to photograph the lamps in the Gustave Collection.

Bette Meich, Paul and Kathy Gresko, John Barker, the daughters of Jody Goyette, Clarence Maier, John Freeman, and Millers' Publication, for the photographs of their lamps.

Alan and Adele Grodsky for their help in identifying the Pairpoint lamps.

The staff at the Corning Museum of Glass library, for help in the research material and photos of some catalogs.

The staff at Gordon's Photo for their courtesy and professional help.

We also want to thank the next two generations of the Ruf family for their encouragement and constructive criticism.

CONTENTS

Plate I

INTRODUCTION

Lighting in the civilized world today is accomplished with such ease and convenience that it is difficult to imagine day-to-day existence a century ago, when the world was lit only by meager, dirty, smelly flickers of light. Who would have imagined that the malodorous lard-burning lamp would have evolved into the beautiful, delicate and fascinating burning devices called "fairy lamps"?

Man's initial excursion into artificial illumination began many centuries ago with the open fire. Improvements came very slowly and in pitifully small steps—from an open fire outside a crude shelter of rocks or inside a hut of hides or branches, to a moveable torch made from a pitchy pine knot, pine splints, or rolled birch bark. By the time of the Mesopotamians and Romans, oils expressed from vegetable matter (especially olives) were burned in small clay or bronze vessels. Hebrew menorahs during this period burned olive oil, which was expensive and available only in the Mediterranean region. This method of lighting persisted from Greco-Roman times to the late 1800s, in the form of non-raisable string wick Lucerne lamps that burned vegetable oil, and the slightly spouted Cruisie and Betty pan lamps that burned fat and lard. More northerly regions were advancing to crude wicks set in shallow pans of expressed blubber or tallow. Wick material ranged from moss and lichens to flax or rush stems. With wick improvements came spout lamps. Another major advance was the supported wick Betty lamp, around 1550.

During the third century A.D., another type of candle was made in which each horizontal rush wick would be drawn repeatedly through a pan of warm tallow. When the tallow hardened, the wick was stuck vertically on a spike (called a 'pricket') and burned as a candle. This was not much of an improvement over the pan lamp because the fuel was the same. The tallow smelled bad when burned, smoked with considerable soot, and was messy. Therefore, these candle holders included a large pan under the candle to catch the overflow and drips.

All of these lighting devices were in use simultaneously from the beginning of recorded time through the 1800s in Western civilization. In contrast to the Western world's lighting during the intellectual Dark Ages which started with the fall of the Roman Empire, the Arab world began producing petroleum oil in the seventh century. Shortly thereafter, around 850 A.D. in the region around Baghdad, the Muslims were batch distilling kerosene for lamp fuel. By the tenth century, records indicate that ninety metric tons of oil were distilled each year to "light the palace of the Caliph" in Persia.[1] Independent of European civilization, the Arab world preceded the West by a thousand years in the production of kerosene and kerosene lighting devices.

Apparently the Crusaders were not impressed enough to bring either the technology of kerosene lamps nor the product itself back to Europe and England from their forages in the Middle East. In all the readily available literature on the development of lighting, the overall consensus is that lard, beeswax, or vegetable oil lamps were used exclusively until the 1860s, when petroleum was discovered in Pennsylvania. Kerosene distilled from this crude oil then became the light of commerce in the West.

Thus man in Europe progressed through the ages. He advanced in art, architecture, mechanics, literature, and warfare, but not illumination. Even in centers of civilization like Paris, where wealth was concentrated, the advances in illumination were more social than technological. In the thirteenth century, guilds were formed for candlemakers. This was a form of quality stratification; tallow guilds selling house-to-house produced a low grade of candle for poor customers, while beeswax guilds made high-grade candles to be sold only in shops to wealthier customers.[2]

Throughout this period, the designation of time was a concern. Since at night one needed light to read time, it was logical that a lighting device be used as a time marker. Charles V of France had such "time candles" constructed, in which a candle of given weight would burn in 24 hours. The candle was marked in twelve equal segments. Accuracy was not the major attribute, as the tallow would burn at a rate affected by wick length and air movements.[3] Another interesting time lamp was made in Western Europe around 1610, using the principle of vacuum-proportioned oil flow into a Betty lamp to indicate hours elapsed (Plate II). The pewter band over the glass oil reservoir is marked in hours. As the oil level lowered, the time could be read by the light of the timepiece's flame.

Plate II

Around 1690, changes began to appear in candle holders.[4] The large drip pan around the base was replaced by a rim around the candle socket because of improved beeswax and bayberry candles, which burned more completely and evenly. The word "wax" should be emphasized at this point; improvements in tallow candles did not appear until later. Tallow candles continued to require a large drip pan until tallow was phased out in the late 1800s.

The first significant advance in tallow candle-making occurred around 1823, or possibly as early as 1811, when a Mr. Chevreul discovered stearine (C^3H^5 [$C^8H^{35}O^2$]^3), animal fat from which glycerine had been removed. It was the glycerine in tallow that was smoky and smelly when burned. Of even greater importance was the fact that stearine has a melting point of 160°F, while tallow melts at a mere 93 to 113°F—so unlike tallow candles, stearine candles could stay upright. Tallow was plentiful and inexpensive to start out with, and to 'add frosting to the cake', it was hydrolyzed to make stearine by boiling it with alkali (wood ashes)—also plentiful and inexpensive.[5]

After this, progress in candle-making occurred rapidly. In 1825 the braided or plaited wick became available, a very important development.[6] A burning candle burns neither the wick nor the solid wax; instead, the flame melts the wax, allowing it to move up the wick by capillary action, whereupon the wax evaporates and then burns. The braided wick resulted in a more uniform capillary movement of the fuel to the flame.

In 1830 paraffin was discovered as a component of wood tar, but it was too soft and flexible to use as a candle. In 1850 James Young of Scotland added stearine in the form of stearic acid to paraffin, and produced a candle that emitted more light than stearine alone. Within a decade, paraffin wax as derived from petroleum oil became plentiful, and thus inexpensive.

ABOUT FAIRY LAMPS

FAIRY LAMP DEVELOPMENT

By 1840, the stage had been set for inexpensive, dependable, and controlled lighting. The dismal darkness of England's night was illuminated by the extensive manufacture of squatty candles. The squatty candle is described as having a cylinder diameter greater than its height. These paper-wrapped candles, set in a shallow saucer with a bit of water, burned the fuel completely and safely. During the 1840s and 1850s, numerous English manufacturers of squatty candles came into existence or expanded. Among these were Price's Patent Candle Company, Childs', and Clarke's Pyramid and Fairy Light Company.

Erroneous conclusions have been drawn about when fairy lamps were introduced because of patents issued to George Clarke in 1844 and Samuel Clarke in 1857. These patents and many later ones covered improvements in candle-making, not in fairy lamp development. The confusion arises from the patent terminology, namely "improvements in night lights." These patents had nothing to do with the lamp which today is called a fairy lamp, but rather with the candle only.

There is mention that the word "Pyramid" as a candle name was used by Samuel Clarke around 1860, but the first association of the Pyramid candle with a receptacle was when S. Clarke registered a hand lamp with a Pyramid candle in 1876.

Continuously improving his candles, Samuel Clarke applied for a patent (U.S. Patent #329536) in 1885, stating

> I overcome these difficulties [of wick placement] by casting the *mass of fatty material* with a wire in place, instead of a wick. I then withdraw the wire and insert a strip of rush...Where considerable light and heat are required—I insert a strip of rush divided down the center. This in burning forms two wicks.

One advantage of the double wick over the single wick is this: when the double wick is lit, the two strips bend away from each other, producing a wide flame with more than one candle-power. The principle was widely used with whale oil and camphene lamps where two separate but close flames would yield 2.5 candle-power. Greater candle-power would permit a more opaque glass to be used for fairy lamp domes.

What was going on in the years between Samuel Clarke's 1857 patent and his 1885 patent (U.S. #329536) for the "Manufacture of Night Lights"? Tibbets[7] reports that the cover of one of Clarke's catalogues mentions awards received in London in 1862, 1873 and 1884; Paris in 1867 and 1889; Moscow in 1872; Australia in 1888 and 1889; and New Orleans in 1884 and 1885. There is no mention, however, of what the awards were for. It would be desirable to know when the fairy lamp as commonly referred to, e.g. a dome on a lamp cup, came into existence.

Geoffrey Godden, in his book *Antique Glass and China,* lists Samuel Clarke's British Registry trade names and trademarks as follows:[8]

1876 Hand lamp with "pyramid" candle
1880 Trade name "Pyramid." A note states that this name (although nonregistered) had been used since before 1856, with other references to its use since 1860.
1884 Trade name "Burglar's Horror"
1885 Trade name "Fairy"
1886 Trademark of fairy with wand
1887 Trade name "Fairy-Pyramid"
1887 Trade name "Wee Fairy"
1889 Trade name "Cricklite"

The words "Burglar's Horror" and "Pyramid" above refer to brands of candles (Appendix C), while "Fairy-Pyramid" pertains to the smaller size fairy lamp registered by Samuel Clarke in 1887.

Godden also lists the British Registry numbers that mark the beginning of each year (Appendix A). These dates, plus others forthcoming, can help collectors to properly date and sequence the introduction of various lamps. While British Registry marks can not authenticate the date of actual manufacture, they do provide the earliest *possible* manufacturing date. These registry numbers occasionally can be found on fairy lamps or their holders. The location and visibility of these marks are variable and elusive. Whenever registry or patent marks are found on the lamps depicted in this book, they are noted in the captions. Fortunately for American researchers without the funds to procure British records, Samuel Clarke secured U.S. patents for the most important developments of his fairy lamp enterprise. Through these patents we can not only accurately date the beginning of a design but also understand the usage of the lamps during the period of their popularity.

With an 1876 British Registry date for a Pyramid "hand lamp" we know that Samuel Clarke was burning his candles in a saucer, perhaps encircled by a glass dome. In all likelihood, the pyramid hand lamp had a brass-handled, perforated base and a porcelain candle dish like that used in the food warmer. In patenting improvements in his "Infant's Food Warmer or Night Light Apparatus," U.S. #334747, 1/1886, he states "preferably a pyramid night light is employed. This is placed in a metallic saucer and covered with a dome-like glass". In the summary description of the invention he reiterates the uniqueness of the dome for funneling the heat to the bottom of the hot-water vessel. The enclosed flame concept received a great boost, since in 1880 the London fire departments were warning of potential conflagration due to open candle flames.

The ugly, prosaic food warmer (Appendix B) was the catalyst for the entire fairy lamp craze, so it is necessary to discuss the "Pyramid Nursery Lamp Food-Warmer" in detail. The Continental tea and food warmers, called veilleuses, had been commonplace in England as well as in Europe since the 1750s.[9] The majority of these veilleuses had a godet, which was a small receptacle in which vegetable oil was burned by a floating wick. The logical step for a candle maker in the 1850s was simply to substitute a candle for the oil and a chimney (of sorts) for the ceramic cylinder which directed the heat to the bottom of the food or beverage container. Samuel Clarke's advertisements for food warmers were prolific and continuous. In the 1898 Pears Christmas Annual, Clarke's advertisement states that

his food warmer "for upwards of 50 years [has been] the Premier Nursery Lamp of the World." Now we know what Clarke had been up to from 1857 to 1885 and later; he was making and selling food warmers. The heating unit of Clarke's food warmer, standing alone, was the prototype of his widely popular fairy lamps.

Clarke's U.S. Patent #352296 seems to be the cornerstone of fairy lamps as we know them today. The patent pertains to a glass cup to support the dome and was filed on December 14, 1885. This item had already been patented in England (Sept. 23, 1885) and in France, Germany, Belgium and Austria according to U.S. filing papers. Clarke states in his application that

by my improvements it will be seen that when the candles are lighted they soon become melted, the glass domes (usually of tinted glass) confining and reflecting heat toward the candles, and light passing through the liquid fatty material and freely through the glass sides and bottoms of the lamps gives a bright luminous appearance to the lamp when viewed from below, which is especially advantageous for decorative purposes.

His claim also describes in detail the construction of the Patent Fairy lamp cup and the construction of chandeliers holding up to twenty-five individual lamps.

The following is another excerpt from U.S. Patent #352296 of November 9, 1886 which covers the corrugated surfaces upon which the dome rests. This was a novel idea for the admission of fresh air for combustion below the flame.

Each of the lamps of a group or cluster of any desired number consists of an outer lamp-cup, A, made of glass, the cavity of which is adapted to receive the short candle in an inner glass cup, D, which is of a capacity suitable for holding the fatty material composing the candle when it becomes melted, as it soon does after lighting the candle. The lamp-cups are provided with horizontal annular flanges B', upon which rest the glass domes B, having open tops. The annular horizontal flanges B' are corrugated upon their upper surfaces, in order that air to supply combustion may be admitted beneath the lower edges of the glass domes.

C are projections standing up from the horizontal flange at its inner surface, to keep the glass dome in place, and for a like purpose each lamp cup A is provided with an upright annular flange, A', surrounding the horizontal surface of the flange B'.

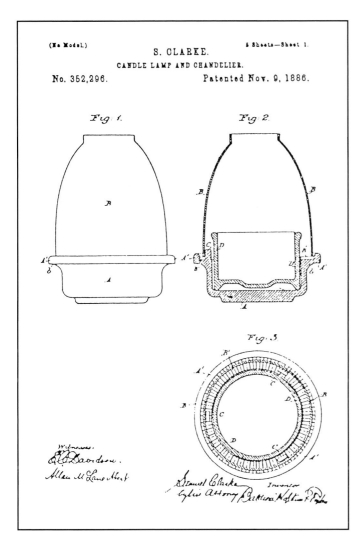

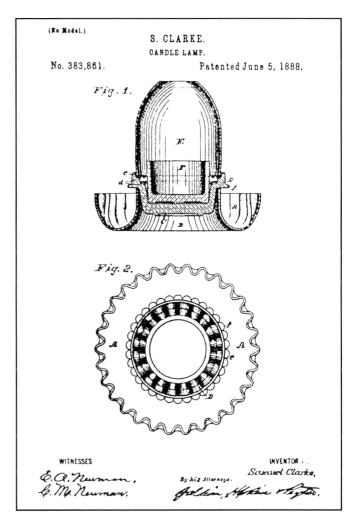

sizes." The next bit of news Clarke gives is that "instead of a continuous flange–an interrupted flange, or one composed of a number of short sections or lugs with spaces between them" is used (Fig. 103).

Any lamp cup with other provisions for fresh air entry is not a Clarke Patent Fairy lamp cup, with the exception of those lamp cups with a hole drilled in the bottom.

In U.S. Patent #383861, granted on June 5, 1888, Clarke states that "the lamps are preferably made of glass, but may be composed of porcelain, or equivalent material, through which light from the candles will pass sufficiently freely to give a bright and luminous appearance to the lamp." It seems that the importance of the lamp is no longer strictly based on its usefulness as an illuminant, but also on its value as a decorative piece.

Patent #383861 contains additional vital news. This is the first mention of "dish-like bases having central tubular posts" (Fig. 567). Certain bases with tubular center posts are reversible (Fig. 577). Generally these are skirted bowls. Figure 575 shows a base with a tubular center post that is not reversible. These bases have either a flared center post or an extended post. The next unique factor is that "instead of the two shoulders (to support domes in the lamp cup) a single shoulder only may be provided. By forming two shoulders, however, provision is made for supporting domes of different

Patent dates are critical to establish when these elegant fairy lamps were made and in vogue. They allow us to say that the lamp shown in Fig. 567 was not available prior to 1888.

An interesting technique for admitting air for combustion is found in the Hobbs, Brocunier "Acorn" lamp (Fig. 634). Here a hole was drilled into the bottom of the lamp cup. The lamp cup contains a candle holder raised on three dimpled feet. The first conclusion one jumps to is that of a patent circumvention of fresh air entry. Wrong: Clarke had this idea covered in U.S. Patent #383862. What's more, Clarke combined this idea with the concept of a menu lamp! This patent also introduces the bowl-shaped base with three points on the circumference pulled inward near enough to support the lamp cup.

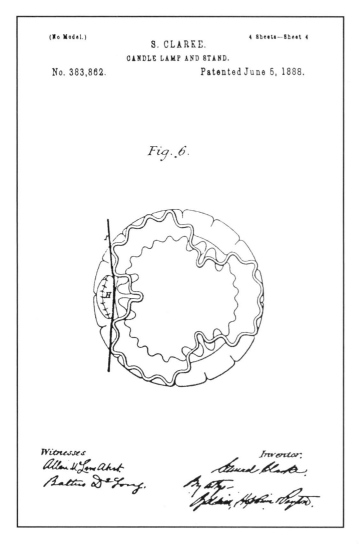

metal hanging or sitting lamp holder (Fig. 285). Quoting Clarke,

> This invention has for its object, improvements in lamp holders or frame designed especially for the class of lamps known as 'Fairy Lamps'. The lamp holder consists of three or more slender uprights at equal distances apart, carrying near their lower ends a support for the glass cup in which the candle *or oil* is to be contained.

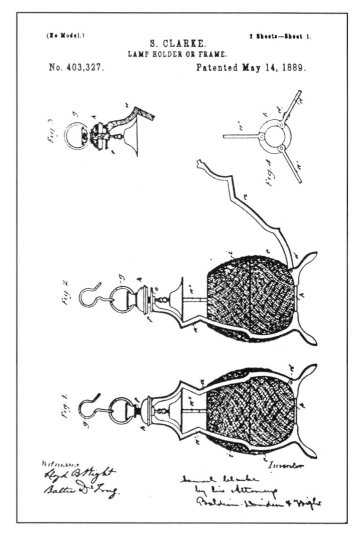

This same U.S. Patent #383862 contains a most interesting statement, which may either end or intensify a debate among today's fairy lamp collectors, some of whom say that fairy lamps burn only candles. Samuel Clarke puts this notion to rest himself: "My invention relates to lamps of that kind in which a short candle or *oil-lamp* is contained within a glass cup, which is covered over with a dome shaped shade, also of glass. These lamps are commonly known as 'fairy' lamps."

The late 1880s were a period of zooming popularity for fairy lamps. Among all the manufacturers of squatty candles and devices in which to burn them, Samuel Clarke must have been the premier promoter, a salesman *par excellence* who understood the power of the press. Extravagant displays of fairy lamps at public events and world expositions resulted in excellent publicity. He followed this up with color advertisements in national magazines at unheard-of expense (Appendix G, H & I). In addition, Clarke understood merchandising by creating a demand for the latest in fashion, even on a month-to-month basis.[10] Even though he garnered awards throughout the world, he did not rest on his laurels. In 1889 he received U.S. Patent #403327 for a small

Apparently, the reference to oil in the 'fairy' lamp statement of #383862 was not a mistake. Many fairy lamps burn oil. The general consensus among previous writers of articles on fairy lamps was that these lamps only burned squatty candles. However, these articles are accompanied by pictures of lamps that burned oil. These lamps burned the oil in a godet as opposed to a raisable wick lowered into a covered font, which would be considered a kerosene lamp. Examples of oil-burning fairy lamps can be seen in Figures 413, 422, 428 and in Plate III. Plate III is an exception to the general use of the open godet; it does include a raisable wick in an enclosed font.

Plate III

THE DEVELOPMENT OF DECORATIVE TECHNIQUES

From 1880 to 1900 there was a convergence of events of cosmic proportions which fueled the fire of fairy lamp popularity. It was the second phase of the Victorian Era, a period replete with extravagant materialism. The glassmaker's art and the chemical knowledge needed to produce magnificent types of glass and pottery were developing at an awe-inspiring rate. This was the period of elegance in candle lighting.

Henry Doulton of Burslem, England developed "a method of ornamenting China and EarthenWare and other Pottery," which he patented in 1882 in England and in 1885 in the U.S. (Pat. #314002). This was done by "impressing textile fabric, such as lace, upon the clay, together with the application of color or colored clay, and pressing the clay so embossed in plaster or other molds...." (Fig. 473). This technique was widely used for the lamp cup/flower bowl combination of many fairy lamp pottery bases.

Another outstanding discovery was described in U.S. Patent #332294, 1886, granted to Frederick S. Shirley of New Bedford, Massachussets. He claimed that he had invented "a mixture for glass in which uranium oxide or its described equivalent coloring agents and prepared gold are both added to glass batch containing alumina or its equivalents...." This became known as Burmese glass. Soon after Shirley patented this process in England, Thos. Webb & Sons purchased a license to produce Burmese glass at their works. This type of glass was greatly admired by Queen Victoria and subsequently was named "Queen's Burmese Ware" by Thos. Webb & Sons.

Burmese glass fairy lamps, both decorated and undecorated, are among the most sought-after types of lamp.

Some other glass developments of the period associated with fairy lamps and their patentees were:

1883	Schierholz – coralene
1883	Locke – amberina
1885	Webb, J. (not to be confused with Thos. Webb & Sons) – techniques for controlled air traps in glass
1885	Northwood – improved machinery for producing threaded glassware and a machine to produce pulled loops and feathers
1886	Hobbs, Brocunier & Co. – Peach Blow (a resurgence of an ancient technique)
1886	Shirley – Pearl Satin Ware

OTHER MANUFACTURERS

Samuel Clarke manufactured the candles, and patented the designs for the domes, lamp cups, bases, holders, hangers, stands, and brackets. Clarke, doing business as Clarke's Fairy and Pyramid Light Co., Ltd., never actually made the lamps or cups he had patented. Instead, he assigned the rights to manufacture the lamps to several companies. Clarke did, of course, manufacture the candles.

Clarke's patents were circumvented in a number of ways by manufacturers who wanted to make fairy lamps without having to acquire rights from Clarke. The lithophane dome in Fig. 444 has air holes through the lower rim. Other lamps have a smooth rim in the lamp cup and a serrated lower dome rim; or a flat, smooth rim with air vents cut into the base of the dome; or perforated lamp cups. Still other forms have no apparent opening for air to enter at the candle level; but since these lamps burn satisfactorily, they must be sufficiently irregular at point of contact or have an opening sufficiently large to accommodate the movement of fresh oxygen around the rising plume of spent air.

There were several planets that revolved around in the cosmos of fairy lamps, manufacturers of other products who saw an opportunity to stimulate the fad. Hobbs, Brocunier & Company has been identified as producing fairy lamps (Fig. 172) in the U.S., as has Hampshire Pottery (Fig. 525). The U.S. also contributed with Central Glass' handled lamp (Fig.140) and Fostoria's answer to the Cricklite (Fig. 744). The Diamond Candle Company, the Blue Cross Safety Lamp Company (Fig. 756), and Pairpoint (Fig. 699) also made and marketed fairy lamps. Candles were made by Will & Baumer in N.Y. and Felix Schmitt in Chicago. On the Continent, lamps were made by Baccarat, Daum, Galle, A d T, KPM, and PPM (Plaue Porzellan Manufaktur). In England the following companies were making fairy lamps and selling direct to retailers: Sowerby's, White House Glass Works, J. Walsh, Walsh, and Copeland. This is not a complete list, especially considering that most fairy lamps found today have no identifying marks.

By 1900 gas light was available in towns, but the magnificent elegance of fairy lamp domes lent an enchantment and mystique provided only by candlelight. The dancing shadows, the subtle hues, and the radiant warmth of candlelight were as seductive in 1900 as they are today, but by 1900 the fairy lamp fad was coming to an end. The flow of new designs and types of glass was ebbing. The clear dome Cricklite fairy lamp on fancy cut-glass standards became *de rigueur* for dining-room lighting (Appendix G & H). In what seems to be an attempt to shore up his slowing sales, Clarke tried a new approach. In 1908, U.S. Patent #896275 was granted to Clarke for a bizarre lamp with an internal chimney that could be raised or lowered by external means. This was the beginning of the end for Samuel Clarke's enterprise. Within two years his empire would become a subsidiary of Price's Patent Candle Co., Ltd.

Price continued the Clarke name and line for many years. Even as late as 1924, a Royal Worcester Cricklite fairy lamp was made from their 1916 mold and sold (Fig. 716). Worcester dated its finished wares with a pattern of dots and stars. This particular statuette of the female lyre player is thus dated 1924. Under the glaze it is also stamped "Cricklite." This lamp is considered Victorian and now raises a question: where should the line be drawn to separate Victorian (read "old") from contemporary (read "new") lamps?

OLD LAMPS & NEW

It is difficult to assign an absolute cut-off date for the Victorian fairy lamp. Certainly it did not end abruptly with Queen Victoria's death, nor does it continue to the present. Fairy lamps made in the 1950s and 1960s certainly did not have the delicacy and character of the lamps made in the 1890s. Considering lamps made only of thin, delicate glass to be Victorian, however, would eliminate the fairy lamps made by Baccarat in 1903 (Fig. 213) and Fostoria in 1909 (Fig. 151). On the other hand, one would hardly expect such a fine lamp as the Royal Worcester, mentioned above, to have been made as late as 1924. A customer buying that lamp in 1924 would be comparable to someone today buying a manual typewriter in the era of personal computers. Such a purchase would be an anachronism attributed to habit or perhaps necessity in a remote location lacking electricity.

With the onset of war preparations in Europe during the late 1930s came the lack of availability of chemicals essential to ornamental glass manufacture, and labor forces were redirected to war or the production of essential goods. By the 1940s all non-essential consumer production had ceased throughout Europe, England, and America.

By the end of World War II, when consumer products could again be produced, the entire world had changed. People's ideas of home decor had changed, production had become all mechanized, and the throw-away attitude of society became entrenched. Consequently, the late 1930s are a good break to define the period between the old and the new in fairy lamps.

FAIRY LAMP 'MARRIAGES'

Not all 'marriages' are made in heaven. Some fairy lamps are assembled from parts in antique shops or collector's homes today, while some became 'marriages' at the point of original purchase years ago—a most interesting source of varying assemblages. Unexpected marriages can even be seen in original advertising; for example, a Roman lamp was pictured with a diamond point dome in one advertisement, with a Christmas tree dome in another, and with a Burmese dome in a third. Taylor, Tunnicliffe

Tapestry Ware bases were also shown or described with a variety of domes. In the October 1967 issue of *Hobbies Magazine,*[11] a blue Webb Cameo lamp is pictured. The dome and base both have flower blossoms. The pink Webb Cameo lamp (Fig. 536), of impeccable provenance, has a dome with open flowers and the skirt with mature fruit. Some collectors might expect these Cameo fairy lamps to have bases and domes in matching patterns. These examples are proof that sometimes an authentic lamp can have patterns that are complimentary, rather than exact matches. Clarke's catalogue of 1887 shows another example: a Burmese chandelier (item #176) with decorated domes and an undecorated skirt and rose bowl.

In virtually all of Clarke's advertising appears the notation "can be obtained from the Patentees and Manufacturers, Clarke's Pyramid and Fairy Light Co." The inference is that a merchant or individual customer could not purchase Burmese fairy lamps from Webb & Sons, for example, even though Webb & Sons made and signed the lamps. All Clarke Patent fairy lamps, regardless of the manufacturer, could be purchased only from Clarke's Pyramid and Fairy Light Co. or their agents. Since Clarke gathered and assembled the component parts from many sources, it is logical that mix and match practices could have been used. Taylor, Tunnicliffe & Co., among others, made and marked a wide variety of flower bowl bases, but so far no Taylor, Tunnicliff domes appear to exist, which proves that at least two manufacturers' components had to be married.

The evidence becomes overwhelming that multiple-piece fairy lamps could have been purchased in a variety of styles, colors and sizes to be assembled over time by the lady of the house, and varied as the decor required. There is documentation that domes were sold independently (Appendix I). Units could be purchased complete but different: for example, the Roman lamps described above. Most convincing of all for salesroom marriage was the fact that Clarke sold the components purchased from a variety of sources.

Not all marriages work. In Appendix D, differences among lamp cups can be observed, but perhaps not to the point of seeing variations in diameters where the dome rests. There are at least five different diameters of fairy-size shades. This is also true of pyramid-size shades; at least seven different shade diameters are known. Plate IV shows the basic three sizes of domes: Fairy, Pyramid, and Wee. Some of the diameter variations are undoubtedly due to manufacturers other than Clarke's patented licensees, but even Clarke lamp cups are of different sizes.

Plate IV

Careful reading of a Clarke advertisement reprinted by MacSwiggen[12] answers a number of questions while raising others. First, it advises the tallow wax usage rather than paraffin with the note "*Caution—all Night Lights made of Paraffine, if burnt in a lamp, become very hot; the material is liable to 'take fire', and very* dangerous." Secondly, conventional wisdom holds that fairy lamps did not produce enough light for any other use than as dim nursery lamps or decorative lighting. However, the advertisement reads "Clarke's double wick "Fairy" Lights are the best for reading...."

LAMP VALUES – THEN & NOW

Fairy lamps were fundamentally useful. Picture a very dark night in a home without illumination—hard to imagine today, because the typical home has a plethora of glowing things (digital clocks, alarm lights, battery chargers, fax machines, alarm systems, coffee makers, thermostats, etcetera). In a very dark room, lighting a five-watt incandescent bulb provides enough light to facilitate many activities. A double wick Cricklite candle in a Cricklite dome is equivalent to a five watt bulb.

Who could afford these lamps? According to contemporary catalogues and literature, everyone! In the United States in 1890, a factory worker earned $1.50 to $8.00 per week, and a typist was paid $6.00 to $15.00 per week—tax free![13] At the exchange rate of those days, a simple lamp selling in England at 6 pence wholesale would have cost $.24 retail in the

U.S.[14]—$5.00 in 1994 dollars, inexpensive enough to have such light in the house today.[15] The more expensive decorated Burmese domes sold for 30 shillings per dozen wholesale,[16] or about $1.20 each in the U.S.—almost a week's wages for a beginning factory worker. The 'power bill' of one shilling for a box of twelve candles works out to a U.S. cost of $.02 a night in 1890 for each light.

Quite literally, there have been thousands of styles, colors, materials, decorations, and combinations of fairy lamps. For the past few years lamps have not been auctioned, traded or sold on a large enough scale to establish a monetary track record for any given lamp. To take a single sale and proclaim that price to be the value of that lamp is irresponsible.

One basic factor in a valuation is the original cost of the item. Godden[17] obtained a wholesale price list of fairy shades (domes) from 1889. Excerpts of this list with 1889 currency conversions are as follows:

clear glass or opal shades	$1.44 U.S./doz
"Cleveland" types	$2.16 U.S./doz
"Satin"	$2.16 U.S./doz
"threaded" type	$2.16 U.S./doz
"Verre Moire" (Nailsea type)	$2.88 U.S./doz
"Silk finish"	$2.88 U.S./doz
"Burmese"	$2.88 U.S./doz
Transparent porcelain, undecorated	$3.84 U.S./doz
Silk finish	$4.32 U.S./doz
Transparent porcelain, decorated	$5.76 U.S./doz
"Burmese," decorated	$7.20 U.S./doz
"Cameo"	$8.64 U.S./doz

Interestingly, it cost $1.92/dozen to decorate porcelain and $4.32/dozen to decorate Burmese. A decorated Burmese shade cost two and a half times as much as an undecorated Burmese, which in turn cost one and a third as much as the threaded, "satin" or "Cleveland" types.

As the design of a lamp becomes more complex, the amount and length of labor becomes greater. Some pieces may require a return to the furnace for reheating one or more times. Another individual may be required to bring additional gathers of glass to form handles, feet, overlays, or edges. Threading, pulling, fluting, crimping, acid treating, and grinding all contribute to the expense involved in making a given lamp.

Air-trap forms of glass, such as diamond quilted, most frequently are unsealed at the edges. These openings allow for soot and dirt to enter and spoil the appearance. High-quality glass of this type had the edges flame burnished in manufacture. This is termed a "rolled edge" and has the advantage of preventing the entry of foreign matter. This additional labor increased the cost of producing these wares, putting them in a more costly range both then and now.

Any collector strives for absolutely perfect specimens. Certainly these command premium prices. Unfortunately, there aren't enough of these items to fill the shelves and egos of every collector. These lamps were used on a daily basis. Removing and replacing the shade at each lighting was certain to cause chips of varying sizes, from chunks to flea bites. These are not as serious as cracks, which have a tendency to run.

LIGHTING YOUR LAMPS

Many collectors wish to light the old elegant lamps to experience the thrill and awe which enchanted the people in the gay nineties. This must be done with extreme caution.

It has been mentioned that paraffin burns brighter than tallow. It also burns *hotter*. Many beautiful fairy lamp shades are cracked because of illumination with modern paraffin votive candles. An interesting observation was made by Howard Seufer of Fenton Art Glass Company.[18] Immediately after lighting, the temperature of the glass dome rises to a very high but brief peak, then drops. Through the entire burn of the candle, the temperature remains constant until just before the last of the fuel is consumed, when the glass temperature rises to an even greater peak before abruptly falling.

These disastrously high temperature fluctuations might be avoided by allowing the candle to burn to a low steady flame before replacing the dome and again removing the dome before the candle is completely burned. The safest way to enjoy the old elegant lamps is to use a candle which burns at a low temperature, comparable to the tallow lights that Clarke and his contemporaries manufactured. In his tests, Seufer used an old Burglar's Horror candle, a new foil-wrapped Price's candle, a fifteen-hour votive as used in modern fairy lamps, and a small aluminum-sheathed candle. The maximum temperatures he recorded were as follows: Burglar's Horror 109° F (possibly understated due to wick deterioration and only 1.25 hours burning time); Price's 245° F; fifteen-hour votive 178° F; small sheathed four-hour candle 161° F.

IN CONCLUSION: MORE ABOUT FAIRY LAMPS

The history of the candle began in association with religious devotional offerings, through a period of simple daily illumination to a stimulant of our basic senses. The warm soft flickering flames in a dimly lit room are commercialized as romantic mood settings. Add spices to activate the olfactory organ and dyes to reinforce the message—a person's attitude can change drastically.

Today the fairy lamp is alive and well. The Fenton Art Glass Company alone has produced more than three hundred shapes, colors, and sizes since 1953. These have been augmented by lamps produced by Westmoreland, L G Wright, Moser, Geo. Davidson (England), Indiana Glass, Viking Glass and Lord Carlton, plus others. These contemporary lamps are becoming very collectable. There will be more yet to come. The candle does not appear ready to be snuffed out!

The prices given in this guide should not be taken as absolute values. Many factors influence the selling prices of a given lamp, including condition, region of the country, type of transaction, and the buyer's personal preference. The authors assume no liability for any losses which may occur as a result of using this guide.

GROUP 1

PYRAMID-SIZE DOMES ON CLEAR CUPS

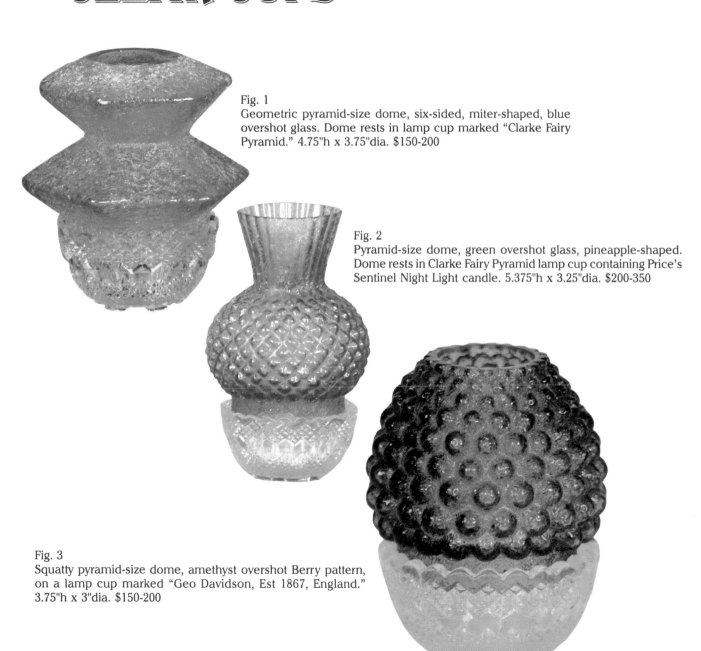

Fig. 1
Geometric pyramid-size dome, six-sided, miter-shaped, blue overshot glass. Dome rests in lamp cup marked "Clarke Fairy Pyramid." 4.75"h x 3.75"dia. $150-200

Fig. 2
Pyramid-size dome, green overshot glass, pineapple-shaped. Dome rests in Clarke Fairy Pyramid lamp cup containing Price's Sentinel Night Light candle. 5.375"h x 3.25"dia. $200-350

Fig. 3
Squatty pyramid-size dome, amethyst overshot Berry pattern, on a lamp cup marked "Geo Davidson, Est 1867, England." 3.75"h x 3"dia. $150-200

Left:

Fig. 4
Pyramid-size dome, reverse swirl embossed, spatter glass with two ground air vents in bottom rim. Dome rests in clear unmarked lamp cup. 3.5"h x 3"dia. $150-200

Fig. 5
Pyramid-size dome, yellow satin with embossed swirl, in clear Clarke lamp cup. 3.5"h x 3"dia. $100-150

Fig. 6
Transparent pyramid-size dome with impressed diamond pattern, on clear Clarke Fairy Pyramid lamp cup. 3.75"h x 3"dia. $50-100

Fig. 7
Satinized, cased, ribbed pyramid-size dome on Clarke Fairy Pyramid lamp cup. 3.75"h x 3"dia. $150-200

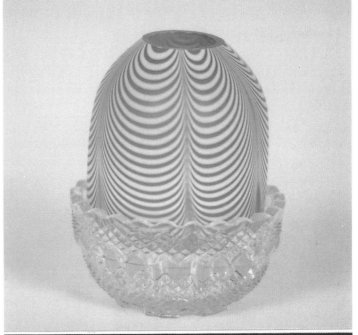

Right:

Fig. 9
Nailsea-type pyramid-size dome with red ground and white looping, on Clarke Fairy Pyramid lamp cup. 3.5"h x 3"dia. $150-200

Fig. 10
A pyramid-size panel dome, vaseline to custard, embossed, in Fairy Pyramid lamp cup. 3.75"h x 3"dia. $150-200

Fig. 11
Amber, opalescent swirl pyramid-size dome, with three ground air vents in bottom rim. Domes rests in Clarke Pyramid lamp cup. 3.75"h x 3"dia. $150-200

Fig. 8
Blue DQMOP pyramid-size cased dome in Fairy Pyramid lamp cup. (#56, Appendix I) 3.75"h x 3"dia. $200-350

Fig. 12
Smocked pattern pyramid-size dome in Eden Light lamp cup.
4"h x 3"dia. $150-200

Fig. 13
Three overshot crown figural fairy lamps commemorating
Queen Victoria's Golden Jubilee. From left to right: cranberry,
cobalt and opaque. Domes rest in Clarke Fairy Pyramid lamp
cups. Each crown is 4.375"h x 3.625"dia. $350-500 each

Fig. 14
Pyramid-size dome, cranberry spangled and threaded with gold
glass, in S. Clarke Fairy Pyramid swirl pattern lamp cup. 3.5"h x
2.75"dia. $200-350

Fig. 15
Blue pyramid-size dome, embossed with four-in-one diamond
pattern, rick rack pattern around both rims and ribbing on bottom rim, in Clarke Fairy Pyramid lamp cup. 3.75"h x 2.875"dia.
$150-200

Fig. 16
Pyramid-size dome in yellow spatter with frosted overlay and
an embossed swirl pattern. Dome rests in lamp cup with
crenelated rim, six dimple feet, and embossed concentric
circles. 3.625"h x 2.875"dia. $200-350

Fig. 17
Ruby pyramid-size dome with embossed swirl, in Clarke Fairy
Pyramid lamp cup. 3.625"h x 2.875"dia. $100-150

Fig. 18
Pyramid-sized dome, teal reverse swirl on white embossed swirl
with clear overlay, in Fairy Pyramid lamp cup. 3.75"h x 3"dia.
$150-200

Fig. 19
Acid Burmese pyramid-size dome in Fairy Pyramid lamp cup.
3.75"h x 3"dia. $150-200

Fig. 20
Pyramid-size dome, embossed with reverse swirl, overshot with
clear overlay. Dome rests in Clarke Fairy Pyramid lamp cup containing Burglar's Horror Fairy Pyramid candle. 3.75"h x 3"dia.
$150-200

Left:

Fig. 21
Opaque pyramid-size dome, waffle impressed, swirled stripes varying from burnished red to burnished gold and outlined in white. Dome rests in Clarke Fairy Pyramid lamp cup. 3.625"h x 2.875"dia. $200-350

Fig. 22
Pyramid-size cased dome, blueberry and white swirl with embossed vertical ribs, in Clarke lamp cup. 3.75"h x 3"dia. $150-200

Fig. 23
Acid Burmese pyramid-size dome, decorated in ivy pattern, in Clarke Fairy Pyramid lamp cup. 4"h x 3"dia. $500-750

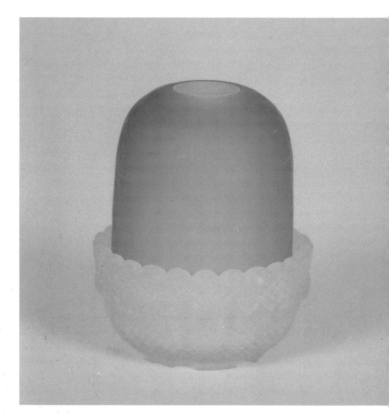

Fig. 24
Green satin, cased pyramid-size dome in opaque S. Clarke Fairy Pyramid lamp cup. 3.5"h x 3"dia. $200-350

24

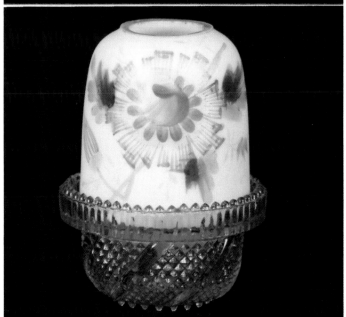

Fig. 25
Pyramid-size dome, light pink satinized, decorated with flowers and foliage on all sides, five air vents in bottom rim. Dome rests in lamp cup marked "Arcadian Light," with flat upward ribbing and horizontal uneven scalloped rim, containing Arcadian ribbed and three-footed candle holder. 3.5"h x 3.75"dia. $200-350

Right:

Fig. 26
Pyramid-size dome, milk glass with satinized exterior, decorated with pansy and foliage, three air vents in bottom rim. Dome rests in Fairy Pyramid lamp cup. 3.375"h x 2.875"dia. $150-200

Fig. 27
Milk glass pyramid-size dome, satinized exterior, yellow top half, decorated with branch of plums in front, branch of cherries in rear. Bottom rim has five air vents and rests in crystal Eden Light lamp cup. 3.375"h x 2.875"dia. $150-200

Fig. 28
Pyramid-size dome of decorated milk glass, with three air vents in bottom rim. Dome rests in swirled and diamond pattern Clarke Fairy Pyramid lamp cup, ribbed and pearled rim, containing a ribbed candle holder with three square feet. 3.625"h x 2.75"dia. $200-350

Fig. 29
Peach Blow pyramid-size dome, cream-cased, decorated in Wild Rose pattern in green, on Fairy Pyramid lamp cup. 3.75"h x 3"dia. $200-350

Left:

Fig. 30
Pyramid-size blue satin dome, white and light blue spatter, in Clarke Fairy Pyramid lamp cup. 3.5"h x 3"dia. $150-200

Fig. 31
Pyramid-size dome, pink ground with white Arabesque design, in Fairy Pyramid lamp cup containing Price's Improved Export Night Light candle. 3.5"h x 3"dia. $150-200

Fig. 32
Pyramid-size cased dome, tan opalescent with embossed scallops in swirl pattern and two ground air vents, resting in Fairy Pyramid lamp cup. 3.625"h x 3"dia. $200-350

Fig. 33
Pyramid-size dome of cream bisque, embossed and decorated with two peacocks, and drilled for light blue opaline glass inserts. Dome marked "Reg N. 147747" and "Made in Austria." Dome sits in S. Clarke Fairy Pyramid lamp cup. 3.5"h x 3"dia. $350-500

Fig. 34
Pyramid-size cranberry dome, embossed rib swirl, Craquelle glass, in Clarke Fairy Pyramid lamp cup. 3.5"h x 3"dia. $150-200

Right:

Fig. 35
Blue pyramid-size dome, alternating pattern of diamond panel and three vertical stripes, scalloped bottom rim in Fairy Pyramid lamp cup. 4.625"h x 2.625"dia. $100-150

Fig. 36
Vaseline pyramid-size dome, paneled and threaded, in Fairy Pyramid lamp cup. 3.625"h x 3"dia. $150-200

Fig. 37
Melon-ribbed pyramid-size dome, honey amber overshot with girdled bottom rim, in Clarke Fairy Pyramid lamp cup. 4"h x 3"dia. $150-200

Fig. 38
Vaseline pyramid-size dome, embossed thumbprint and impressed square grid pattern, in Clarke Fairy Pyramid lamp cup. 3.375"h x 3"dia. $150-200

Fig. 39
Pyramid-size dome, blue shading to white, cased, irregular scalloped top rim, decorated with Wheat pattern in Coralene. Girdled bottom rim of dome rests in Clarke Fairy Pyramid lamp cup. 5.25"h x 3.125"dia. $350-500

Left:

Fig. 40
Triple-waisted dome of green and white glass on opaque ground, resting in a ribbed, slightly flared lamp cup with integral recessed candle holder marked "Eclipse Patent Lights." 5.25"h x 3.25"dia. $100-150

Fig. 41
Clear dome with embossed flame pattern, girdled bottom rim, resting in oversize Fairy Pyramid lamp cup. 5"h x 3.25"dia. $100-150

Right:

Fig. 42
Pyramid-size dome, cranberry overshot with shell embossed pattern, in clear lamp cup containing Burglar's Horror candle. 4"h x 3.5"w. $200-350

Fig. 43
White to yellow porcelain rose petals with shaded green porcelain leaves applied to a porcelain band which forms the smooth bottom rim of dome. Rim is marked "Made in Germany" but all other marks are covered by leaves. Rose sits in Fairy Pyramid lamp cup, with ribbed and crenelated top marked "92571." 4.375"h x 4"w. $350-500

Fig. 44
Pyramid-size dome, floral pink porcelain, in Clarke Fairy Pyramid lamp cup. 3"h x 2.875"w. $200-350

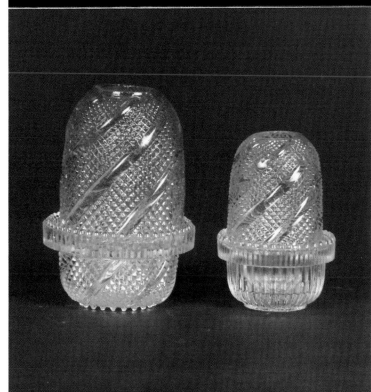

Fig. 45
(At left) Pyramid-size dome, teal diamond point and plain swirled rib pattern, in clear Clarke Fairy Pyramid matching lamp cup with pearl drop feet and base ray design. 4"h x 3" dia. (At right) Matching wee fairy dome in ribbed pattern and pearl topped wee lamp cup with ray design. 3.125"h x 2.25"dia. $200-350 each

Fig. 46
Nailsea-type wee-size dome with a red ground, in clear swirl and diamond pattern lamp cup marked "Clarke's Patent Wee Fairy." 3"h x 2"dia. $350-500

Fig. 47
Acid Burmese wee-size dome in clear ribbed lamp cup with pearled rim. 3.375"h x 2.25"w. $350-500

Fig. 48
Acid Burmese wee-size dome, decorated in woodbine pattern, in lamp cup containing clear ridged candle holder and candle marked "Clarke's Patent Wee Fairy." 3.125"h x 2.125"dia. $750-1000

GROUP 2

FAIRY-SIZE DOMES ON CLEAR CUPS

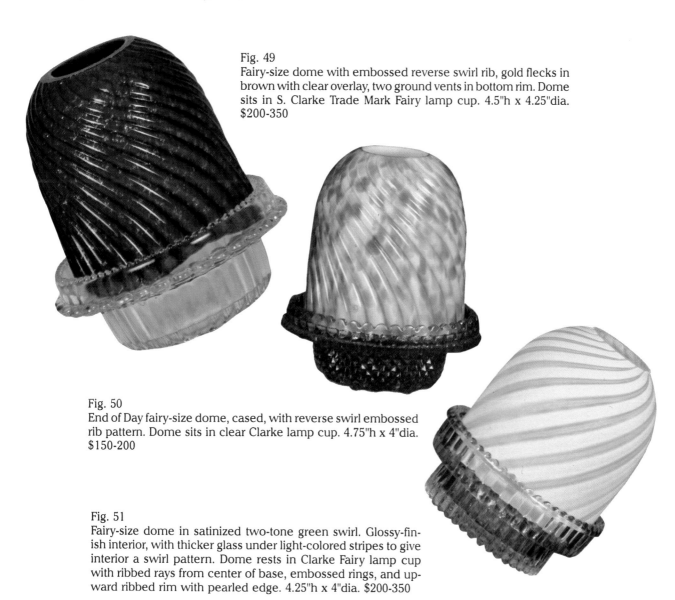

Fig. 49
Fairy-size dome with embossed reverse swirl rib, gold flecks in brown with clear overlay, two ground vents in bottom rim. Dome sits in S. Clarke Trade Mark Fairy lamp cup. 4.5"h x 4.25"dia. $200-350

Fig. 50
End of Day fairy-size dome, cased, with reverse swirl embossed rib pattern. Dome sits in clear Clarke lamp cup. 4.75"h x 4"dia. $150-200

Fig. 51
Fairy-size dome in satinized two-tone green swirl. Glossy-finish interior, with thicker glass under light-colored stripes to give interior a swirl pattern. Dome rests in Clarke Fairy lamp cup with ribbed rays from center of base, embossed rings, and upward ribbed rim with pearled edge. 4.25"h x 4"dia. $200-350

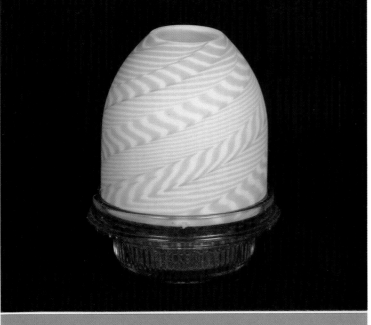

Left:

Fig. 52
Fairy-size dome, white ground with horizontal citron stripe pattern which increases in thickness in reverse swirl bands before returning to stripe pattern again. Dome sits in smooth-edged, two-shoulder lamp cup with ribbed sides, marked "S. Clarke Patent Trade Mark Fairy," containing clear candle holder. 4.75"h x 4"dia. $200-350

Fig. 53
Fairy-size dome, satinized cobalt blue, glossy rims and Greek Key design with two rings above and below design. Dome sits in ribbed lamp cup with smooth rim and top, marked "Clarke Trade Mark Fairy" and containing a candle marked "Co Op Night Light 8 hr." 4.5"h x 3.75"dia. $200-350

Fig. 54
Fairy-size dome, swirl Cleveland pattern in citron, white, and opaque, with embossed ribs. Marked "Rd 50725" and "Trade Mark Fairy" up the ribs. Dome rests in a Clarke Trade Mark Fairy lamp cup. 4.5"h x 4"dia. $200-350

Fig. 55
Red mother-of-pearl fairy-size dome, ribbon satin swirl with air trap, cream-cased, inward-crimped top rim, resting on four bars on shoulder of lamp cup. The lamp cup has an impressed four-in-one diamond pattern and scalloped top, 1.875" deep, marked "S. Clarke Trade Mark Fairy," with fairy (one hand up, the other down with a wand), and rayed or starred pattern impressed in exterior. 4.875"h x 3.375"dia. $200-350

Fig. 56
Fairy-size dome with citron, white, and opaque Cleveland swirl pattern, in Clarke Fairy lamp cup. 4.625"h x 4"dia. $200-350

Fig. 57
Tortoiseshell End of Day fairy-size dome with glossy overlay and embossed ribs, cased, in Clarke Trade Mark Fairy lamp cup. 5"h x 4"dia. $200-350

Right:

Fig. 58
Fairy-size dome, embossed ribs, blue with reverse swirled white spatter design, in Clarke Patent Fairy lamp cup. 4.5"h x 4"dia. $200-350

Fig. 59
Tall fairy-size dome, Mother-of-Pearl striped ribbon satin, pinched top rim, scalloped bottom rim. The dome rests on shoulder of lamp cup with horizontal scalloped rim. Base of cup marked "Br Clarke SGDG, Portieux." 5.25"h x 5"dia. $200-350

33

Fig. 60
End of Day fairy-size dome, cased, with embossed ribs, in Clarke Cricklite lamp cup. 5"h x 4"dia. $150-200

Fig. 61
Green fairy-size dome, rib and smock embossed, in clear Clarke Fairy lamp cup. 4.75"h x 4"dia. $200-350

Fig. 62
Fairy-size dome, blue, white, and opaque striped Cleveland pattern, embossed ribs (one of which is marked "Rd 50725"), in a clear Clarke lamp cup. (#2, Appendix I) 4.875"h x 4.125"dia. $200-350

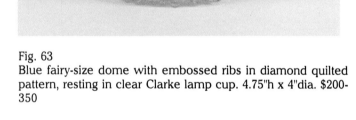

Fig. 63
Blue fairy-size dome with embossed ribs in diamond quilted pattern, resting in clear Clarke lamp cup. 4.75"h x 4"dia. $200-350

Fig. 64
Fairy-size dome in golden to chocolate brown, reverse drape pattern, cased, embossed on outside bottom rim, with "Rd 62029," with "S. Clarke's Patent Trade Mark Fairy" etched inside. Dome rests in clear crystal double-shouldered lamp cup with ribbed and scalloped horizontal rim. Cup is marked "Br Clarke, SGDG, Portieux." 5.25"h x 5.25"dia. $350-500

Right:
Fig. 65
Fairy-size dome, frosted with a reverse drape pattern shading from deep rose to white, in Clarke lamp cup containing clear, rimmed candle holder. 5.5"h x 4"dia. $200-350

Fig. 66
Fairy-size dome in red, diamond embossed with multi-faceted bottom rim, in clear lamp cup marked "Geo Davidson, Est 1867, England," with horizontal rolled rim, and containing ribbed candle holder. 5.375"h x 4.25"dia. $150-200

Fig. 67
Nailsea-type fairy-size domes in blue, white, red, green, citron and dark blue with white loopings, resting in crystal Clarke lamp cups. (#5-8, #87 & #89 Appendix I.) Courtesy of Authors. $200-350

Left:

Fig. 68
Orange fairy-size dome, diamond point, marked "S. Clarke Patent Trade Mark Fairy" halfway down the interior surface, with multifaceted smooth bottom rim, in clear Clarke lamp cup. 5"h x 4"dia. $150-200

Fig. 69
Brown fairy-size dome in cut-velvet type pattern, in clear Clarke lamp cup. 4.75"h x 4.25"dia. $200-350

Fig. 70
Gold fairy-size dome in cut-velvet type pattern, on double shouldered lamp cup marked "S. Clarke Patent Trade Mark Fairy." 4.75"h x 4"dia. $150-200

Fig. 71
Elongated fairy-size dome with flared bottom rim, embossed and satinized, in double-shouldered lamp cup marked "S. Clarke Patent Trade Mark Fairy, U.S. Pat. Nov. 9, 1886, #352296." 5.5"h x 4"dia. $200-350

Fig. 72
Pink fairy-size dome, cased, in embossed honeycomb pattern.
Dome rests in Patent Trade Mark Fairy lamp cup containing a
clear-footed Price's Palmitine candle holder. 5.5"h x 3.875"dia.
$200-350

Fig. 73
Fairy-size dome, vaseline to custard in pattern of raised diamonds and impressed chevrons and stars, scalloped bottom
rim, resting in Clarke lamp cup. 4.125"h x 4"dia. $150-200

Right:

Fig. 74
Fairy-size dome, Russian-cut, cranberry to clear, in clear lamp
cup containing interior ridges to hold the candle holder. 4.75"h
x 4"dia. $200-350

Fig. 75
Clear fairy-size dome in Thousand Eye pattern, in clear Clarke
lamp cup. 4.75"h x 4"dia. $150-200

Fig. 76
Red DQMOP fairy-size dome, cream-cased lining, on clear Clarke lamp cup holding clear Clarke candle holder. (#57, Appendix I) 5"h x 4"dia. $200-350

Fig. 78
Tall fairy-sized DQMOP dome, cone-shaped and cased, shading from rose to white, with slightly pinched top rim. Dome rests in Clarke Patent Trade Mark Fairy lamp cup. 6.5"h x 4"dia. $200-350

Fig. 77
Cylindrical DQMOP fairy-size dome shading from yellow to white, waisted, horizontal piecrust top rim. Dome rests in Trade Mark Fairy lamp cup containing a clear candle holder and Burglar's Horror candle. 5.375"h x 4"dia. $200-350

Fig. 79
Gold DQMOP fairy-size dome, cased, in double-shouldered Clarke Trade Mark Fairy lamp cup. (#60, Appendix I) 4.75"h x 4"dia. $350-500

Fig. 80
White filigree cane glass fairy-size dome in Clarke lamp cup.
3.625"h x 4"dia. $150-200

Fig. 81
Acid Burmese fairy-size dome in Clarke Cricklite lamp cup.
4.75"h x 4"dia. $200-350

Fig. 82
White acid Burmese fairy-size dome, decorated in hops pattern, in clear Clarke lamp cup. 5"h x 4.25"dia. $500-750

Fig. 83
Acid Burmese fairy-size dome, decorated in woodbine pattern, in clear Clarke's Trade Mark lamp cup. 4.75"h x 4.125"dia. $500-750

Fig. 84
Peach Blow fairy-size dome, cream-cased, pinched top rim, in Clarke Pyramid Trade Mark Fairy lamp cup. (#13, Appendix I) 4.5"h x 4"dia. $200-350

Fig. 85
Fairy-size dome with acid-etched leaves and raindrops, flashed pink satin with two rings cut to glossy, one near bottom, one near the top vent, which is surrounded by small notches. Dome sits in double-shouldered crystal lamp cup marked "Br. Clarke, SGDG, Portieux" with horizontal scalloped rim, impressed dots, and pearled upper edge. 4.875"h x 5"dia. $200-350

Fig. 86
Satin fairy-size dome, green shading to opaque, decorated with etched medallions, ribbons, and garlands. Top rim is flared, bottom rim is scalloped. Dome rests in Clarke lamp cup containing a candle holder. 5.75"h x 4"dia. $200-350

Fig. 87
Glossy light blue dome, cased, in the "Verre de Soie" with air traps pattern (diamonds with crosses inside), bulbous with flared ribbon top rim. The dome rests in S. Clarke Patent Trade Mark Fairy double-shouldered lamp cup containing Burglar's Horror Pyramid candle. 5.625"h x 4.125"dia. $350-500

Fig. 88
Fairy-size cased dome, green marbleized, in clear Clarke lamp cup. 4.75"h x 4"dia. $150-200

Right:

Fig. 89
Bulging fairy-size dome, blue swirled opalescent glass, with waisted top and scalloped rim, in clear Clarke lamp cup. 6.5"h x 4"dia. $150-200

Fig. 90
Tall fairy-size satin dome, dark to light gray, cased in pale blue, waisted with fluted and ruffled top rim edged in opaque glass. Bottom rim has four air holes and rests in Clarke Patent Trade Mark Fairy lamp cup. 6"h x 4"dia. $200-350

Fig. 91
Fairy-size dome, blueberry blue to white, cased, decorated with English robin in flight and stylized foliage, in clear Clarke lamp cup. 5"h x 4"dia. $200-350

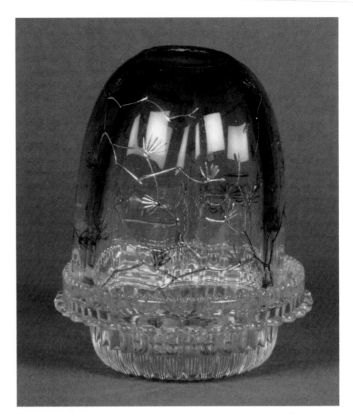

Fig. 92
Paneled fairy-size dome, shading green to clear, with heavy gold enameling in larch branch design, resting in clear Clarke lamp cup. 4.875"h x 4.25"dia. $200-350

Left:

Fig. 93
Fairy-size dome, citron satin decorated in ivy with butterfly on rear, very tightly crimped white-crested upper rim. Dome rests in clear Clarke lamp cup containing ribbed candle holder. 5"h x 4"dia. $200-350

Fig. 94
White Bristol glass fairy-size dome, decorated on both sides with gold band, polychrome thistle flowers and foliage, with four air vents in bottom rim. Dome rests in clear Clarke lamp cup. 5"h x 4"dia. $200-350

Fig. 95
Fairy-size dome, satin citron, cased, decorated in Lace pattern, on Clarke lamp cup. 5"h x 4"dia. $200-350

Fig. 96
Fairy-size dome with white arabesque pattern on citron ground, in Clarke Trade Mark Fairy lamp cup. 4.75"h x 4"dia. $200-350

Right:
Fig. 97
Engraved half Emu egg dome. Lithophane depicts Lyre bird with foliage background. Dome sits on flared rim of glass lamp cup containing candle. 3.25"h x 4.5"dia. $100-150

Fig. 98
Porcelain sawtooth-edge petals applied on bottom band. Petals decorated in shades of pink underneath and antique gold on top edges. Dome in S. Clarke Trade Mark Fairy lamp cup. 5"h x 5"w. $200-350

Fig. 99
Porcelain petals and leaves applied to band that sits in clear pressed crystal lamp cup with integral small flower bowl. Cup is marked Clarke Patent Trade Mark Fairy. 5.5"h x 7"dia. $200-350

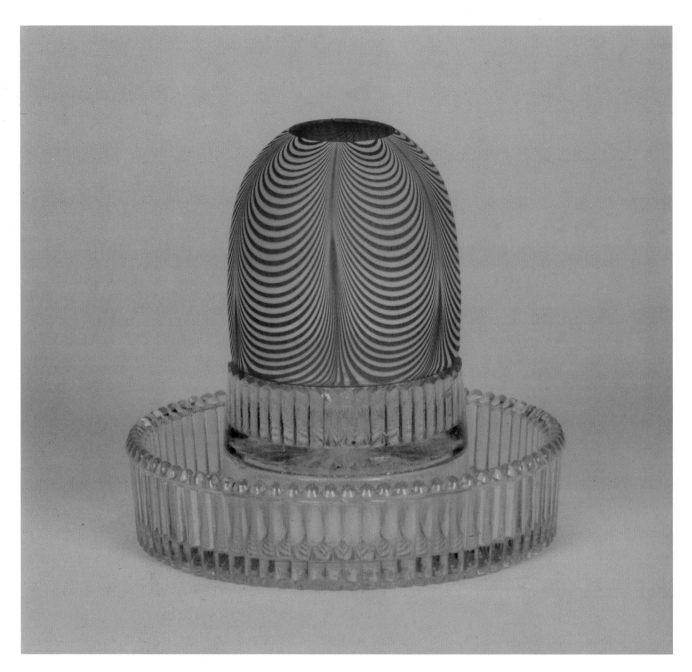

Fig. 100
Nailsea-type fairy-size dome, red ground with white looping. Dome rests on very heavy pressed crystal flower bowl base, tiered and ribbed, with integral lamp cup, marked "S. Clarke Trade Mark Fairy." Base designed with three small pegs on cup rim to hold and align inner surfaces of dome. 5.5"h x 6.25"dia. $200-350

Fig. 101
Nailsea type fairy-size dome with very dark blue ground. Dome rests on ribbed inner shoulder of integral lamp cup, in a ribbed flower bowl of crystal pressed glass, in diamond and star design with scalloped top rim. Base marked "S. Clarke's Trade Mark Fairy." 4.75"h x 7.25"dia. $350-500

GROUP 3

PYRAMID-SIZE DOMES ON SIMPLE MATCHING BASES

Fig. 102
Paneled pyramid-size dome, green marbleized, in clear ribbed flower bowl base, dimpled feet, with integral lamp cup marked "S. Clarke Trade Mark Fairy Pyramid" in candle recess. 4.5"h x 4.625"dia. $200-350

Fig. 103
Pyramid-size dome, ribbed, clear crystal, supported by three interior vertical bars in matching ribbed lamp cup containing Clarke's Pyramid candle. 4.25"h x 2.375"dia. $50-100

Fig. 104
Amber pyramid-size dome in raised swirl and diamond pattern with pearled bottom rim, on corrugated shoulder of matching lamp cup with pearled edge and bottom surface and impressed ray. 3.875"h x 2.875"dia. $150-200

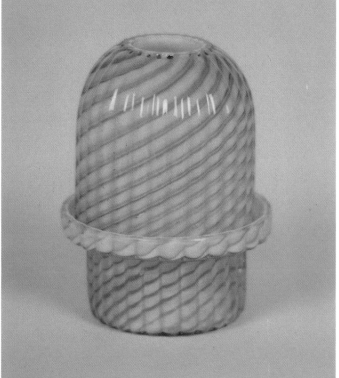

Fig. 105
Green opalescent pyramid-size dome in petal pattern with two ground air vents, in matching ribbed lamp cup. 3.375"h x 2.75"w. $200-350

Fig. 106
Tortoise shell End of Day dome, cased, pyramid-size, embossed reverse swirl in matching lamp cup base. 3.5"h x 2.75"dia. $150-200

Fig. 107
Pyramid-size dome with pink ground, peppermint swirl, ribbed, with gold dots surrounding top vent, in matching lamp cup. 3.5"h x 2.75"dia. $200-350

Fig.108
Pyramid-size dome in satinized swirl pattern, cased, with three air vents in bottom rim, on matching lamp cup base. 3.5"h x 3"dia. $150-200

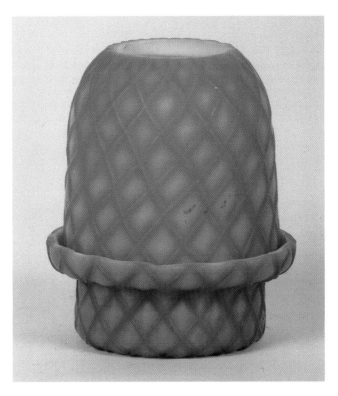

Fig. 109
Pink Diamond Quilted Cut Velvet pyramid-size dome on shoulder of matching lamp cup containing Price's Improved Export candle. 3.25"h x 2.75"dia. $200-350

Right:

Fig. 110
Blue pyramid-size dome in hobnail pattern, marked "Rd 109531," in matching lamp cup with ribbed crenelated rim, concentric circles embossed in bottom, and six dimple feet. 3.875"h x 3"dia. $100-150

Fig. 111
Diamond and ribbed teal dome with scalloped bottom rim, on matching lamp cup, footed and ribbed with crenelated rim. 4"h x 3"dia. $350-500

Fig. 112
Green pyramid-size dome in cut-velvet type pattern. The green lamp cup is marked "S. Clarke Fairy Trade Mark"; inside this circle of words is written "Brevete SGDG." On the outside of cup is marked "Manuf at Baccarat France." 3.625"h x 3"w. $100-150

Fig. 113
Pyramid-size dome, pink and blue striped frosted, girdled and flared piecrust top rim, two air vents in bottom rim, resting on smooth shoulder in matching bulbous footed base with outward flared piecrust rim. Base holds clear glass candle holder and Price's Sentinel Night Light candle. 5.75"h x 5.375"dia. $500-750

Fig. 114
Blue Thousand Eye pyramid-size dome rests in tall matching lamp cup, lightly paneled and footed with flared ribbed rim. "S. Clarke Trade Mark Pyramid" is marked in base. Three deep ribs terminate in depressions on the corrugated shoulder of the cup and receive three small feet on base of dome. 4.5"h x 3.25"dia. $150-200

Fig. 115
Vaseline pyramid-size dome with embossed thumb print and impressed square grid, on shoulder of vaseline lamp cup marked "S. Clarke Trade Mark Fairy Pyramid" on interior, floral impression on exterior. Cup has ribbed and flared rim and foot and four interior bars. 4"h x 3.5"dia. $150-200

Fig. 116
Green glass pyramid-size dome. The applied top rim is clear to opaline, hand-tooled into eight tiered, 'ribbon candy'-type loops; bottom rim has three air vents. Dome rests on smooth shoulder of matching, faintly ribbed green lamp cup. 5"h x 5"dia. $200-350

Fig. 117
Pyramid-size dome with lavendar ground and ten rows of clear tooled loopings, resting in lavender paneled lamp cup containing ribbed candle holder. 5.5"h x 3.5"dia. $350-500

Fig. 118
Transparent green conical dome with embossed flame design, in matching lamp cup base with interior ridge and corrugated horizontal rim. Cup embossed with four stylized "Mother Sun" designs. 4.75"h x 2.75"dia. $150-200

Right:

Fig. 119
Pyramid-size dome in pink, white, and opaque swirled Cleveland pattern, with square flared top rim and slightly flared bottom rim. Dome rests on shoulder of matching lamp cup with slightly inward-turned rim. Cup holds a Burglar's Horror candle. 3.5"h x 3"dia. $200-350

Fig. 120
Pyramid-size dome, pale gold with amber bars, cased and ribbed, on matching lamp cup holding Price's Childs' Night Light candle. 3"h x 3"dia. $200-350

Fig. 121
Pink porcelain pyramid-size dome embossed in coral and shell pattern with scalloped top rim, in matching base. 3.25"h x 2.75"dia. $200-350

Fig. 122
Porcelain-petaled rosebud with sawtooth-edged calyx in conforming porcelain saucer. Inside of base is painted green, with ribbon-like handle. 3.5"h x 4"w. $350-500

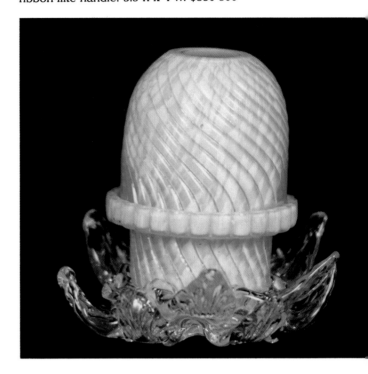

Fig. 124
Pyramid-size dome in pink and white spatter glass, embossed reverse swirl, with two ground air vents in bottom rim, resting on smooth shoulder of matching lamp cup. Two rows of applied, clear, tooled petals point upward from base of cup. 3.875"h x 4.25"w. $350-500

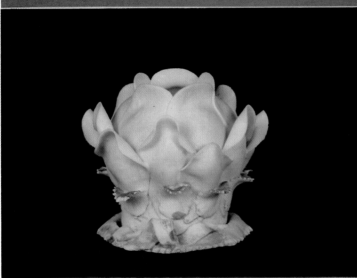

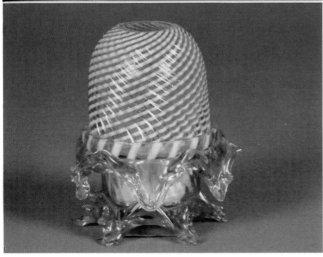

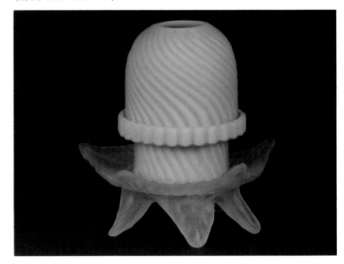

Fig. 123
Pyramid-size dome, white swirl on light amber with reverse swirl embossed, in matching lamp cup with row of applied amber icicles around cup rim and another row on bottom as feet. Cup contains white swirl candle holder and Price's Childs' candle. 4"h x 3.25"w. $200-350

Fig. 125
Pyramid-size dome with reverse swirl embossed pattern, clear frosted overlay, two ground air vents in bottom rim. Dome rests in matching lamp cup, with five applied points of frosted glass coming up from base of cup and five tooled and applied frosted feet below. 4.25"h x 4"w. $350-500

Fig. 126
Apricot overshot pyramid-size dome with embossed shell pattern, in matching ribbed lamp cup with tooled petaled feet. 4.75"h x 3.25"w. $200-350

Fig. 127
Cranberry overshot pyramid-size dome with embossed petal pattern. Dome rests in ribbed cranberry overshot lamp cup with six applied clear leaf feet tooled in the wishbone pattern. Cup holds a Gouda Apollo ribbed candle holder. 4"h x 3.675"w. $350-500

Fig. 128
Cranberry overshot pyramid-size dome, rib embossed, two ground air vents in bottom rim. Dome rests in matching ribbed lamp cup with two rows of upturned applied and tooled clear leaves arising from cup base. 4"h x 3.675"w. $350-500

Fig. 129
Green overshot pyramid-size dome with embossed petal pattern, two ground air vents in bottom rim. Dome rests in matching ribbed lamp cup, decorated with fluted, downward-turning red rim, applied and tooled. 3.5"h x 3.75"w. $200-350

51

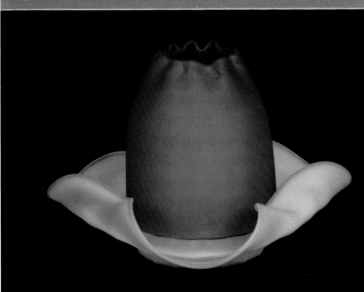

Fig. 130
Amber pyramid-size dome with embossed crosses surrounded by diamonds. Three dimples on bottom rim elevate dome for air ventilation. Dome rests on smooth shoulder of lamp cup in matching color with swirl pattern, marked "Rd 176239." Row of opposing tooled petals are applied around cup rim. 3.625"h x 3.875"w. $200-350

Left:

Fig. 131
Pyramid-size dome with green ground, pulled top rim, and three rows of tilted, tooled, applied clear leaves. Dome rests in matching lamp cup with one row of tooled, applied clear leaves at top of cup and one around the bottom. Cup holds ribbed, dimple footed Ibbetson candle holder. 4"h x 4"w. $500-750

Fig. 132
Cranberry satin pyramid-size dome with puckered upper rim, resting in recessed center of satin pond lily base with tricorn rim. 3.25"h x 4.75"w. $350-500

Fig. 133
Floral-shaped dome of vaseline opalescent glass, with three rows of applied, tooled clear leaves, resting on cluster of amber leaves that form the lamp cup. Cup is attached to bent stem-like arm decorated with tooled vaseline leaves, which is inserted into scalloped base through another cluster of amber leaves. 4.75"h x 5.375"w. $350-500

GROUP 4

FAIRY-SIZE DOMES ON
SIMPLE MATCHING BASES

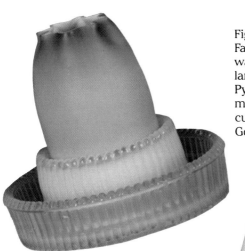

Fig. 134
Fairy-size dome, medium green to pale satin, cream-cased, inward-crimped top rim. Dome rests in yellow opalescent ribbed lamp cup with integral flower bowl. Lamp cup contains Clarke's Pyramid Trade Mark candle in ribbed Clarke candle holder. Base marked "S. Clarke's Patent Trade Mark Fairy" in recess of lamp cup. (Dome #16, Appendix I) 5.5"h x 6"dia. Courtesy of D. & N. Gole Collection. $350-500

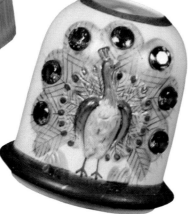

Fig. 135
Fairy-size dome, embossed and decorated with two peacocks and drilled for faceted, transparent green inserts. Dome marked "Reg No. 147747" and "Made in Austria." Dome rests in matching low saucer with integral candle holder containing Burglar's Horror candle. 3.875"h x 3.625"dia. $350-500

Fig. 136
Fairy-size dome, embossed and decorated with two Christmas trees and drilled for transparent jeweled ornaments. Dome rests in low matching saucer base with integral candle holder. 4"h x 4.625"dia. $350-500

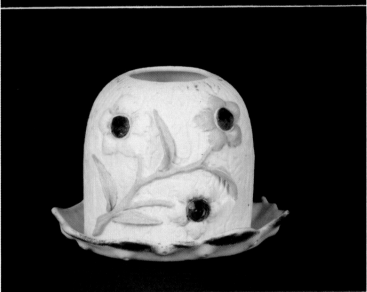

Left:

Fig. 137
Pink fairy-size dome with mica texture, with four jeweled crosses and jeweled ring near dome vent. Dome rests in low matching saucer with integral candle holder. Jewel pattern seen in varying primary colors. 4"h x 3.75"dia. $200-350

Fig. 138
Bisque dome with embossed foliage and three drilled flowers with faceted blue jewel centers, in irregularly shaped bisque saucer with integral candle holder containing Price's Sentinel Night Light. 3.25"h x 4.5"w. $350-500

Fig. 139
Bulbous and waisted fairy-size dome, shading from white to bright rose, decorated with Coralene in branching pattern, with deeply ruffled and fluted top rim. Dome rests in bright rose lamp cup. 5.25"h x 3.75"dia. $350-500

Fig. 140
Fairy-size dome, frosted blue with embossed ribbing and finely scalloped bottom rim. Dome rests on the smooth shoulder of handled lamp cup, which has flared, ribbed rim and base. Chrysanthemum and diamond pattern in bottom of cup. Lamp often referred to as "Central Glass Lamp." 5"h x 4.25"w. $150-200

Fig. 141
Fairy-size dome in yellow, white, and opaque striped Cleveland pattern, in matching opaque footed lamp cup. (Dome #3, Appendix I) 5.25"h x 3.5"dia. $350-500

Right:

Fig. 142
Pink satin Bristol fairy-size dome decorated with veranda scene in the cameo, three air vents in bottom rim. Dome rests in matching lamp cup holding clear candle holder. 4.75"h x 3.625"dia. $350-500

Fig. 143
Cream-color Bristol fairy-size dome, cased and decorated, with six notched air vents in bottom rim, resting in matching lamp cup base. 4.75"h x 3.75"dia. $200-350

Fig. 144
White satin Bristol fairy-size dome, decorated with encircling flowers and foliage, six air vents in bottom rim. Ring of brown with gilt tortoiseshell pattern around top of dome and on rim of lamp cup, with stripes around base. 4.5"h x 3.5"dia. $350-500

Fig. 145
White Bristol fairy-size dome decorated with bird and heavy enameling on the nest to make it three-dimensional. Dome has six air vents in bottom rim and rests on smooth shoulder in matching lamp cup. 4.5"h x 3.875"dia. $350-500

Fig. 146
White glass dome with heavy gilt enamel in Arabic-style design on matching waisted base containing 2.5"h x 2.25"dia crystal candle or float holder. 6.5"h x 4"dia. $200-350

Fig. 147
Fairy-size dome, satinized pink with embossed reverse swirl, resting in matching lamp cup base. 4.75"h x 3.75"dia. $150-200

Fig. 148
Satin porcelain fairy-size dome, very translucent, decorated with forest green band accented with gilt around top vent; chipmunk, acorn and fall foliage on one side, mother robin feeding young on other. Porcelain is thin, so bottom rim has internal lip which rests on shoulder in low dish-shaped base decorated in matching green and gilt. 5"h x 5.25"dia. $350-500

Fig. 149
Blue etched fairy-size dome, decorated with angels and birds, on horizontal scalloped rim of blue lamp cup with interior raised ring and impressed pinwheel in bottom. 5.5"h x 4.25"dia. $200-350

Fig. 150
Cut crystal fairy-size dome, four-in-one diamond pattern. Dome rests in matching lamp cup with cut pattern on all exterior surfaces, marked in interior "S. Clarke Patent Trade Mark Fairy," containing Clarke Fairy ribbed candle holder and Price's Sentinel Night Light. 4.375"h x 3.675"dia. $350-500

Right:

Fig. 151
Pink impressed fairy-size dome resting in matching pattern satin glass lamp cup, six air holes just below top rim. Fostoria Glass Co. 4.625"h x 4.75"dia. $350-500

Fig. 152
Fairy size-dome, blue shading to clear, overshot, with four air vents in bottom rim. Dome rests in blue lamp cup marked "S. Clarke Trade Mark Fairy," embossed four-in-one diamond pattern, scalloped top and three internal posts that support dome. 6.875"h x 3.375"dia. $200-350

Fig. 153
Honey amber dome, curved pressed stripes with floral design alternating with smooth stripes, scalloped bottom rim, resting on horizontally flared scalloped rim of matching lamp cup signed "Bayel." Dome is held by an interior raised ring. 4.75"h x 4.25"w. $200-350

Left:

Fig. 154
Frosted rubina fairy-size dome, embossed with trees and low shrubs, resting in frosted embossed lamp cup shading from ruby to clear. Cup holds clear Clarke candle holder. 5.25"h x 3.75"dia. $200-350

Fig. 155
Fairy-size dome, striped pink, white, and opaque Cleveland pattern, embossed rib, marked "Rd 50725" and "Trade Mark Fairy" up the outside of ribs near the bottom. Dome rests on shoulder of matching (but not ribbed) lamp cup with upright piecrust rim. 4.5"h x 4.25"dia. $350-500

Fig. 156
Flashed green dome with religious scene depicting Zarathustra (or Zoroaster), a philosopher of ancient Persian religion. Dome has three air vents in bottom rim, and rests in matching lamp cup with gold edge. 4.75"h x 3.5"dia. $150-200

Fig. 157
'Mary Gregory'-type fairy-size dome, lightly paneled, in blue with three air vents in bottom rim. Dome rests in matching lamp cup, with white enamel trim and gilt around top, containing Price's Palmitine Star candle holder. 4.5"h x 3.375"dia. $350-500

Fig. 158
'Mary Gregory'-type fairy-size dome, with gilt on top rim and two air vents in bottom rim. Dome rests on horizontal petaled rim, outside of retaining ring of blue ribbed lamp cup with chrysanthemum impressed bottom. 5"h x 4"dia. $350-500

Fig. 159
Flashed pink fairy-size dome, painted in enamel with blue flowers, green leaves, and heavy gold accents, with three deeply cut air vents in bottom rim. Dome is held by interior retaining ring and rests on smooth rim of matching lamp cup. 5.25"h x 4"dia. $350-500

Right:

Fig. 160
Blue satin fairy-size dome, decorated in Florentine enameled foliage, four vents in bottom rim. Dome rests on smooth shoulder of matching lamp cup containing candle marked "Field's 'Safe' Night Light, Made in England, 8 HRS" in clear candle holder. 4.125"h x 3.625"dia. $200-350

Fig. 161
Fairy-size dome, Florentine enameled in white and gilt, with two air vents in bottom rim. Dome rests on smooth shoulder of matching lamp cup with gilt trim on top of rim. Cup contains ribbed candle holder. 4.75"h x 3.375"dia. $200-350

Fig. 162
Satin cranberry fairy-size dome, white Florentine enameled decorations, scalloped bottom rim, in matching lamp cup base. 4.75"h x 3.5"dia. $200-350

Left:

Fig. 163
Daum Nancy French-type Cameo dome, carved in a winter scene, 2"dia. opening in top rim, four rounded air vents in bottom rim, resting in matching lamp cup with wide rim decorated with winter decorations. Cup holds clear candle holder and Burglar's Horror Pyramid candle. Cup exterior is marked with the words "Daum Nancy" and a line with two crosses equidistant from the ends. 4.25"h x 5.375"dia. $7500-10,000

Fig. 164
Orange fairy-size dome with three rows of upturned applied tooled floral petals. Top rim of ground pulled inward to form bud. Dome sits in lamp cup marked "S. Clarke Fairy" with row of upturned clear tooled applied leaves on top rim and another at bottom of cup, with third row of larger leaves going down to form feet. 5"h. x 5.125"w. $350-500

Fig. 165
Fairy-size End of Day dome, cased, embossed reverse swirl with clear overlay, two ground air vents in bottom rim, resting on shoulder in matching lamp cup which holds clear straight-sided candle holder. 4.5"h x 3.75"dia. $200-350

Fig. 166
Frosted half-sphere–shaped dome, ground shading from pink to clear, decorated with brown and gilt chrysanthemums and green foliage, resting in clear base with impressed square pattern inside retaining ring which holds dome. Base has horizontal ribbed rim. 3"h x 4.875"dia. $200-350

Fig. 167
Dome with pink to clear ground, cased, with three rows of tooled vaseline petals, the top row of which are longer. Dome rests in vaseline base with integral candle holder and eight tooled leaves twisted to left. 2.75"h x 3.125"dia. $200-350

Fig. 168
Amber fairy-size dome, raised diamonds and impressed chevrons and stars, scalloped bottom rim. Dome rests in depressed ridge of amber ribbed lamp cup with scalloped upper rim. Cup contains candle holder with repeating pattern of three ribs and smooth panel. 4.5"h x 3.75"dia. $200-350

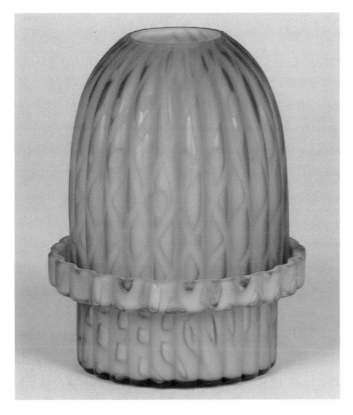

Fig. 169
DQMOP fairy-size dome with embossed ribbing and four air vents in bottom rim, in matching lamp cup base. 5"h x 3.75"dia. $200-350

Right:

Fig. 170
Elongated fairy-size dome, raspberry with clear glossy overlay and two air vents in bottom rim, in matching lamp cup. 5.75"h x 3.375"dia. $200-350

Fig. 171
End of Day fairy-size dome, clear satin overlay, embossed reverse swirl rib pattern, cased, two ground air holes in bottom rim, resting on shoulder of matching lamp cup. 4.625"h x 3.75"dia. $200-350

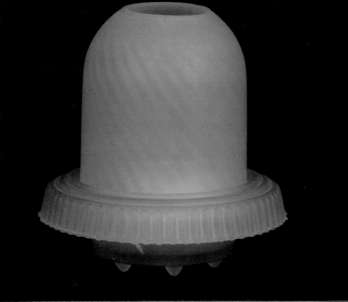

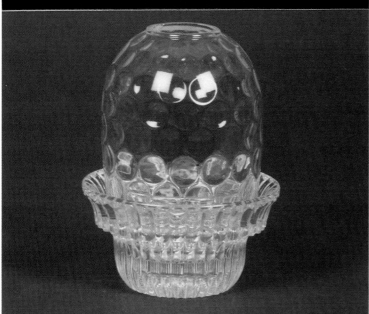

Fig. 172
Frosted fairy-size dome, lightly swirled, light green. Dome sits in vertically ribbed rim base with six dimpled feet. Lamp cup base has hole drilled in center to allow air to enter under candle holder's three dimpled feet, and contains Price's Sentinel candle. Lamp manufactured by Hobbs, Brocunier, & Co. of Wheeling, West Virginia. 5"h x 5"dia. $350-500

Fig. 173
Vaseline balloon-shaped dome in thumbprint pattern, on deeply recessed corrugated shoulder of lamp cup. Cup has ribbed, stepped and flared rim and integral smooth candle holder. 5.5"h x 4.25"dia. $350-500

Fig. 174
Waisted cylindrical dome, cased, satin glass shading from blue to almost white, fluted and heavily ruffled top rim edged in opaque glass. Dome sits on smooth shoulder of satin lamp cup, darker shade of blue on interior. 6.75"h x 3.75"dia. $200-350

Fig. 175
Millefiori cone-shaped dome, clear satin-cased, with waisted and fluted top rim. Dome sits on shoulder of matching stepped base containing Clarke Trade Mark ribbed candle holder in base recess. Base shoulder also holds milk glass inner dome. 5.875"h x 4.5"dia. $200-350

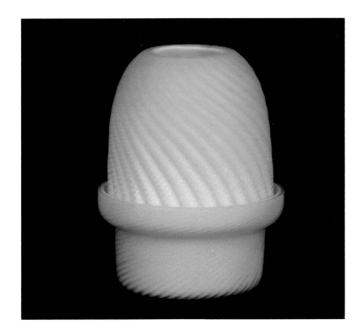

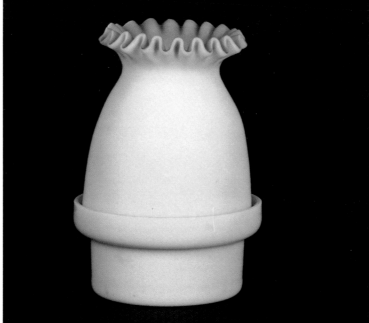

Fig. 176
Fairy-size dome with embossed reverse swirl rib, Mother-of-Pearl swirl ribbon satin, cased, shading from golden yellow to white. Markings on dome ribs make this a zipper-swirl pattern. Dome has two air vents in bottom rim, and sits on shoulder of matching (but not embossed) lamp cup containing Clarke candle holder and Price's Childs' Night Light candle. 4.375"h x 3.875"dia. $200-350

Right:

Fig. 177
White satin fairy-size dome, butterscotch-cased, piecrust flared top rim, four air vents in bottom rim. Dome rests on smooth shoulder in matching cased lamp cup containing clear glass candle holder with flared rim. 5"h x 3.75"dia. $200-350

Fig. 178
Tall lime-green fairy-size dome, Craquelle glass, eight air vents in bottom rim. Dome rests on shoulder of matching round footed lamp cup, with upright rim containing Fairy Pyramid candle holder. 5.5"h x 3.75"dia. $200-350

Fig. 179
Elongated fairy-size dome, pink DQMOP, cased, many air vents around bottom rim, resting on shoulder of low matching lamp cup. 5"h x 3.625"dia. $350-500

Left:

Fig. 180
Satinized fairy-size dome, embossed reverse swirl, cased in pink to rose, four air vents in bottom rim. Dome rests on shoulder of smooth rim of lamp cup in matching color. 4.875"h x 4.625"dia. $200-350

Fig. 181
Fairy-size cased dome, satin shaded from deep rose to white, impressed six pointed stars with gilt dot in center of each, rims decorated in gilt. Bottom rim has three air vents and rests on smooth shoulder of matching base. 4.625"h x 3.75"dia. $350-500

Fig. 182
A ball-shaped fairy-size dome, yellow shading to white and Mother-of-Pearl Herringbone pattern, cased, decorated with English robins and gold foliage, girdled bottom rim with four air vents. Dome rests in matching decorated base, bulbous and waisted with smooth upright rim. 5.25"h x 4"dia. Courtesy of The Burmese Cruet. $1000-1500

Fig. 183
Pink dome shading lighter, opalescent, with double row of clear rigaree around top rim, two air vents in bottom rim. Dome rests on lightly paneled shoulder in interior of matching lamp cup base with two rows of rigaree. Candle and rayed candle holder contained within. 5"h x 4.5"dia. $500-750

Fig. 184
Frosted pear-shape dome, girdled lower rim with three air vents. Dome has applied colored flower and green leaves and rests in frosted tapered base, tooled and applied frosted leaves around rim, holding clear candle holder with Price's Sentinel Night Light candle. 6.25"h x 5.5"w. $350-500

Fig. 185
Elongated pink dome with mica texture, one red faceted jewel in bright ormolu setting, two air vents in bottom rim, resting on smooth shoulder of matching lamp cup. 5.5"h x 3.75"dia. $200-350

Fig. 186
Pale blue fairy-size dome, diamond-shaped, faintly paneled, and decorated with pressed cross-hatching. Dome rests on a ribbed lamp cup base with wide horizontal rim terminating in pearled drop edge. Dome is held by an interior raised ring. Bottom of base has embossed cross (three knobs on ends) and holds a tall clear candle holder with two embossed crosses. Depth of candle holder suggests use as vigil candle or float. 5.5"h x 4.25"dia. $200-350

Fig. 187
White satin fairy-size dome with embossed ribbing and applied red peppermint swirl threading, marked "Rd No 50725" and "Trade Mark Fairy," in matching lamp cup with 2"dia. white foot. Cup holds ribbed candle holder. (Dome #54, Appendix I) 5.25"h x 3.75"dia. $500-750

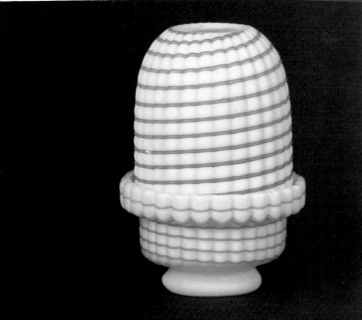

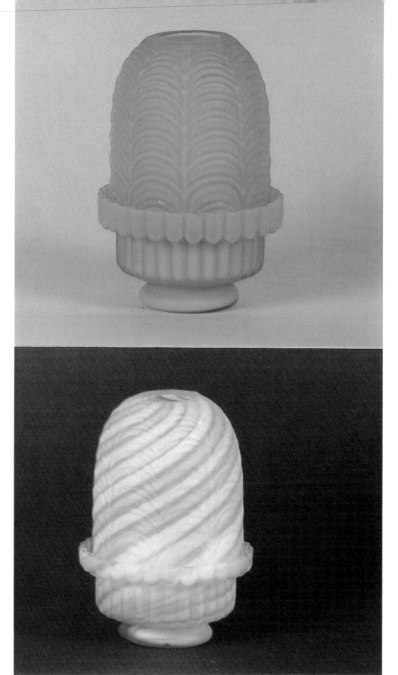

Left:

Fig. 188
Light blue satin fairy-size dome with embossed reverse drape pattern, lightly cased. Dome rests on serrated shoulder of ribbed, cased lamp cup with 2"dia. foot. Cup contains clear candle holder. 5.5"h x 3.75"dia. $350-500

Fig. 189
Fairy-size dome in citron, opaque, and white Cleveland swirl, embossed reverse drape pattern, marked "'Rd' 59136, Patent 'Fairy'." Dome rests in matching ribbed lamp cup with 2"dia. bulbous foot, signed "Clarke's Patent 'Fairy'" around bottom of cup. 5.125"h x 3.75"dia. $350-500

Fig. 190
Aquamarine dome with embossed rib, cased, marked "Rd 50725, Trade Mark 'Fairy'" on ribs, resting on ribbed shoulder of matching round footed lamp cup. Cup interior marked "Clarke's Patent Fairy." 5"h x 3.875"dia. $350-500

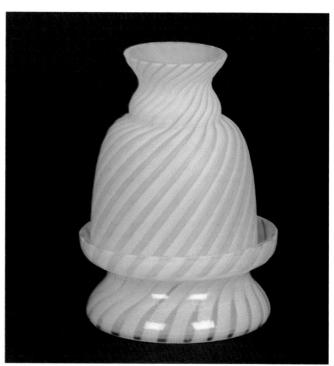

Fig. 191
Dome with satin citron ground and opaque stripes applied in swirl pattern, waisted and bulbous with flared top rim, four air vents in bottom rim. Dome sits on smooth shoulder of glossy base in matching colors. 5.5"h x 4"dia. $350-500

Fig. 192
Fairy-size dome in glossy pink shading to white, partially cased. Dome sits in lamp cup with applied gilt-trimmed ring, slanting ribs that allow air to enter through serrations, containing Clarke candle holder and candle. Cup has pink applied horizontal ribbon rim, and gilt edge embossed with design resembling half wagon wheels and scrolls. 5.25"h x 7.25"dia. $1500-2000

Right:

Fig. 194
Sombrero-style dome, light pink ground with deep pink Northwood pull-up-type pattern. Underneath bottom rim is marked "Rd No 44546" in triangle with double line below, with "Blumberg" on one side, "Limited" on the other. Dome sits on round matching fluted frosted base with integral candle holder containing Clarke's Pyramid Trade Mark candle. 5.625"h x 6"dia. $500-750

Fig. 195
Egg-shaped fairy-size dome, pink DQMOP, cased, pinched and twisted top rim, resting in matching base with horizontal fluted rim with opaque crest. 3.375"h x 6.125"dia. $350-500

Fig. 196
Satinized cranberry dome, slightly bulbous with waisted, flared and scalloped top rim, etched design, decorated in black. Dome sits on a heavy ruffled base with integral candle holder. 5"h x 4.75"dia. $350-500

Fig. 193
Lotus-type dome, pinched-in top rim with clear crested edge, reddish-brown coloring that runs down into the globe. Dome rests in matching saucer base with ribbing on widely flared and ruffled rim. Base has green cast in coloring to resemble foliage, and holds Price's Sentinel Night Light candle. 4"h x 6.875"dia. $500-750

Left:

Fig. 197
DQMOP dome shaded from blue to white, cased, top rim waisted, flared and fluted, with air vents in bottom rim. Dome sits on shoulder in low blue-cased base with downturned ribbon rim. Base contains Fairy Pyramid candle holder. 5.25"h x 6"dia. $350-500

Fig. 198
White satin fairy-size dome, cased in butterscotch satin, shading light to dark, with four air vents in bottom rim. Dome rests on smooth shoulder in white satin stepped base with flaring fluted rim. 5"h x 5.5"dia. $200-350

Fig. 199
White satin dome, cased blue, with waisted and flared piecrust top rim and four air vents in bottom rim. Dome rests on smooth shoulder in matching stepped base containing Clarke clear candle cup. Base has flared piecrust rim. 5.125"h x 5.625"dia. $350-500

Fig. 200
Cone-shaped dome in white satin glass, cased in pink shading to white, with piecrust flaring top rim and four air vents in bottom rim. Dome rests in matching cased footed lamp cup with flaring piecrust rim. 4.5"h x 5.5"dia. $350-500

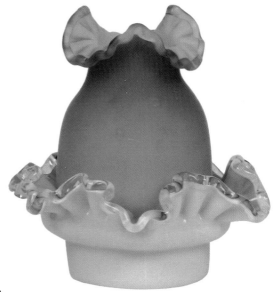

Fig. 201
Cone-shaped satin dome shading from rose to pink, cased, fluted and ruffled top rim edged in opaque glass. Dome rests on shoulder of glossy pink cased base with ruffled and fluted rim edged in clear glass. 5.5"h x 6"w. $200-350

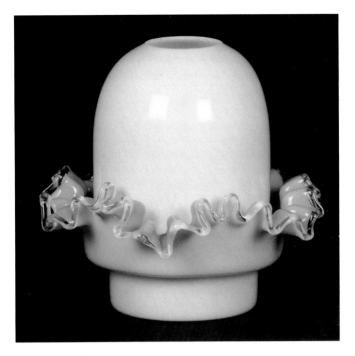

Fig. 202
Fairy-size milk glass dome with two air vents in bottom rim, resting on smooth shoulder of blue-cased lamp cup, with ruffled and fluted rim with clear crest. 4.75"h x 5.25"w. $200-350

Right:
Fig. 203
Light blue satinized fairy-size dome, glossy interior, with three air vents in bottom rim. Dome rests on shoulder of glossy white pedestal base with blue piecrust flared rim. 4.75"h x 5.5"dia. $350-500

Fig. 204
Glossy fairy-size cased dome, shading from dark green to white, fluted and ruffled top rim edged in clear green glass, four air vents in bottom rim. Dome sits on smooth shoulder of matching ruffled lamp cup. 5.375"h x 5.25"w. $350-500

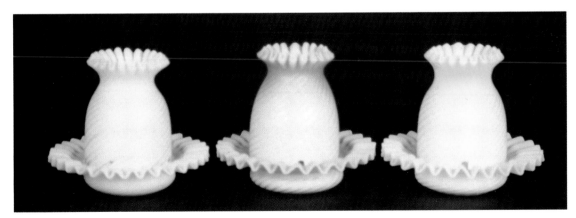

Fig. 205
Three cylindrical, cased fairy-size domes with waisted, flared piecrust top rims, satin ribbon swirl in (from left to right) butterscotch, blue, and yellow, all shading to almost white. Each dome has two air vents in bottom rim and rests on smooth shoulder in round footed matching base. 5"h x 4.75"dia. $350-500 each

Fig. 206
Rose to light pink Mother-of-Pearl dome in swirled ribbon satin, cased, outward piecrust top rim, with two air vents in bottom rim. Dome rests in low matching base containing Clarke candle holder. 5.5"h x 5.5"dia. $350-500

Fig. 207
Cranberry overshot fairy-size dome, embossed reverse swirl pattern, with two ground air vents in bottom rim. Dome rests on smooth shoulder of bulbous waisted overshot base, shading to cranberry, flared and fluted rim. 4.5"h x 5.5"dia. $350-500

Fig. 208
Blue conical fairy-size dome in DQMOP, cased, with flared piecrust top rim. Dome rests on shoulder of matching bulbous footed base with upward fluted and ruffled rim. 5.125"h x 5.625"w. $500-750

Fig. 209
Opalescent to clear dome with interior honeycomb pattern, waisted piecrust flared top rim with color crest. Dome sits on shoulder above waist in matching bulbous base with outward fluted rim. Base contains clear Clarke candle holder and Clarke Pyramid candle. 4.5"h x 5.5"dia. $500-750

Fig. 210
Cranberry overshot fairy-size dome in matching lamp cup with applied clear petals around rim. 4.625"h x 4.5"dia. $350-500

Right:

Fig. 211
Cased dome in a pulled feather pattern, with flared piecrust top rim and two air vents in bottom rim. Dome rests on shoulder of bulbous, footed matching base with horizontal fluted rim. 5.25"h x 6.25"dia. $350-500

Fig. 212
Cone-shaped dome, lightly ribbed blue and opaque stripes, piecrust flared top rim, with three air notches in bottom rim. Dome rests in very low, footed, bulbous matching base with piecrust flared rim. 4.75"h x 6"dia. $200-350

Fig. 213
Rose teinte dome in Helical Twist pattern, crown shape with flaring top rim. Dome rests in low, footed matching saucer with two raised rings, between which is marked "Baccarat Deposé." 4.25"h x 5.25"dia. $350-500

Fig. 214
Baccarat's Pinwheel fairy-size dome of clear pressed crystal, with five air vent notches in bottom rim. Dome rests in matching dish-like base, scalloped and upwardly flared, marked "Baccarat Deposé." Interior of the base contains two raised rings: the outer to contain the dome, the inner to retain the candle. 4"h x 5.5"dia. $200-350

Fig. 215
Baccarat's Pinwheel fairy-size dome in blue pressed crystal, with five air vent notches. Dome rests in matching low swirl pattern base with horizontally flared scalloped rim. Interior of base contains two raised rings: the outer to contain the dome, the inner to contain the candle. Base marked "Baccarat Deposé" between rings. 4.5"h x 5.75"dia. $350-500

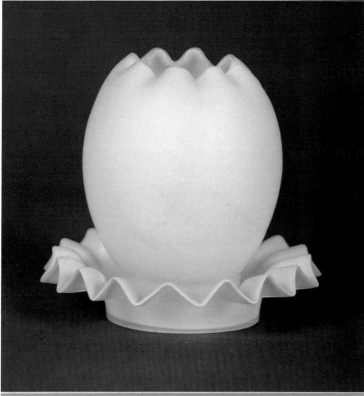

Left:

Fig. 216
Dome in bright pink satin shading to frost, egg-shaped, pinched at top, waisted bottom rim with two air vents. Dome rests in matching low saucer with flaring ribbon edge. 5.75"h x 6.25"dia. $200-350

Fig. 217
Conical, cased dome shading from rose to light pink, scalloped top rim, decorated with Coralene in Wheat pattern. Dome rests in pink-cased white base with fluted and heavily ruffled rim. 4.25"h x 6.25"w. $350-500

Fig. 218
Egg-shaped squatty dome, white satin, butterscotch-cased. Dome rests in butterscotch to white saucer with ruffled and fluted rim. 3.75"h x 5.75"w. $350-500

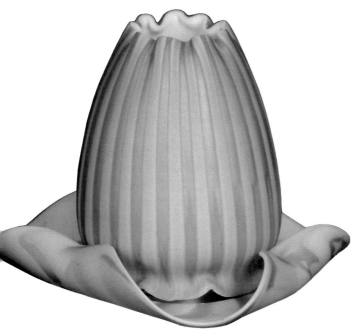

Fig. 219
Fairy-size dome, red Mother-of-Pearl ribbon satin stripe, cased, with puckered top rim and scalloped and flared bottom rim. Dome rests in tricorn green striped pond lily base with recessed center. 4.75"h x 5.5"w. $500-750

Right:

Fig. 220
Balloon-shaped dome, pink shading to opalescent, decorated in white enamel and gilt, with inward-crimped top rim and three air vents in bottom rim. Dome rests in matching base with low foot. Base contains candle holder with three square feet, marked "Waxine Licht" with "T" in center. 4.75"h x 5"dia. $350-500

Fig. 221
Rounded dome with scalloped top rim, blue milk glass decorated with monogram in ring of enameled flowers, three air vents in bottom rim. Dome rests in matching base with horizontal ribbon rim. 5.25"h x 6"dia. $350-500

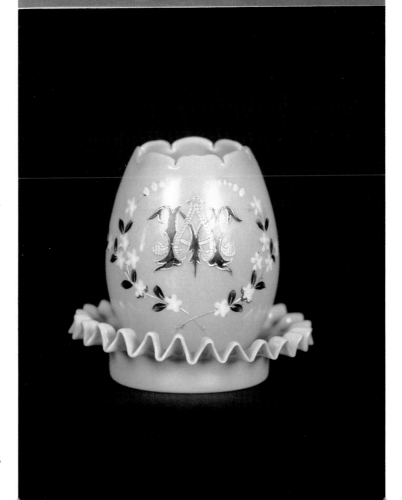

Fig. 222
Bulbous dome, lime green shading to apricot, heavily embossed, with fluted and widely ruffled top rim and wedged bottom rim with four air vents. Dome rests in low base shading from apricot to green with fluted and widely ruffled rim. 6"h x 7.25"w. $350-500

Left:

Fig. 223
Fairy-size cased dome with square flaring piecrust top rim, blue shading to very light blue, transparent red, green, amber, and blue jewels in ormolu setting, with three cut air notches in bottom rim. Dome rests in matching piecrust edge saucer. 5.5"h x 6"dia. $200-350

Fig. 224
Blue satin dome, cased, top rim pinched inward, four openings with ormolu frames holding faceted jewels in various colors, with two air vents in bottom waisted rim. Dome sits in matching base with outward fluted rim. 5.25"h x 5.625"dia. $200-350

Fig. 225
Satinized globular dome, flashed pink, severely pinched top rim with clear applied crest, girdled bottom rim with three air vents. Decorated with four jewels (blue, amber, green, and red) in brass fittings. Dome rests in matching base with horizontal ribbon rim showing remnants of gilt. 5.5"h x 6.25"dia. $200-350

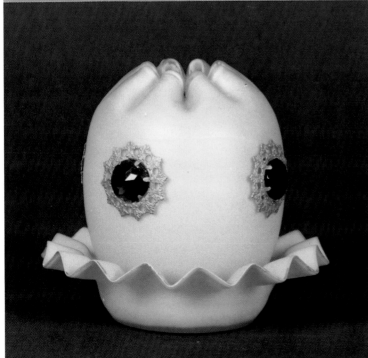

Fig. 226
Satin glass dome shading from blue to almost white, cased, with fluted and deeply ruffled top rim, cut air vents in bottom rim, four jewels in decorated brass retainers. Dome rests in pale blue satin lamp cup, waisted with upright smooth rim. 7.25"h x 4.5"dia. $200-350

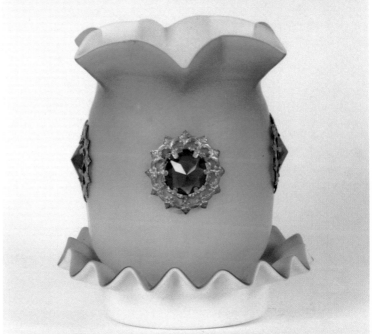

Right:

Fig. 227
Ball-shaped opaque dome with canes of white in oversize repeated W pattern, four colored jewels set in ormolu sunbursts, waisted and ruffled auburn-color top rim, girdled bottom rim. Dome rests in shallow matching saucer. 6.5"h x 6.5"w. $200-350

Fig. 228
Lightly cased dome, blue satin shading lighter, tooled and flared top rim in form of six-pointed star, four blue transparent faceted jewels in ormolu frames, two air vents in girdled bottom rim. Dome rests in low matching saucer base with outward ribbon rim. 5.875"h x 5.25"dia. $200-350

Fig. 229
Fairy-size dome, satinized white to red, piecrust flared top rim, diamond pattern, four air vents in bottom rim. Dome rests on shoulder in matching, bulbous, 2.5"-dia. footed base, containing clear candle holder and Burglar's Horror candle. Base has outward flaring piecrust rim. 6.25"h x 5.25"dia. $500-750

Left:

Fig. 230
Conical dome, Craquelle glass in teal blue shading to clear, with fluted, ruffled, and flared top rim. Dome rests in matching ruffled base with applied tooled clear feet. 6"h x 6"w. $350-500

Fig. 231
Amber fairy-size dome in pressed diamond design, scalloped bottom rim. Dome rests on smooth ridge inside amber lamp cup with scalloped rim and small amber tooled feet. 4.5"h x 4"dia. $200-350

Fig. 232
Fairy-size dome, blue ground with white mottled or iced surface (called "Arabesque"), two ground air vents in bottom rim. Dome rests in matching lamp cup with applied tooled blue feet. 5.25"h x 5.875"w. $350-500

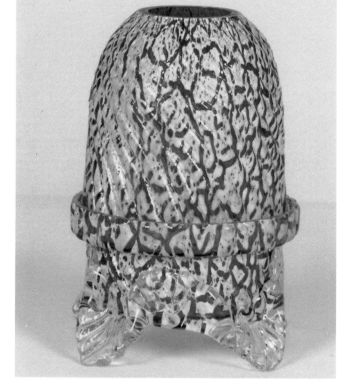

Fig. 233
Fairy-size dome, cranberry ground, Arabesque, embossed reverse swirl rib. Dome rests on ribbed shoulder of matching lamp cup, which has alternating applied clear tooled leaves, four up the sides of cup, four forming cup feet. 5.375"h x 4.25"w. $350-500

Fig. 234
Fairy-size pink opalescent dome, impressed diamonds and faint paneling on interior surface, resting on shoulder of matching lamp cup with applied clear tooled feet. 5.375"h x 3.625"w. $350-500

Fig. 235
Short cylindrical dome, shading from lime green to clear, embossed with random scales, waisted, flared and fluted, tooled and threaded top rim, ribbed and girdled bottom rim. Dome rests in matching low base with applied tooled feet. 5.875"h x 7"dia. $350-500

Fig. 236
Fairy-size dome in yellow and white spatter, clear overlay, embossed reverse swirl, wide ground air vents in bottom rim. Dome rests in matching lamp cup with petticoat of clear tooled leaves applied to top rim and matching applied feet. Cup holds candle marked "Price's Patent Candle Co Limited" in ribbed holder. 5.25"h x 5.25"w. $350-500

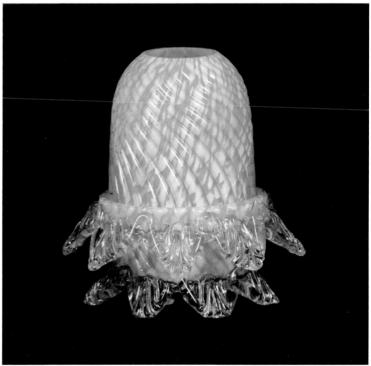

GROUP 5

CHIMNEY- STYLE LAMPS

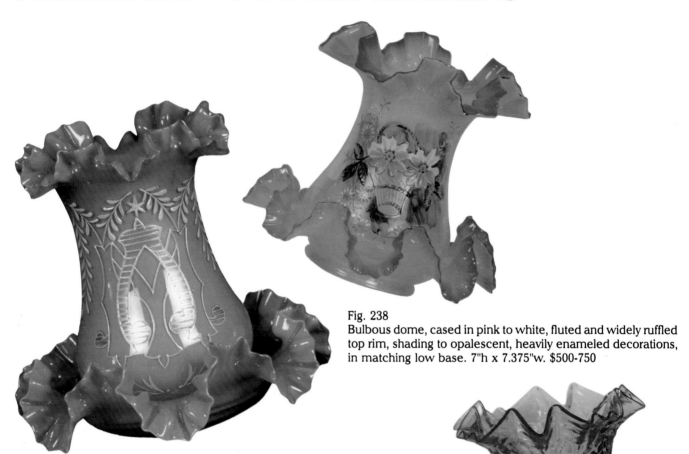

Fig. 238
Bulbous dome, cased in pink to white, fluted and widely ruffled top rim, shading to opalescent, heavily enameled decorations, in matching low base. 7"h x 7.375"w. $500-750

Fig. 237
Slightly bulbous dome, pink decorated with monogram and foliage in gold enamel, fluted and ruffled horizontal top rim, three air vents in bottom rim. Dome rests in matching stepped saucer base with fluted and deeply ruffled rim. 7.25"h x 7.5"w. $500-750

Fig. 239
Blue bulbous dome with impressed honeycomb pattern, waisted and flared top rim with alternating single and double folds. Bottom rim slightly girdled, with two ground air vents. Dome rests in matching low saucer holding Clarke Pyramid candle. 6"h x 5.5"dia. $350-500

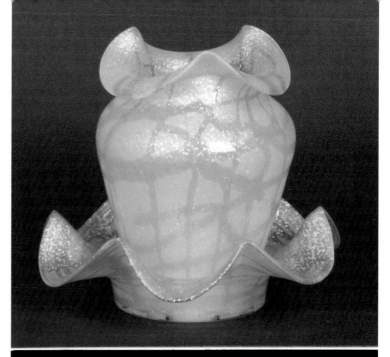

Fig. 240
Vase-shaped glossy dome with citron net design, mica flakes applied to interior; waisted, pulled and wavy top rim, four air vents in bottom rim. Dome rests in low matching base containing clear ribbed candle holder. 6"h x 6.75"w. $350-500

Fig. 241
Egg-shaped dome, clear frosted Craquelle glass with embedded gold threads and zigzag top rim. Dome rests in matching saucer with outward zigzag rim. 7"h x 6"dia. $200-350

Fig. 242
Slightly bulbous dome, light blue milk glass decorated with gilt monogram and enamel flowers, scalloped top rim with evidence of gilt. Dome rests in a matching saucer base with horizontal fluted rim with evidence of gilt. 6"h x 6.25"dia. $500-750

Fig. 243
Pear-shaped dome, embossed floral design, golden brown shading to opaque. Top rim pulled to six-pointed star. Bottom rim waisted and contains two air vents. Dome rests in matching low base with flared ribbon rim. 6.5"h x 6.5"dia. $350-500

79

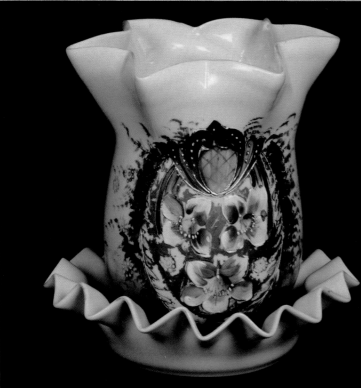

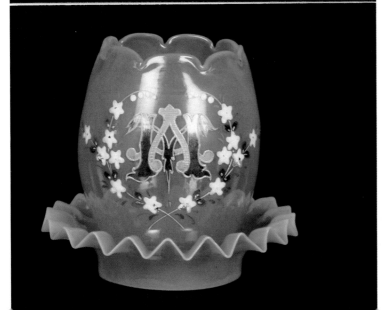

Left:

Fig. 244
Corseted ribbed dome, green band at top changing first to opalescent, then to clear glass. Top rim pulled into eight points, two air vents in bottom rim. Dome rests in matching ribbon-edged base. 6"h x 6.5"dia. $200-350

Fig. 245
Slightly bulbous dome, light green milk glass, decorated with heavy enameled cameo of flowers with surrounding gilt flowers and foliage. Top rim pulled into six-pointed star, bottom rim painted dark green and has two air vents. Dome sits in matching base with dark green painted interior and flared ribbon rim. Base holds pearl-footed, ribbed candle holder with heavy rim, embossed "Diamond Candle Co Inc, Brooklyn, NY." 5.875"h x 6"dia. $200-350

Fig. 246
Blue opaline rounded dome with scalloped top rim, monogram in gold and enameled flowers, four air vents in bottom rim. Dome rests in saucer base with horizontal ribbon rim. 5.5"h x 6.5"dia. $500-750

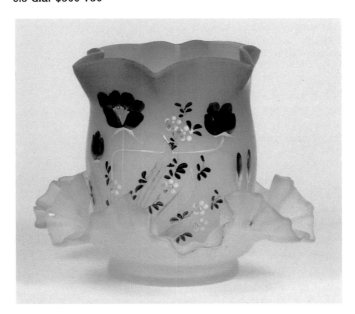

Fig. 247
Slightly bulbous dome shading from blue to opaque, decorated with brown flowers and cattails, top rim pulled into six-pointed star, two air vents in bottom rim. Dome rests in deeply ruffled saucer with blue edge. 5.5"h x 7.5"w. $350-500

Fig. 248
Bulbous embossed opaque dome with fluted and deeply ruffled pink top rim. This pattern is embossed four times on the lamp, one decorated in green, gold, and blue. Dome rests in matching low base. 6"h x 7.25"w. $350-500

Right:

Fig. 249
Bulbous, melon-ribbed dome with waisted, fluted and deeply ruffled gilt-trimmed top rim, expanded bottom rim with three air vents. Satin dome shades from pink to clear, decorated and signed by artist on bottom rim. Dome rests in low matching saucer with deeply ruffled, gilt-trimmed rim. 5.25"h x 6.25"w. $350-500

Fig. 250
Pear-shaped dome, faintly paneled, decorated in heavy white and gilt flowers, ruffled and fluted top rim, girdled bottom rim. Dome rests in matching stepped base. 7.5"h x 6.75"w. $350-500

Fig. 251
Blue cylindrical dome with waisted, fluted and ruffled top rim, decorated in Mary Gregory style. Dome rests in low matching base decorated with white dots below the fluting and gold trim near bottom. 6.25"h x 7"w. $500-750

Fig. 252
Translucent pink cylindrical dome with waisted, fluted, and downward-pulled ruffled rim, decorated with gilt monogram and enameled flowers, two air vents in bottom rim. Dome sits on shoulder in matching footed base containing clear candle holder and Childs' Night Light candle. 7.5"h x 6"w. $500-750

Fig. 253
Cylindrical dome, waisted and faintly scalloped horizontal top rim, three air vents in bottom rim. Dome decorated with cameo of young lady with bouquet of flowers, surrounded by pink flowers and green leaves. Dome rests on smooth shoulder of deeply ruffled and fluted footed base. 8.75"h x 6.75"w. $200-350

Fig. 254
Cylindrical vaseline dome with waisted, fluted and outward ruffled top rim. Interior of dome heavily ridged, giving optic effect. Dome rests on shoulder of matching bulbous footed base. 7.5"h x 7.125"w. $350-500

Fig. 255
Pink to opaque cylindrical dome, waisted, fluted, and deeply ruffled top rim, decorated with gold monogram and enameled flowers. Dome rests in matching footed base containing Clarke's Burglar's Horror candle. 7.5"h x 6.5"w. $500-750

Fig. 256
Paneled, cylindrical, green opalized dome, decorated with fired-on gold monogram and flowers, with waisted, ruffled and fluted top rim. Dome has three air vents on bottom rim, which rests on shoulder in wide footed base with widely ruffled and fluted rim. 7.75"h x 6.25"w. $500-750

Fig. 258
Cylindrical milk glass dome, decorated with female bust in diamond cameo over green stripe and red flowers on yellow band encircling dome, with waisted, fluted and heavily ruffled top rim. Dome rests in milk glass base with horizontal fluted rim. Base holds ribbed candle holder. 6.5"h x 6"dia. $350-500

Fig. 257
Bulbous dome with ruffled, fluted and waisted top rim, flared bottom rim. Dome decorated with gilt-framed cameo of two women and child, surrounded by trees and pink flowers. Ruffled and fluted saucer has matching deep green paint inside. 7.5"h x 6.25"w. $200-350

Fig. 259
Cylindrical dome shading from pale yellow to butterscotch with waisted, ruffled and fluted top rim, decorated with bronze colored flowers, two air vents in bottom rim. Dome sits on smooth shoulder in butterscotch base with ruffled and fluted rim. 6.5"h x 6.25"w. $200-350

Fig. 260
Blue pear-shaped decorated dome, fluted and ruffled gilt-trimmed top rim, three air vents in waisted but flared bottom rim. Dome rests in matching base with gilt decorated rim. 8"h x 8"w. $500-750

Fig. 261
Acid-etched dome, shading from pink to frosted, decorated with embossed design and fired-on gold, fluted and widely ruffled top rim, three air vents in bottom rim. Dome rests on shoulder of matching base. 9"h x 5.5"dia. $500-750

Fig. 262
Blue satin bulbous dome, decorated with enameled flowers and foliage, fluted and deeply ruffled top rim. Dome rests in matching base with applied tooled clear petal feet. White enameling of grass also found inside base. 6.5"h x 7"w. $500-750

GROUP 6

LAMPS WITH METAL HOLDERS

Fig. 263
Yellow satinized fairy-size dome, decorated in shades of orange and brown. Dome is fitted into silver-plated, handled base, with ring of air holes around side and inner ring that holds Price's candle and supports dome. Base marked with shield containing man shooting arrow and "7796" below. 4.125"h x 4.25"w. $350-500

Fig. 264
Nailsea type pyramid-size dome, red ground with white looping. Dome rests in silver-plated, handled base with crenelated rim, air holes around bottom edge, depressed candle holder. Base impressed on exterior bottom with man shooting arrow inside crest and "7796." 3"h x 4.25"w. $200-350

Fig. 265
Fairy-size cased dome shading from pink to white, decorated in gold Coralene in Wheat pattern, irregular scalloped top rim, girdled bottom rim, in handled metal base. Base contains metal-encased candle embossed "Milly Nachtlichter, Sarg's Patent, Wien, Beim Gebrauche Auf Porzellan Zu Stellem." 4.75"h x 4.75"w. $500-750

Left:

Fig. 266
Decorated frosted dome. Top rim is amber, waisted, fluted and ruffled; bottom rim is clear and waisted. Dome rests on four inward prongs that also are air vents in metal lamp cup marked "Gesetzlich / Geschutzt." Footed base is ornated with copper domes. 6.125"h x 4.625"dia. $150-200

Fig. 267
Pyramid-size dome, diamond pattern, resting in silver-plated lamp cup with slotted openwork design and depression for candle. 4.25"h x 3"dia. $150-200

Fig. 268
Pyramid-size dome, waffle embossed, with five-prong applied pewter ring around top vent. Dome fits into pewter lamp cup with simple applied handle and openwork in stem above saucer base. 3.75"h x 4.75"w. $200-350

Fig. 269
Crystal pyramid-size dome, cut in four-in-one diamond pattern, in crystal lamp cup marked "S. Clarke Fairy Pyramid Trade Mark" on interior and "Manufr at Baccarat" on exterior bottom. Cup holds Price's Export Night Light candle. Cup sits in a ring on the metal frame, and spring steel leaves clasp the dome on two sides to hold it firmly. Below the lamp cup can be seen an embossed flower, growing from the stemlike handle of the frame. Handle marked "J.N." and bottom of frame marked "Br SGDG." 4.625"h x 6.125"w across handle. $750-1000

The dome is shown tipped here to demonstrate how the supporting ring can swing in the metal frame, which allows the lamp to be used in two different ways. First, it can be set on all four feet (as shown) with the embossed flower below the lamp. Second, it can be hung as a wall-hanging lamp by using a ring (hidden here) opposite the handle. Used this way, the flower is behind lamp, the handle hangs down, and the feet act as wall supports.

Fig. 270
Satin Peach Blow cased fairy-size dome, waisted, fluted and heavily ruffled top rim with opaque crest, four air vents in bottom rim. Dome rests on smooth shoulder of matching lamp cup with fluted and heavily ruffled rim with opaque crest. Cup contains candle holder and Price's Sentinel candle, and sits in ring in low ormolu stand with leaf foot design. 6.5"h x 5.625"dia. $350-500

Right:

Fig. 271
Two-color Intaglio dome, white with tan overlay, in matching cased lamp cup containing Price's Sentinel Night Light candle. Cup rests on rim of light tan cased glass base with heavy white enameling, attached to three-footed ormolu stand marked "162" on bottom of feet (with paper sticker reading " -raus"). 5.5"h x 3.625"w. $750-1000

Fig. 272
Gold satin Raindrop Mother of Pearl fairy-size cased dome, four air vents in bottom rim. Domes rests on smooth shoulder in matching lamp cup, fitted into three-footed cast ormolu frame. 6.125"h x 3.875"w. $350-500

Fig. 273
Pear-shaped dome, white ribbed swirl, flared and scalloped top rim, round 2"dia. opening on bottom that fits over integral candle holder on metal frame. Frame is a branch forming five feet and decorated with metal leaves and metal flowers. 5.625"h x 5.25"w x 7.25"l. $350-500

Fig. 274
White satin pyramid-size dome decorated in green Wild Rose pattern. Dome rests in Clarke pyramid lamp cup supported on embossed ormolu frame. 5"h x 4"w. $200-350

Left:

Fig. 275
Fairy-size dome, frosted shading to red ground, two-color intaglio. Dome rests in clear Clarke Fairy lamp cup, which is supported by beaded ring on three-legged, ball-footed ormolu stand. Stand has six-petaled flower where legs supports meet. Legs are decorated with long-beaked bird. 6.375"h x 4.125"dia. $750-1000

Fig. 276
Nailsea-type fairy-size dome with red ground and deep red interior. Dome sits in Clarke lamp cup containing a ribbed candle holder. Cup rests in footed holder marked "Quadruple Plate, Van Birch Silverplate Co, Rochester, NY., #3657." Silver base holds cup very securely; users need to tip cup to get it in. 6.375"h x 3.875"w. $350-500

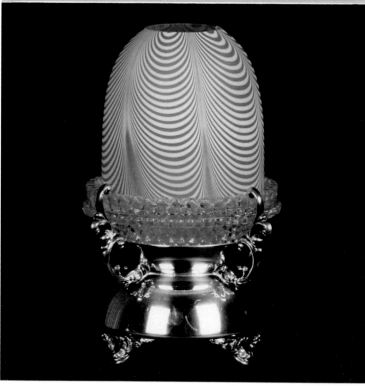

Fig. 277
White fairy-size dome, gilt around top vent and around cameo of winter scene, surrounded by pink poppy-like flowers and green foliage. Dome rests in ormolu stand with four dolphin feet. 6.5"h x 6.5"w. $350-500

Fig. 278
Acid Burmese fairy-size dome in Clarke lamp cup, resting on upright piecrust rim of matching Burmese base. Base is attached to a short silver-plated flared pedestal with three feet. 7.25"h x 4.5"dia. $500-750

Right:

Fig. 279
Fairy-size cased dome, green and pumpkin-color swirl with air traps, puckered top rim. Dome rests in double-shouldered Clarke Patent Fairy lamp cup marked "American Patent, Nov. 9 1886, #352296." Cup rests in ormolu frame with three paw feet. 5.5"h x 6"w. $350-500

Fig. 280
Pyramid-size dome in rainbow swirl impressed waffle pattern. Dome rests in lamp cup with concentric rings and six dimples on bottom, ribbed dentate upper rim, containing Waxine Licht candle holder marked "T" in middle with three nubbins on base. Lamp cup sits in silver-plated stand with three maidens serving as feet, holding baskets of fruit over their heads. 5.125"h x 3"dia. $350-500

Fig. 281
Pyramid-size dome, satin Peach Blow, cream-cased, resting in creamware lamp cup marked "S. Clarke Trade Mark Fairy Pyramid" in black in candle recess and "Taylor, Tunnicliffe & Co." in black on bottom. Cup rests in ring of ormolu stand, decorated with red and turquoise beads, with six loops as feet and double loop for handle. 4.375"h x 6.25"w. $350-500

Fig. 282
Fairy-size dome with three-color Intaglio (clear, white and red) depicting garlands of flowers. Dome rests in creamware lamp cup marked "S. Clarke Patent Fairy" in the recess, and "Taylor, Tunnicliffe & Co." and "369" (script) on the bottom. Cup contains Clarke ribbed candle holder and Burglar's Horror candle, and rests in foliage-enhanced ormolu frame on four ball feet. 5.125"h x 6"w. $750-1000

Fig. 283
Pyramid-size dome with reverse thumbprint, shading from clear to lemon yellow and decorated with enamel, with ribbed and scalloped bottom rim. Dome rests in clear lamp cup with smooth top containing a diamond and paneled candle holder marked "The Venus Nacht Licht"; across the center is "Palmer Co. Ltd." with the letter "D" above "Palmer." Cup sits in holder on short pedestal of footed and handled brass base marked "Gesetzlich Geschutzt." 5.5"h x 4.25"w. $350-500

Fig. 284
Peach Vasa Murrina dome, bulbous and cased, with girdled, flared and ruffled top rim, girdled bottom rim with four air vents. Dome rests on smooth shoulder in matching base, which is fitted into the ormolu frame. Frame has four feet, medallions in frame above feet, dragon head on one side and handle with ball on opposite side. 7.875"h x 7.25"w. $1500-2000

Fig. 285
Acid Burmese pyramid-size dome resting in S. Clarke Fairy Pyramid pegged lamp cup. Cup is set in brass frame consisting of top hook for hanging, subtended by brass smoke bell suspended in tripod brass frame. To remove lamp from frame, top collar is unscrewed and one arm hinges out to release restrained dome. Base ring of tripod marked "Fairy Pyramid, Rd No 95261." Frame is U.S. Patent 403327. 7"h x 3.25"w. $500-750

Fig. 286
Cased satin pyramid-size dome, decorated in black in Lace pattern. Dome rests in Clarke Pyramid Fairy lamp cup held in simple three-footed ormolu stand. 5"h x 4"w. $200-350

Fig. 287
Pyramid-size dome, cream-cased, satin Peach Blow decorated in foliage pattern. Dome rests in Clarke Fairy Pyramid lamp cup containing ribbed candle holder marked "Trade Mark Fairy Pyramid" with star in center and candle with wrapper reading "Sceid's 'Safe' Night Light, Made in England, 8 Hr." Cup held in three arms of ormolu frame with ball calyx forming feet and holding three opaque tooled leaves. 5.375"h x 4"w. $750-1000

Fig. 288
Pyramid-size dome, red DQMOP, cased. Dome rests in Clarke Pyramid lamp cup holding ribbed Price's Palmitine Star candle holder with three dimpled feet. Cup fits in ring of ormolu stand attached to beveled mirrored plateau raised on three half round metal feet. 5.5"h x 4.5"dia. $350-500

Fig. 289
Bisque rose with thirteen applied tooled petals and seven green calyx leaves all applied on band. Rose dome is atop an ormolu stand. 5"h x 3.25"w. $200-350

Fig. 290
Blue satin opalescent dome embossed with tulip petals, set in brass lamp cup on central stemmed brass tri-corn base, etched with birds in flight and trees, with lion handle. Cup contains metal-encased candle embossed "Milly Nachtlichter, Sarg's Patent, Wien, Beim Gebrauche Auf Porzellan Zu Stellem." 6.5"h x 3.75"w. $200-350

Fig. 291
Acid Burmese fairy-size dome in clear Clarke pegged lamp cup. Cup rests on footed cast brass stubby candlestick. 8"h x 4.25"sq. $200-350

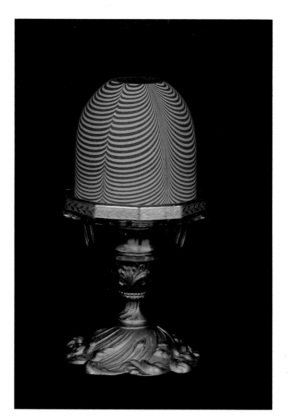

Fig. 292
Nailsea-type fairy-size dome with white loopings on red ground, resting in ten-sided gilt and embossed-edge pegged lamp cup. Cup is inserted in ormolu metal base signed "Pairpoint Mfg. Co., New Bedford, Mass., #31, QUADRUPLE PLATE." Paper sticker reads "The finish on this article will prevent all tarnish. Clean only with a soft damp cloth." 7.25"h x 4.125"w. $350-500

Fig. 293
Blue satin fairy-size dome, decorated in white Florentine floral pattern, four air vents in bottom rim. Dome rests in base of matching lamp cup with matching double stripe. Cup held by ring in two-arm ormolu frame. 7.5"h x 6.125"w. $350-500

Fig. 294
Lightly paneled fairy-size dome, Florentine decoration on two sides in white and gilt, two air vents in bottom rim. Dome rests on smooth shoulder of matching green lamp cup with gilt top, containing clear ribbed candle holder with Price's Night Light candle. Cup held in ring on bright ormolu frame, swirl paneled clear glass foot, decorated in heavy gilt enameling. 7.25"h x 5.125"w. $350-500

Fig. 295
Teal fairy-size dome with pressed diamond alternating with four-in-one diamond pattern, marked "Rd No 92571" inside top vent, ribbed and scalloped bottom rim. Dome rests in matching lamp cup with ribbed and round crenelated top rim marked "Rd No 92571" under rim. Cup rests in removable ring, which has a bar on each side that fits into double prong on both arms of heavy cast base. 8.75"h x 5"w. $200-350

Fig. 296
Pyramid-size dome, white milk glass, decorated both sides with thistle flowers and multicolored foliage. Dome rests in pegged Clarke Fairy Pyramid lamp cup, which is inserted into ormolu stand with green bead grapes and ormolu grape leaves and tendrils. 6.75"h x 3.625"w. $350-500

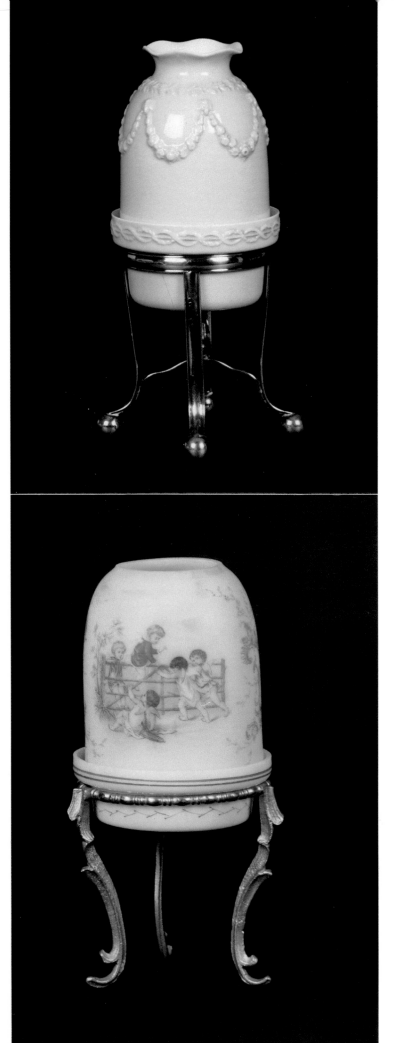

Fig. 297
Light blue translucent porcelain dome with white lining, flared wavy top rim and embossed swags of flowers. Dome rests on shoulder in matching lamp cup, inserted in four-legged, ball-footed silver frame. 8"h x 4.5"w. $200-350

Fig. 298
White Bristol fairy-size dome, decorated with five cherubs on garden gate framed by scrolls, with three air vents in bottom rim. Dome rests in matching lamp cup decorated in brown and holding clear candle holder. Cup fits into ormolu tri-footed stand. 7.25"h x 4.625"w. $350-500

Fig. 299
Acid Burmese fairy-size dome, decorated in ivy pattern and highlighted in silver. Dome in S. Clarke Patent Trade Mark Fairy lamp cup resting in three-legged, ball-footed cast brass stand. 8.5"h x 3.375"dia. $500-750

Fig. 300
Amber pyramid-size dome, embossed diamond and swirl pattern, pearl-textured bottom rim, in pierced brass lamp cup containing clear ribbed candle holder. Cup supported by brass pedestal on enameled base with three brass ball feet. Base marked "25292." 7"h x 4.75"w. $750-1000

Fig. 301
Oversize dome (4"dia.), cased glossy Peach Blow shading from rose to light pink, in white milk glass lamp cup with recess for candle, rolled ring and wide shoulder to hold dome. Cup fits into ormolu stand attached to plush mirrored plateau. 8.875"h x 4.875"dia. $350-500

Fig. 302
Pink satin pyramid-size dome with embossed petal pattern, two ground air vents in bottom rim, sitting in matching ribbed lamp cup. Lamp cup rests in ormolu standard with twisted tendrils up the lamp, three spades hanging down with three grape leaves below. Footed standard is supported on three feet. 7.5"h x 3.5"dia. $350-500

Fig. 303
Pyramid-size dome with purple ground and pulled white thread, set in Clarke Fairy Pyramid lamp cup containing Burglar's Horror Pyramid candle. Cup inserted into ring on gilded brass frame. 9.5"h x 5.5"w. $200-350

Left:

Fig. 304
Fairy-size dome in yellow, white, and opaque striped Cleveland pattern, set in matching pegged lamp cup containing Clarke Fairy candle holder and Burglar's Horror candle. Cup is inserted in heavily embossed, footed brass candle stick. 12.5"h x 4.125"sq. $500-750

Fig. 305
Pyramid-size cased dome, yellow diamond-quilted and decorated with Coralene, two air vents in bottom rim. Dome is set in Clarke Fairy Pyramid lamp cup, resting in ring of elaborate ormolu frame. 10.75"h x 3.125"w. $350-500

Fig. 306
Cranberry cylinder inserted into silver handled tankard, shield above handle, flared foot, containing Price's Sentinel candle. Tankard has bracket on side for holding handled cone-shape snuffer marked "Rd No 328312." 3.875"h x 4.375"w across handle. $350-500

Fig. 307
Jeweled ormolu dome consisting of eight diamond-shape shields soldered together. Dome rests on four points of shields in leaf-handled round base decorated in Persian flower motif. Base has integral candle holder. 3.5"h x 5"w across handle. $150-200

Fig. 309
Cradled, jeweled ormolu dome with open top, attached to leaf-handled square base decorated in Persian flower motif. Small ring on handle allows lamp to be hung and dome swings down. 3.75"h x 5.5"w. $150-200

Fig. 308
Jeweled ormolu dome in three-footed, thumb-handled matching base. Dome twists to lock into base. Rimmed spun brass candle holder fits into circular opening in base. 4"h x 6"w. $150-200

Fig. 310
Dual-purpose jeweled ormolu lamp on round footed standard. Removable top has fitting for taper candle. 6.5"h x 3.25"w. $150-200

GROUP 7

NURSERY LIGHTS

Fig. 311
Beautiful little child in bisque with green transparent eyes, holding cattails. Top opening slants downward. Rear impressed with woodsy design. 3.5"h x 3.25"w. $350-500

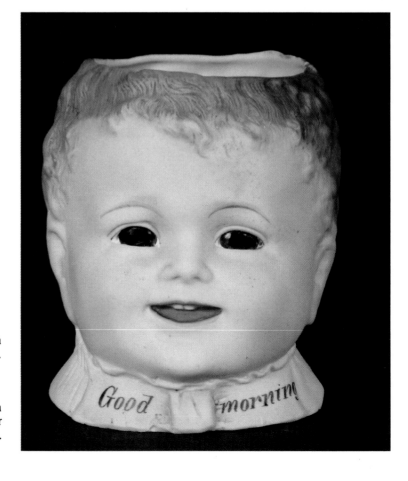

Fig. 312
Figural angel nursery light, three-footed, painted bisque with transparent brown glass eyes. Top opening slants downward. 3.75"h x 5.5"w. $350-500

Fig. 313
Young smiling boy with neat hair, transparent amber eyes with black centers, marked "Good Morning" on collar. One of a pair of figural lamps. "Made in Germany" printed on the bottom. 3.625"h x 3.75"w. $350-500

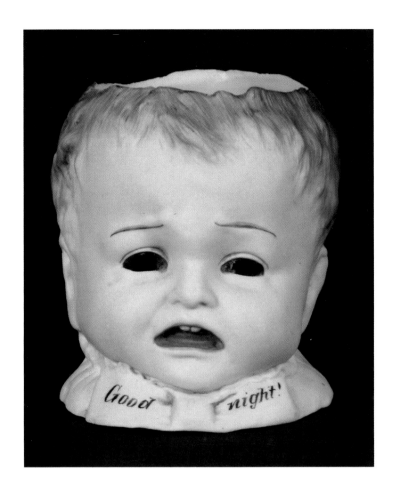

Fig. 314
The second in the pair, the boy's other self shows messed hair and portrays him crying. Marked "Good Night" on the collar, "Made in Germany" printed on bottom. 3.625"h x 3.75"w. $350-500

Fig. 315
Painted bisque black man with transparent brown eyes. 3.5"h x 3.5"w. $750-1000

Fig. 316
Lady's head with pretty blue eyes and three pink feet (front one covered by blue bow). Top opening slopes to rear. 3.5"h x 4"w. $350-500

Fig. 317
Painted porcelain lady with fine detail, two small air holes in top of head; two flowers (one on each side of head) are open, 1.75"h x 2.25"w candle opening in rear. Base marked in green with acorn and rustic "W," impressed with numbers "422," "11" and "4." 4.75"h x 3.625"w. $350-500

Left:

Fig. 318
Young girl's head in painted bisque, blonde and blue eyed, with textured cap. 3"h x 3.25"w. $350-500

Fig. 319
Painted bisque cherub, white transparent eyes with black center, waisted bottom rim, inserted in open filigree lamp cup of brass handled base marked "Gesetzlich Geschutzt." 6.25"h x 4.375"w. Courtesy of D. & N. Gole Collection. $350-500

Fig. 320
Red frosted dome in shape of monk's head, top opening, resting on ribbed shoulder in clear frosted base in shape of cowl. Base has integral candle holder marked "Clarke Fairy Pyramid" in recess and contains Clarke's Pyramid Trade Mark candle. 4.125"h x 4.375"w. $350-500

Fig. 321
Old Man in the Moon wearing stiff collar with pin, translucent, top opening slants downward. 3.75"h x 3"w. $350-500

Fig. 322
Head of child decorated as jester, light amber transparent eyes with dark center, rear decorated in animal fur pattern. 3.625"h x 3.375"w. $350-500

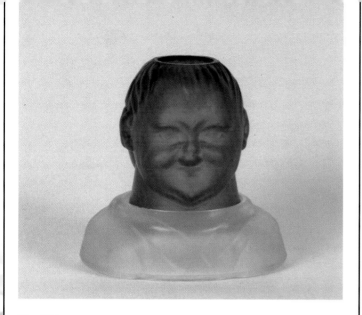

Fig. 323
Cranberry satinized dome shaped like a male child's head, smiling on one side and crying on the other. Dome sits in frosted base shaped as cowl. Base has integral candle holder marked "Clarke Fairy Pyramid" in recess. 4.375"h x 4.375"w. $350-500

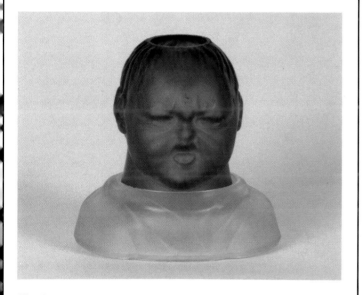

Fig. 324
Reverse of Fig. 323.

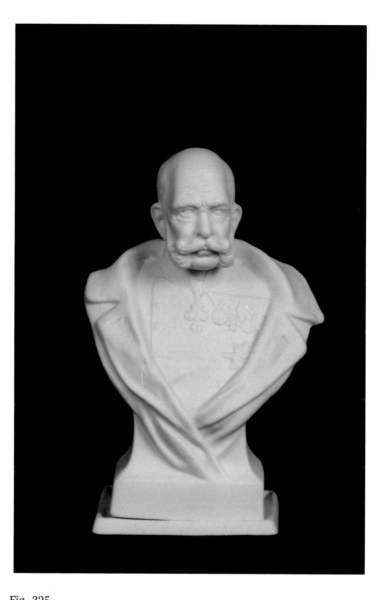

Fig. 325
Parian bust of Franz Joseph. Rectangular open bottom, vented below collar and between shoulders, and two holes near bottom opening. Bust sits in matching ridged plinth with overshot interior to hold shade, containing Burglar's Horror candle. 7.125"h x 3.375"w x 4.625" across shoulder. $500-750

Fig. 326
Translucent porcelain figural skull in shades ranging from gold to brown. Marked "3" on bottom. 3.25"h x 3.25"w x 5"l. $350-500

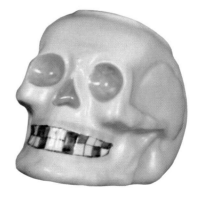

101

Left:

Fig. 327
One side of two-face figural, showing man in flesh tones with light yellow transparent eyes and removable hat. Figure rests on four blue feet, two of which appear as neckties on the two collars. 5.25"h x 5"w. $500-750

Fig. 328
Other side of Fig. 327, showing monkey in shades of brown with transparent amber eyes. Rim inside head opening accepts the perforated pink hat with open top. 5.25"h x 5"w. $500-750

Fig. 329
Monkey playing mandolin, pierced stars and Man in Moon watching. Painted bisque lamp with impressed fleur-de-lis on unpainted back. 4.625"h x 3.5"w x 4.375"l. $350-500

Fig. 330
Unpainted translucent bisque monkey head. 3"h x 4"w. $200-350

Fig. 331
Figural bisque monkey in shades of brown with transparent amber glass eyes. 3.5"h x 3.75"w. $350-500

102

Fig. 332
The first side of a triangular unpainted bisque figural, showing a monkey with amber transparent eyes. Fur frames a face on each of the three sides, with a double rope around bottom and tassels under each chin. 3.875"h x 4.75"w. $350-500

Fig. 333
The second side of the unpainted bisque figural, showing a Pekinese dog with amber and black transparent eyes. $350-500

Fig. 334
The third side of the unpainted bisque figural, showing a lion with green transparent eyes. $350-500

Fig. 335
Three-faced cat in painted bisque, light green transparent eyes with black centers, pink rope with pink and gold tassels in front of each face, and a blue base. 3.625"h x 4"w. $350-500

Fig. 336
Figural cat, green transparent eyes, pale pink rope and tassels. Marked on base with "I" in red. 3.375"h x 3.625"w. $200-350

Fig. 337
Bisque cat with green transparent eyes, two ropes around neck and two tassels under chin. 3"h x 3.625"w. $200-350

Fig. 338
Unglazed white bisque cat, green transparent glass eyes, embossed twisted rope around neck and tassels under chin. 3.5"h x 3.5"w. $200-350

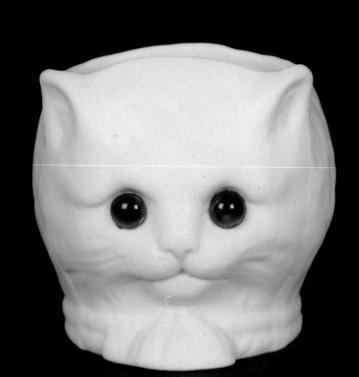

Fig. 339
Figural three-faced kitten, painted bisque, with green transparent eyes, pink rope, gold tassels and blue at base. 4"h x 4.25"w. $350-500

Fig. 340
Three-faced bisque hanging figural: dark gray cat with green glass eyes, tan dog with amber glass eyes, and light gray owl with amber eyes. All figures have transparent eyes, bows, and common pink ribbon. Left ear of each animal was factory pierced for hanger. Base incised with "X," "97" is written, and "KPM" is stamped. 4"h x 4"w. $350-500

Right:

Fig. 341
Figural lamp in shape of cat's head in shades of gray, with black nose, yellow and black transparent eyes. 3.25"h x 3.375"w. $350-500

Fig. 342
Bisque painted cat with big pink bow, black transparent eyes, back embossed as fur. 3.75"h x 3.25"w. $350-500

Fig. 343
Figural bisque cat in shades of gray, green transparent glass eyes, and rope collar. Two other sides of three-footed triangular lamp have embossed cream-color basketweave design. Marked "44" in script and impressed "3439," "6" and "81." 4"h x 4"w. $350-500

Left:

Fig. 344
Bisque painted cat in gray tones, transparent blue and black eyes, blue rope and tassels in front, and blue panel with impressed fleur-de-lis in rear. 4.25"h x 4"w. $350-500

Fig. 345
Bisque painted cat in gray tones, transparent green eyes, blue rope and tassels in front, and blue panel with impressed fleur-de-lis in rear. 3.5"h x 3.375"w. $350-500

Fig. 346
Bisque figural cat in shades of brown, amber transparent eyes, blue rope, and tassels. Blue rear panel with impressed fleur-de-lis. 3.75"h x 3.375"w. $350-500

Fig. 347
Gray bisque figural cat with highlights in peach, blue-green eyes with black centers, single pink rope and sprinkling of gold on tassels. 3.5"h x 3.25"w. $350-500

Fig. 348
Smirking bisque cat painted in gray tones, light blue transparent eyes with black centers, and bow off to side. 3.875"h x 3.625"w. $350-500

Fig. 349
Figural cat in shades of black and gray, transparent green and black eyes, double collar of pink rope and tassels under chin. Base impressed "3832" and "41" and painted "33." 3.25"h x 3.75"w. $350-500

Fig. 350
Painted porcelain lamp drilled for insertion of multi-colored, multi-faceted transparent jewels, surrounding embossed cat caught in the cookie jar. Fern impression on two sides. 3.25"h x 3.5"w. $350-500

Right:

Fig. 351
Two-faced figural cat and owl. 1.25"dia hole in center of re-movable hat, holes around crown, fits onto shoulder inside top rim of lamp. Cat has transparent light blue eyes. Owl has transparent marbleized eyes. Pink ribbing between faces and on top and bottom rims. Base incised "36," "78" and "21." 5.25"h x 4.625"w. $350-500

Fig. 352
White bisque owl, transparent aqua eyes with black centers, impressed fleur-de-lis on rear. 3.5"h x 3.25"w. $200-350

Fig. 353
Pink cased triangular three-faced owl, triangular top vent, in Clarke Cricklite lamp cup. 4.5"h x 4.25"w. $200-350

Fig. 354
Unglazed white bisque owl, amber transparent glass eyes, embossed twisted rope around neck, and tassels under chin. 3.5"h x 3.75"w. $200-350

Fig. 355
Triangular figural owl in shades of gray, transparent amber eyes. Three feet resemble cut branches, and other two sides of lamp are patterned to resemble bark of tree in brown. Burglar's Horror pyramid candle inside. Base marked "B440," "25," and in script "56." 4.125"h x 4"w. $350-500

Fig. 356
Figural bisque owl in shades of gray, yellow transparent eyes and light blue ribbon and bow. Blue rear panel impressed with fleur-de-lis. 3.5"h x 3.125"w. $200-350

Fig. 357
Figural ceramic owl, shades of gray and green, transparent red eyes, and yellow feet. 4"h x 3.5"w. $100-150

Fig. 358
Wee hanging fairy figural, two-faced, made of bisque. Owl in shades of gray with transparent amber eyes; cat in shades of gray with transparent green eyes. Pink rope around base. Marked "3061" and "79." Old wire hanger may or may not be original. 2.5"h x 2.75"w. $350-500

Fig. 359
Embossed two-faced owl in frosted dark green glass with red painted eyes, resting in oversize Clarke pyramid lamp cup. 4.5"h x 4"w. $200-350

Right:
Fig. 360
Bisque owl in shades of gray, clear transparent eyes with black centers, blue ribbon with bow under beak, blue rear panel with impressed fleur-de-lis. Marked "K" on bottom. 4.375"h x 4"w. $350-500

Fig. 361
White china owl with transparent amber eyes. Face decorated in pink and gilt. Marked "Rudolstadt," "Ernest Bohne," and "B." 3.125"h x 3.375"w. $350-500

Fig. 362
Figural bisque owl in shades of gray, transparent brown glass eyes, and blue bow tied around neck. Blue rear panel with impressed fleur-de-lis. 3.5"h x 3"w. $350-500

Left:

Fig. 363
Three-faced triangular figural owl in shades of gray, transparent amber eyes, pink ribbon around base with three pairs of tassels forming feet. Marked "SPS" over large "X," "EM" over "X," and in script the number "2." 4"h x 4.25"w. $350-500

Fig. 364
Two-piece porcelain owl, transparent amber glass eyes, vent in rear between shoulders. Matching base resembles tree trunk, integral holder for small taper, two air holes. Base marked with "*" over "RS" in open wreath and "Germany." Dome and base loosely lock together. 5" x 2.875"w. $200-350

Fig. 365
Bisque triangular three-faced figural with open eyes: owl in black and gray, cat in black, and dog with tan accents. Faces have common flared blue base with 1"dia. hole through center. Base marked "3241" and "75." 3"h x 3.25"w. $350-500

Fig. 366
Four-faced figural lamp; two cats in black tones with green or amber eyes and blue bows, and two bulldogs in brown tones with brown or yellow eyes and pink bows. Bottom marked "31" in red and impressed "103." 3.625"h x 5.75"w. $500-750

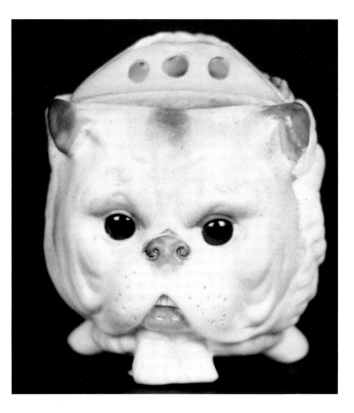

Fig. 367
Triangular three-faced bisque figural, all faces (cat, dog, and owl) with colored transparent eyes. Pink rope circles base and three pairs of tassels form lamp feet. Top rim of lamp has depressed smooth shoulder and holds removable, vented, triangular cover with colors matching animals. Base is embossed "2377," "69" and in script "49." 4.75"h x 4.25"w. $350-500

Right:

Fig. 368
Three-faced unpainted bisque triangular figural: pug dog with amber transparent eyes, cat with green and black eyes, owl with yellow and black eyes. 3.875"h x 4.25"w. $350-500

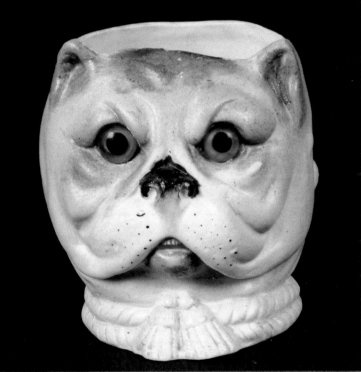

Fig. 369
Figural bulldog in shades of brown, black nose, amber and black transparent eyes, double collar of pink rope and tassels under chin. Base impressed "333" and "23" and painted "52." 3.5"h x 3.75"w. $350-500

Fig. 370
Painted bisque three-faced triangular lamp: green eyes on gray cat, light amber eyes on gray owl, light brown eyes on brown dog. Pink rope base with tassels forming feet under each face. Base marked "KPM" (in blue), cross, incised cross, and "4" (in red). 4"h x 4.625"w. $350-500

Left:

Fig. 371
Painted bisque three-faced triangular lamp: dog, cat and owl with transparent eyes, pink rope and tassels. Base incised "61." 3.25"h x 3.5"w. $350-500

Fig. 372
Bisque three-faced triangular figural lamp: cat with teal eyes and black centers, owl with amber eyes, and bulldog with brown and black eyes. Single rope encircles base and tassels are feet. Base incised "2577." 4"h x 4"w. $350-500

Fig. 373
Figural bisque bulldog in shades of tan and brown, transparent brown glass eyes. Two sides of three-footed triangular lamp are a doghouse with horizontal impressed wooden boards. Impressed "3638" on base and marked "89." 4.25"h x 4.25"w. $350-500

Fig. 374
Figural bulldog with transparent amber eyes with dark centers, pink double rope and tassels. "56" printed in black on bottom. 3.25"h x 3.625"w. $200-350

Fig. 375
Brown bisque Pekinese, brown transparent eyes, black leather collar around neck. 3.875"h x 3.5"w. $350-500

Fig. 376
Brown bisque Terrier, blue rope around front of neck, blue panel on rear impressed with fleur-de-lis. 3.5"h x 3.625"w. $350-500

Right:

Fig. 377
Larger size of Terrier figural, blue rope and blue rear panel with impressed fleur-de-lis. Marked "21" in blue on bottom. 4.25"h x 4"w. $350-500

Fig. 378
Figural dark brown werewolf, brown transparent glass eyes, four sharp teeth with opening from candle chamber to interior of mouth. Bottom embossed "BRETBY," "1258," "England." (Not exactly what we'd think of as a nursery light.) 3.75"h x 4.5"w. $200-350

Fig. 379
Unpainted bisque ram's head, 1.125" hole between horns on rear, resting on matching base with form-fitting rock-impressed rim tapering inward. 5.125"h x 4.75"w. $200-350

Fig. 380
Painted bisque bison, transparent orange eyes with black center. 4.25"h x 4.75"w x 4.125"across horns. $350-500

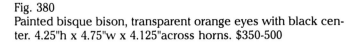

Fig. 381
Figural lion in shades ranging from gold to white, dark amber transparent eyes, red mouth, blue rear panel with impressed fleur-de-lis. 3.5"h x 3.125"w. $350-500

Fig. 382
Figural translucent lion's head in shades ranging from brown to cream, "2" written into glaze on base. 3.5"h x 4.625"w. $200-350

Fig. 383
Three-dimensional porcelain rabbit with red eyes. Figure painted in shades of brown. Small oval vent between ears approximately .625" in size. Figure's bottom is completely open. 5"h x 9.5"w nose to tail. $350-500

Fig. 384
Painted porcelain lamp drilled for insertion of multi-colored, multi-faceted transparent jewels around embossed pheasant. Ferns impressed on two sides. 3"h x 3"w. $350-500

Fig. 385
Figural frog in shades of green, with amber eyes and sloping rear opening. 3.25"h x 4.25"w. $350-500

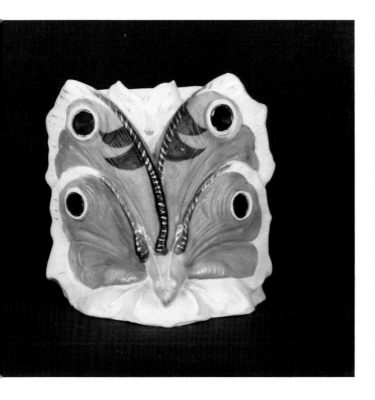

Fig. 386
Porcelain figural lamp, embossed and decorated as butterfly, wings drilled for insertion of four faceted blue jewels. 4.375"h x 5"w. $350-500

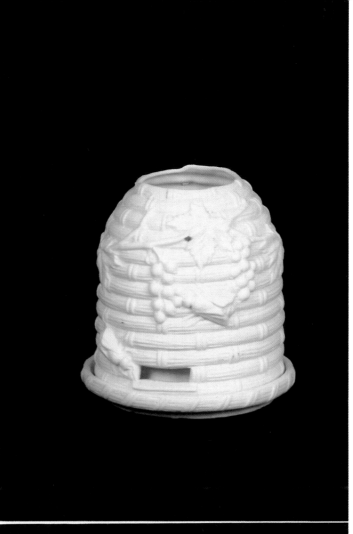

Right:

Fig. 387
White bisque dome resembling old straw beehive, embossed with bees and grapes, resting in matching base with integral candle holder. 4.75"h x 3.75"dia. $350-500

Fig. 388
Porcelain dome, marked "Copeland," depicting pile of clam shells with scroll reading "Please Remember the —-" over 1"h x 1.25"w candle opening. Dome rests on three stanchions on round brickwork-embossed base. Candle holder is formed by cup within base. Base embossed "COPYRIGHT RESERVED COPELAND." 4.75"h x 4"dia. $350-500

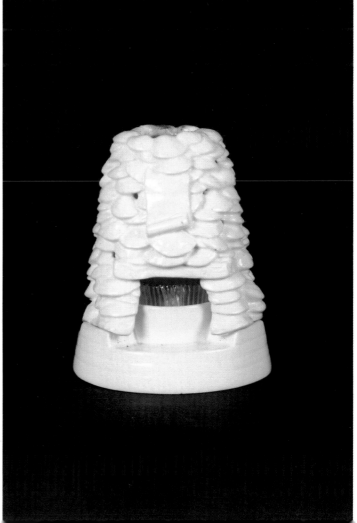

115

GROUP 8

HOUSES & BUILDINGS

Fig. 389
Bisque house with thatched roof, incised "4648" and "II," 1.5"h x 1.75"w candle opening in rear. 4.75"h x 3.25"w x 6.25"l. $350-500

Fig. 390
Bisque Alpine-style house painted in earth tones, with 2"h x 2.25"w candle opening in rear. 5.5"h x 2.625"w x 4.25"l. $350-500

Fig. 391
Glazed and painted porcelain nightlight, full-length model of building, marked "W H Goss, Rd No 225833, Model of Shakespeare's House" on bottom. 1.5"h x 2"w candle opening, 1"dia. opening in back of roof, and two open chimneys. 3.625"h x 2.875"w x 7.25"l. $350-500

Fig. 392
Glazed porcelain model of English cottage with "Ann Hathaway's Cottage" plaque on front. Base marked "W H Goss" with shield, line with dot on either side, and "Model of Ann Hathaway's Cottage Shottery near Stratford-on-Avon, Rd No 208047." Open front door and chimneys, .75"dia. hole in back of roof, and 1.75"h x 2"w candle opening. 4"h x 2.875"w x 5.875"l. $350-500

Fig. 394
Unglazed porcelain painted model of building, marked "Robert Burns' Cottage" by front door. Marked on rear "Robert Burns the Ayrshire poet was born on the 25th. January A.D. 1759 died 21st. July A.D. 1796 aged 37 1/2 years." Chimneys open, and .875"dia. opening in rear roof. Under rear 1.375"h x 2.875"w candle opening is marked "Model of Burns' Cottage, W H Goss, Rd No 211037." Base impressed "Goss," line with two dots on either side. 3.25"h x 3"w x 5.75"l. $350-500

Fig. 393
Glazed porcelain painted nightlight, tied thatched roof, .75"dia opening in rear, open chimney and 1.375"h x 2"w candle opening. Bottom marked "W H Goss, Model of Manx Cottage, Rd No 273243." 3.625"h x 3.125"w x 4.75"l. $350-500

Fig. 395
House with plaque reading "First and Last House in England" on side by taller chimney. Base marked "Rd No 521645, W. H. Goss," vertical slash with two dots on each side. Limited painted decoration, extension on back side, 1"dia. vent in back roof, and 1.5"h x 1.75"w rear candle opening. 4.5"h x 4.125"w x 5"l. $500-750

Fig. 396
Painted bisque English cottage wth thatched roof, open chimney vents, 2.25"h x 2.5"w candle opening in rear. "#1705" impressed on side roof peak. 6"h x 4.25"w x 6.5"l. $350-500

Fig. 397
Two-piece white bisque English-style house, open door and chimney, in foundation-fitting square base with integral candle holder. 4.25"h x 4"w. $350-500

Fig. 398
Painted bisque building with the date "1575" on front, chimney and some windows open, 1.75"h x 2"w rear candle opening. 3.25"h x 3.625"w x 4"l. $350-500

Fig. 399
Painted china two-story house, pierced windows, 1" x 1" roof vent, and 1.75"h x 2"w rear candle opening. 3.75"h x 2.75"w. $350-500

Fig. 400
Painted bisque chalet, stairs leading to second story, bird in tree on front right corner. Roof has 1.125" opening, and 2"h x 1.75"w arched rear candle opening is framed by bent trees. 5.875"h x 3.125"w x 3.125"l. $350-500

Right:

Fig. 401
Painted bisque building with 1.75"h x 2.25"w rear candle opening plus some open windows and chimney. Incised "Germany" on bottom. 4"h x 3.75"w x 5.25"l. $350-500

Fig. 402
Cast iron chalet with interior clips holding green glass which covers front windows and door. Rear hinged door 2.5"h x 3.25"w. Recess in floor for candle holder. Assembled with hand-cut nuts. 6.5"h x 5"d x 6.375"l. $200-350

Fig. 403
Painted bisque Russian architecture building with walking bear crest over doorway. Open vent measuring .75"l x .375"w in roof, and 2"h x 2"w rear candle opening. 7"h x 3.75"w. $350-500

Fig. 404
Painted bisque building with painted lithophane of castle on a hill. 2"h x 2.25"w rear candle opening. Chimney and windows open. 6.25"h x 3.5"w x 4"l. $350-500

Fig. 406
Painted bisque castle with 2"h x 2.125"w arched candle opening in rear. 8.375"h x 3.125"w. $500-750

Fig. 407
Painted bisque church, 1.5"h x 2"w rear candle opening and "683" impressed on rear bottom. 6.5"h x 3.625"w x 4.75"l. $350-500

Fig. 405
Painted china castle with open windows, three triangular openings in roof, 2"h x 2"w arched candle opening in rear. 6"h x 3.125"w x 3.125"l. $350-500

Fig. 410
Bisque castle figural night light, one turret seriously leaning, mold mark "1694" under arched 2.125"h x 2.25"w rear candle opening. 7"h x 4.125"w. $350-500

Fig. 408
Painted bisque castle, all windows open, with chimney and roof vents. Impressed "#1167" above 1.75"h x 2.375"w rear candle opening. 5.75"h x 3"w. $350-500

Fig. 409
Painted bisque castle with 2"h x 2.125"w arched rear candle opening. 8.375"h x 3.125"w. $350-500

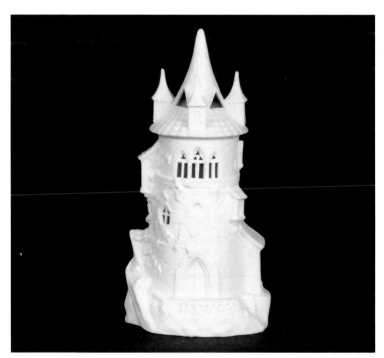

Fig. 411
Porcelain castle embossed with large cross on door. Window openings in gothic style, spire roof with four triangular air vents and four turrets. Came from Australia. Handwritten note inside reads "Castle, 18th of September 1863, married Arthur Jercoe, Great Grandma Eatwell (Newman)," signed "Maryann Eatwell." 1.75"h x 2.125"w candle opening in rear. 7.75"h x 3.5"dia. $350-500

Fig. 412
Two-piece castle with 1"sq. opening in center tower, open windows, and girdled bottom rim which fits into earthtone colored base, eight air holes and depressed center for candle. Marked "Oliver K Whiting & Co., Regent St., W. 1." 5.75"h x 4.75"dia. $500-750

Fig. 414
Brown, stained, unglazed castle marked "Round Tower Windsor," with 2.25"dia hole in roof, door in rear open, hole in tower with "Rd No 209991" on remaining surface. Building fits into form-fitting base marked "W H Goss, Round Tower Windsor, Rd No 209991." 5.75"h x 5.75"dia. $1000-1500

Fig. 415
White bisque two-piece round castle, front windows open, embossed windows in rear, two balconies with turret roofs and finials, three dormers, and a clock tower in rear. Roof and turrets have embossed tiles and castle has embossed vines. Roof has 2.25" diameter vent. Embossed base has retaining ring for castle and contains ribbed candle holder. Base is marked but unreadable. 8.75"h x 5.75"dia. $500-750

Fig. 413
Round two piece castle, red cut to clear glass, alternating etched patterns, variously decorated with frosted and polished areas. Top rim of dome and base have matching dentate pattern. Center of base has integral stemmed small candle or float holder. Possibly Baccarat. 7.25"h x 5.375"dia. $750-1000

Fig. 417
Pyramid-size dome in shape of small green house with waisted bottom, inserted into a darker green lamp cup in shape of hill. Base impressed "S. Clarke's Fairy Pyramid," designed with steps up one surface, depression for candle, and ribbing at top to support dome. 4.75"h x 4.25"sq. $500-750

Fig. 416
Painted bisque two-piece castle, open windows and circular roof vent. Seven gilded pontils on turrets. Base depicts hill and foundation with interior raised retainer. Bottom of base marked "#1698." 6.75"h x 4.125"w. $350-500

Fig. 418
Glazed and painted English cottage, open door and windows, 1.75"dia. roof vent, resting on green saucer base with candle depression. Bottom of base marked "Made in England." 3.5"h x 5"w. $100-150

Fig. 419
Glazed porcelain English cottage, rectangular, with open doors, windows, and roof vents, on green oval base with candle depression. 3.5"h x 4.125"w x 7.5"l. $150-200

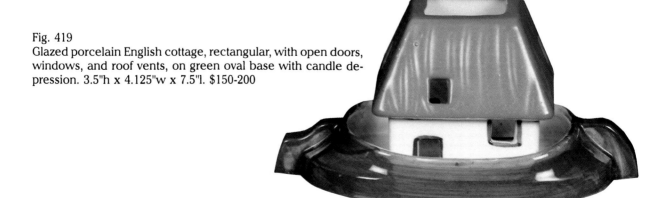

Fig. 420
Cranberry embossed lighthouse on green hill base marked "S. Clarke Fairy Pyramid" in ribbed candle recess. 4.5"h x 3.875"sq. $350-500

Fig. 422
Collection of lighthouses in a variety of colors: (from left to right) pink satin, gold milk glass, blue shaded, opaque, blue, and pink milk glass. 8.25"h (top of ring) x 3.5"w. $200-350 each

Fig. 421
Two-piece Copeland lighthouse raised on three tiers of bricks. Base with interior retaining ring for candle and holding dome, embossed with garlands and rings for tying boats. 6.5"h x 3.5"dia. $350-500

Fig. 423
White opalescent glass lighthouse, brick embossed sides, three embossed windows, tile embossed roof (nearly flat) containing three air vents, topped by embossed silver vent cover and silver carrying ring. 1.5"h x 1.75"w rear candle opening. 8" to top of ring x 3.5"dia. $200-350

Fig. 424
Shaded pink circular building, cased, with embossed brickwork and steeply sloping ribbed roof. Dome rests in unmarked crystal lamp cup, embossed in stonework pattern, which rests in central post arising from matching base with piecrust rim. Lamp cup holds a ribbed Clarke Fairy candle holder. 7.5"h x 6.25"dia. $500-750

Right:

Fig. 425
Cased dome, blue shading lighter, in shape of square house with .75"dia. open chimney. Dome rests in square lamp cup embossed to resemble stonework, with three air holes. Base of cup is round and contains Price's Sentinel Night Light candle. Cup sits in tapered center post of DQMOP cased base with short upturned piecrust rim. 7.75"h x 6.75"dia. $500-750

Fig. 426
Eight-sided white milk glass building. Three sides have embossed window pattern, others have brickwork. Embossed shingled roof has four ridges ground at bottom for air vents. Top opening has metal cover and ring for hanging or carrying. 1.75"h x 1.75"w candle opening. 7.5"h x 3.5"w. $200-350

Fig. 427
Red frosted six-sided building, woven pattern walls, ribbed roof with six vents and top opening, five glossy windows, 1.875"h x 1.625"w candle opening. 6.5"h x 3.75"w. $200-350

Fig. 428
Honey amber transparent glass lighthouse, embossed windows and doors, six air vents on sides and one on top of embossed shingled roof. Lighthouse contains original handled godet, containing metal covered, circular cork float wick with tab for lifting and impressed iron cross centered around wick opening. 6.5"h x 4"w. $200-350

Fig. 429
Two-piece six-sided buildings in blue milk glass and honey amber transparent. Each has embossed windows, door, and shingle roof, on conforming bases with stone block motif and integral candle cup. 6"h x 4"w. $200-350 each

Fig. 430
Cranberry English-style telephone booth, embossed shingled roof, paneled sides, and dimpled feet. 1.75"h x 1.75"w candle opening. 6.5"h x 3.5"w. $200-350

Fig. 431
Pink milk glass Russian-style building, onion turret top, three embossed panels as shown, four diamond air vents in roof, topped by embossed silver cap with ivory carrying or hanging ring, signed "Deposé Pantin" on bottom. 8"h (top of ring) x 4"w. $350-500

Fig. 432
Blue porcelain handled lantern, impressed waffle-pattern panels, twelve air vents in yellow roof with knurled top. 2.25" x 2.25" Arabesque-style candle opening. 6.75"h x 3.5"w. $350-500

Fig. 433
Porcelain footed and handled lantern with two silhouettes, sailing boat with sail partially down by the shore of a lake illuminated by full moon; slight variation on other side. Four slit air vents in roof, four holes in top open knob. 2.25"h x 1.75"w Arabesque-shaped candle opening with candle depression in base interior. 7"h x 4.125"w. $350-500

Fig. 434
Porcelain handled lantern-style lamp, pierced roof and top of sides, impressed wire fence pattern around base, birds painted by 3.125"h x 2.5"w candle opening. Candle depression in base interior. 6.875"h x 3.75"sq or 5"w. with handle. $350-500

127

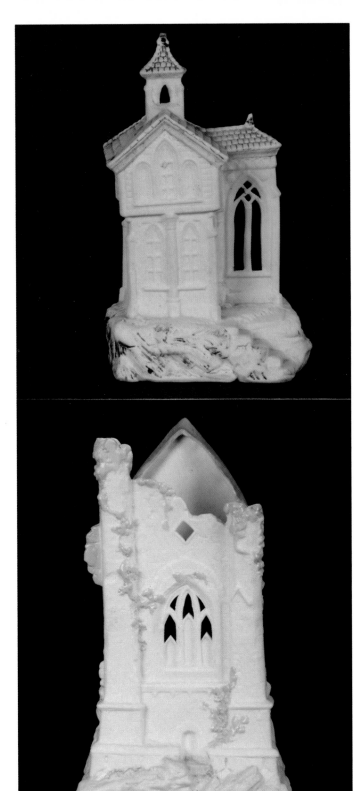

Fig. 435
Painted bisque church, open Gothic window and belfry, 1.375"h x 2"w candle opening in rear. 6.5"h x 2.75"w x 4.125"l. $350-500

Fig. 436
Figural lamp depicting church in ruins. Candle opening in rear 2"w x 3"h (at highest point in double arch). 7.5"h x 4.25"w. $350-500

Fig. 437
Porcelain replica of London Daily Mail building. Air holes found above columns, in gilted roof dome, along roof ridges and roof lettering, and below the ball on top. Embossed "Paris" over left window, "London" over center, and "Overseas" over right. 2"h x 1.5"w candle opening in rear. 5"h x 5.25"dia. $500-750

Right:

Fig. 438
Blue to opaque frosted iceberg with 2"h x 2.25"w candle opening. 6.5"h x 4.25"w. $200-350

Fig. 439
Ribbed bird cage, shading from apricot to almost white, with two circular bands and protruding feeders. Roof has three vents and top opening. 2.25"h x 2"w arched candle opening. 5.5"h x 4.25"w. $200-350

GROUP 9

LITHOPHANES

Fig. 440
Two-piece porcelain lithophane, signed "AdT." Enameled crenated projections on rim, 1.75"-dia. top air vent surrounded by six .375" holes, resting on a low footed base with six holes. Scenes depict typical Tyrolean cottage surrounded by snow capped peaks, mosque by lake with palm trees and small boat, small dhow on lake near castle and pine trees. 5.75"h x 4"dia. $500-750

Fig. 441
Lighted scene of mosque on porcelain lithopane shown in Figure 440.

Fig. 442
Pair of lithophane newel post domes, multiple air holes in bottom rim, center post tapered to insert in stairway newel post. One dome depicts lady in window and cavalier outside, lady by well, lady in Dutch door talking to another lady outside in the wind. The second depicts man with sword talking to boy and girl, girl with three small children and dog kneeling at her feet, girl child with younger boy carrying book with two other children in background. 3"h x 3"dia. $350-500 each

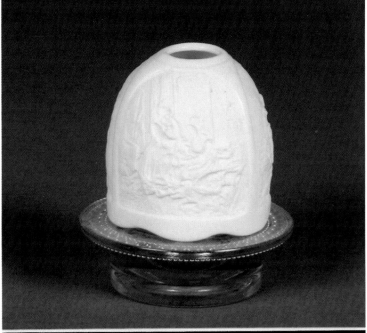

Fig. 443
Three-paneled lithophane with scalloped bottom rim, on un-marked clear beaded-rim lamp cup with interior retaining ridge which also forms candle holder. Scenes depict frightened boy and girl, mother and young girl sitting in cottage, boy leaning against wall and girl kneeling. 3.5"h x 3.5"dia. $350-500

Fig. 444
Painted lithophane fairy-size dome with gold accents, depicting boy and girl reclining in garden, girl peering from window, girl carrying basket and pole, boy and his dog. Four small (.125"dia) holes drilled near base. Clear glass lamp cup. 4"h x 4"dia. $750-1000

Fig. 445
Painted porcelain panoramic scene on lithophane dome, depicting two deer drinking water from lake, one bear watching another bear killing deer, mother fox by den with her kits. Bright gold border around both rims. Dome rests in Clarke lamp cup. 4.25"h x 4"dia. $750-1000

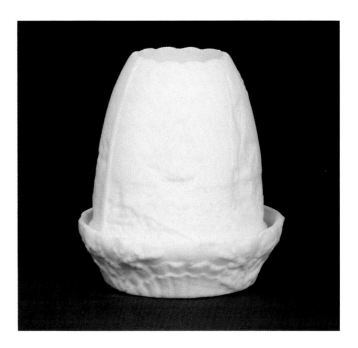

Fig. 446
Porcelain lithophane dome with slightly scalloped top rim, two scenes depicting two sailing ships and a windmill. Dome rests on shoulder in low base impressed with sea shells and coral. 3"h x 2.875"dia. $500-750

Fig. 447
Three-panel colored lithophane fairy-size dome with gilt band around top rim. Scenes depict boy pretending to photograph young girl, policeman with sword talking to young girl and boy with puppy, girl with younger brother walking through woods in winter. Dome rests in Clarke Fairy lamp cup containing Clarke candle holder and candle. Cup rests in center post of white satin reversible style base. 4.75"h x 6.375"dia. $1000-1500

Right:

Fig. 448
Handled porcelain lithophane lantern depicting mother talking to older child, mother holding infant, and angel in upward flight holding infant. 1.785"h x 1.75"w candle opening. 6.5"h x 3.5"w. $500-750

Fig. 449
Clear diamond point pyramid-size dome in Clarke Fairy Pyramid lamp cup. Lamp sits in raised retaining ring on bronze three-footed frame, heavily embossed with vines and berries. Frame has rear clips holding porcelain lithophane depicting young boy and girl being frightened by defending mother hen. Lithophane marked "PPM 808." Frame impressed "Verlag Bei F.O. Zimerman, Hanau." 8.75"h x 3.5"w. $500-750

Fig. 450
Squatty round footed lithophane tea warmer with removable grated cover. Base signed "Von Schierholz." Four scenes depict young boy taking picture with simulated bellows camera, older boy and girl walking in the woods, two girls with shepherd's crooks, and older boy and girl in conversation on a bridge. Porcelain teapot not original to warmer. 6.25"h x 5.625"w. Warmer 3.75"h x 5"dia. $750-1000

Fig. 451
Two-piece porcelain lithophane square veilleuse, crenelated top rim, pegged squatty porcelain teapot with recessed cover. Footed lithophane fits inside top rim of square porcelain base marked "Motrahedeh." Lithophanes depict cavalier with three women and a child, man sitting and two women standing (one partially disrobed), two women in mountains with shepherd's crooks, three women (one nude) and a man offering an apple to the nude. 10"h x 5.5"sq. $750-1000

Fig. 452
Square lithophane dome decorated with gilt, removable cover over central vent. Cover is gilt-trimmed, with two rows of perforations and open center flower bud knob. Scenes depict girl sitting next to mother, woman sitting on step holding infant while visiting with neighbor lady, mother teaching child how to write in a tablet, female sitting by river watching male about to sail a boat. Dome rests in matching base with four fan-shaped feet and four air holes, containing white porcelain candle holder and Price's Sentinel candle. 8.5"h x 4.875"sq. $1000-1500

Fig. 454
Two-piece porcelain oriental temple, decorated in gilt and blue, with six air holes in top. Six air holes in three-footed base decorated in same colors. Girdled bottom rim of lithophane cylinder recesses into base with nubbins that center the lithophane. Scenes depict oriental village, two warriors standing near scholar with stick, oriental woman holding child's hand while maid holds umbrella on long pole over woman's head. 7.75"h x 5.5"w. $1000-1500

Fig. 453
Two-piece painted porcelain castle turret in Moorish architecture style, with young lady leaning out window. Three lithophane panels depict two ladies talking, cavalier courting, and soldier talking to girl by fence. Porcelain base embossed but unreadable. 9.25"h x 5.25"w. $3000-5000

Fig. 455
Two part lithophane lamp. Shade panels depict girl and boy talking across the fence, fellow walking away and girl looking back at him, and the first scene repeated but with figures in very close proximity to one another. Shade is impressed "Francaise Lithophanie" in a circle. Cylindrical lithophanes depict draped buxom lady smelling a flower, man and dog confronting three kneeling children, and angel ascending with child and flowers. Lithophanes are held in four-footed ormolu frame in a handled bamboo design, marked "Long—" (covered by fitting), and "M, #2, 4.83.." Blue flowered cloisonne bowl fitted in base. 10"h x 6.375"w. $1000-1500

Fig. 456
Porcelain lamp, embossed grapevine, grapes, and gilt highlights on all sides, holding porcelain candle cup. Removable painted lithophane of religious statue in background, angel and two children in foreground. Font in front below panel. 6.25"h x 4"w x 5.125"l. $1000-1500

Fig. 458
One-piece porcelain sedan chair with painted lithophanes depicting lovers in swing, man with flowers peering around corner at female, and man and lady running through woods with drape overhead. Four square air vents in top, depression for candle inside bottom. Opening on fourth side is 3.5"h and varies from 1.5" to 2.25" in width. Base marked "12" with two sticks in one direction and one stick crossing near the top. 8"h x 7.5"w. $3000-5000

Fig. 457
Painted tramp standing on square of cobblestones, carrying two picture frames with straps over his shoulders, top slots for raising lithophane panels for candle insertion, and four bottom air vents. Painted lithophane depicts grandmother holding child while making house of cards, "437" impressed in back of panel, sickle and "PR" with another mark above. Second panel on back side depicts grandfather with Russian-style fur hat holding his watch to ear of blonde child. Green cistern water pump in left rear is supporting back lithophane. Under raised arm and on other side are V-shaped vents; top of hat is also vented. Raised hand is about to insert or remove pipe from mouth. Figure contains Price's Sentinel Night Light. 9.875"h x 5"w. $5000-7500

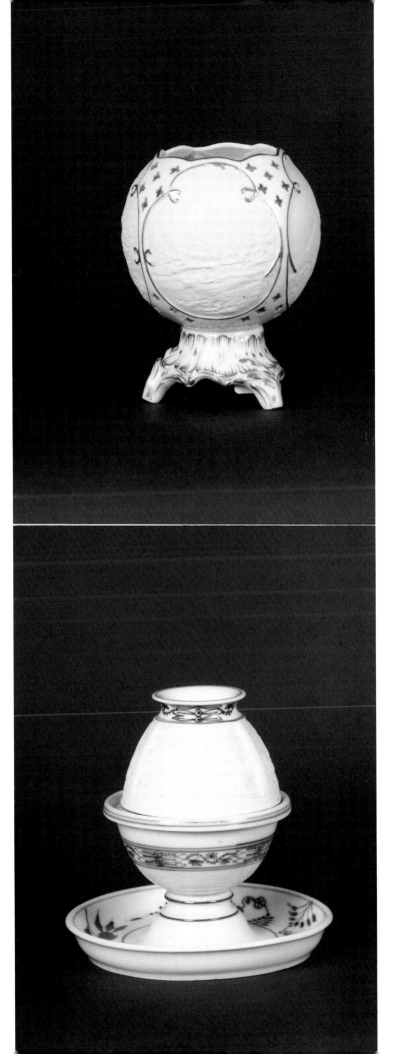

Fig. 459
Two-piece painted porcelain lithophane, French, with young lady peering through door window of beach cart. Three lithophane panels depict two ladies talking, cavalier courting lady, and lighthouse. Porcelain base has four wheels, platform, and two steps. Base has candle depression and four air holes. Cart and base marked with sickle with "PR" inside the curve. 7"h x 3.5"w x 4.75"l. $1500-2000

Right:

Fig. 460
One-piece ball-shaped lithopane dome on three-legged, gilt-decorated porcelain stand. Colored crosses on dome are glass screening which is applied to interior surface. Four scenes depict four different castles. 4.875"h x 4.125"w. $1000-1500

Fig. 461
Meissen onion pattern lithophane lamp, depicting inn with mountains and river, multiple-story buildings in village with three men standing by lake, mountain scene with tree in foreground and two people and horse in the background. Glossy porcelain is decorated in blue. Dome rests on shoulder in matching pedestal porcelain lamp cup containing white porcelain candle holder with Clarke candle. Swords marked on bottom in blue. 6"h x 6"w. $1500-2000

Fig. 462
Painted ball-shaped lithophane dome on heavily embossed footed metal standard with air vents in top cup where dome rests. Scenes depict young boy wearing Pilgrim hat and sword, with his dog holding leash in its mouth, girl by piano sitting on floor with pet, girl sitting at piano trying to get the pet to play the piano, and older girl looking out window with potted plants below. 9"h x 4"dia. $1000-1500

Fig. 463
Four-panel lithophane impressed "Germany 42" on interior. Scenes depict woman by bench in woods; woman with basket picking fruit; woman with long braid and hat held on her elbow by ribbon, raising her arms as if defending herself from insect; and matronly woman in doorway with dog in front of her. Oversize 4"dia. dome. Bottom rim sits on smooth shoulder in impressed rayed lamp cup with beads around horizontal rim. Cup contains Clarke ribbed candle holder and Price's Improved Export Night Light candle. Cup rests in squat Tapestry Ware base with polychrome flowers signed "Taylor, Tunnicliffe & Co." 4.75"h x 5.375"dia. $1000-1500

Fig. 464
Fairy-size painted porcelain lithophane dome with pink trim, French. Scenes depict angel holding child outside of window, angel appearing to woman in prayer, and angel ascending with child and flowers in her arms. Dome marked with a sickle. Dome rests in pegged Clarke lamp cup with heavy serrated rim, containing Clarke candle. Cup is inserted in ormolu frame with three arms that end in open balls, forming calyx in which three frosted leaves are inserted. Leaves support lamp. 7.875"h x 5.375"w. $1000-1500

Fig. 465
Three-panel colored lithophane fairy-size dome decorated in pink porcelain around rims and between scenes. Scenes depict standing man carrying bag with white dog and three children sitting around him, man scolding two boys while writing them a ticket for fishing in posted pond, girl with younger brother walking through woods in winter. Dome rests in matching pink scrolled base containing six air holes and holding candle holder and Burglar's Horror candle. 4.75"h x 4.75"w. $3000-5000

Fig. 466
Porcelain two-panel lithophane dome known as "Little Miss Muffet" but depicting female child scared by a frog in her dish and same child sitting happily in woods watching rabbit. Four notched air vents on bottom rim. Low matching saucer base with integral candle holder. 4.25"h x 4"dia. $500-750

Fig. 468
Fairy-size painted lithophane dome with panoramic scenes of fox and her kits, deer eating in a meadow, and deer being killed by bear. Dome rests in Trade Mark Fairy lamp cup containing ribbed candle holder and Burglar's Horror candle. Cup is held by twining gilt branches to which are attached four porcelain bud vases, each with two applied flower buds. The branches continue on to form feet. Base is marked "Moore." 5.75"h x 7.375"sq. $1000-1500

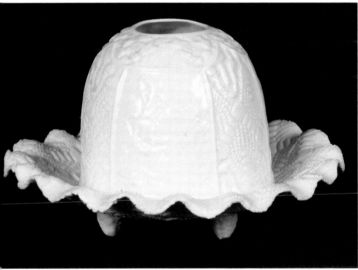

Fig. 469
Porcelain fairy-size dome, three-panel lithophane with scenes depicting mother fox by den holding kits, deer grazing by pond, and bear killing deer. Dome rests in integral lamp cup of bluish-gray 'Aladdin's lamp'–style base trimmed in gilt. "S. Clarke Patent Trade Mark Fairy" in blue marked in bottom of cup, which holds ribbed candle holder and Burglar's Horror candle. Base marked "Rd No 93321" and in script "1528." 5.5"h x 9.5"l. $750-1000

Fig. 467
Cream-colored glazed porcelain lithophane dome depicting two children with basket of fruit on balcony dropping the fruit into horizontal skirt of young girl below, little boy in Pilgrim hat and his dog with leash in his mouth, and matron looking at thorn in reclining boy's foot while girl is checking out his ear. Random pattern of embossed bead and stepping-stone-like design on dome is repeated on three-footed base. Base holds low porcelain candle holder marked "For Clarke's Patent Pyramid Night Lights, Trade Mark Pyramid, Rd US Patent Office," holding a Saml Clarke Pyramid candle. Base marked with three green dots, "Adderly & Lawfon, Provo Patent." 4.25"h x 7"dia. $1000-1500

Fig. 470
Painted lithophane dome depicting romantic scenes: boy and girl running through woods with drape over their heads, boy and girl on swing, and couple walking through woods. Dome rests on majolica-type base with integral lamp cup on short pedestal with multiple holes just below top rim of cup. Lamp called "Fanning the Flames of Love." The monkey dressed in a gold-buttoned double-breasted jacket is working the bellows to do just that. 5.25"h x 8"w. $3000-5000

Fig. 471
Lithophane with panorama of three love scenes: man and woman in close proximity walking through woods, man and woman running through woods with drape of her gown over her head, man and woman in swing. Dome rests in handled pottery base decorated with paisley-style flowers, on smooth rim with twelve air holes just below rim but above candle holder portion, containing ribbed S. Clarke Trade Mark Fairy candle holder holding Price's Improved Export Night Lights candle. Base signed "Sarrequemines." 4.25"h x 4.25"w x 6"l. $1500-2000

Fig. 472
Fairy-size lithophane dome depicting young boy with sword and his dog with leash in his mouth, girl looking out window with plants in window box below, and two boys going over a wall. Dome sits on shoulder of integral lamp cup of Tapestry Ware spade-shaped base decorated with gold cording and tassels, marked "Doulton Burslem," numbered "9993-" and inscribed with "4" and a square. 5.25"h x 7.75"w. $1000-1500

GROUP 10 POTTERY LAMPS

Fig. 473
Doulton Burslem Tapestry Ware base of Figure 474, turned to show details. Note gold cord with alternating pairs and single tassels around edge and marking in integral lamp cup. This is one of twelve Doulton tassel designs for fairy lamp bases. 2.25"h x 6"w x 8.25"l.

Fig. 474
Acid Burmese fairy-size dome resting on ribbed shoulder in Doulton Burslem Tapestry Ware handled base, signed and marked "US Patent 314002." Tapestry Ware base is decorated with impressed floral pattern, gold cord and tassels, and gold fire-breathing serpent encircling the integral lamp cup. Cup marked "S. Clarke's Patent Trade Mark Fairy" inside candle depression containing Clarke Pyramid candle. 5.875"h x 6"w x 8.25"l. $1000-1500

Fig. 475
Acid Burmese fairy-size dome, decorated in prunus pattern, on ribbed shoulder of Tapestry Ware lamp cup marked "S. Clarke's Patent Trade Mark Fairy" in black, containing Clarke candle holder and Clarke candle. Cup is integral to small flower bowl elevated on taper above larger flower bowl. Handled base decorated with gold rope and single and double tassels, and marked "Doulton Burslem, US Patent 314002, Rd. No. 99929," and "6" in front of box. 8"h x 8"dia. $1500-2000

Left:

Fig. 476
Acid Burmese fairy-size dome, decorated in woodbine pattern, on ribbed shoulder of Tapestry Ware lamp cup, marked "S. Clarke's Patent Trade Mark Fairy" in black, containing ribbed Clarke candle holder and Burglar's Horror candle. Cup is integral to heart-shaped handled base decorated with gold rope and single and double tassels. Base marked "Doulton Burslem, US Patent 314002, Rd. No.99934," impressed "Doulton Slater Patent." 5.625"h x 7.5"l. $1000-1500

Fig. 477
White acid Burmese fairy-size dome, decorated in hops pattern. Dome rests on ribbed shoulder of integral lamp cup, marked "S. Clarke's Patent Trade Mark Fairy" in black, containing Clarke ribbed candle holder and Clarke's Burglar's Horror candle. Cup is on Tapestry Ware handled bowl with three pulled spouts, on standard attached to flower bowl below. Both bowls are decorated with gold cord and single and double tassels. Base marked "Doulton Burslem, US Patent 314002," "8" in front of "Rd No 99930." 9"h x 8"dia. $1000-1500

Fig. 478
Acid Burmese fairy-size dome, decorated in woodbine pattern, on ribbed shoulder of Tapestry Ware lamp cup marked "S. Clarke's Patent Trade Mark Fairy" in black, containing ribbed Clarke candle holder and Burglar's Horror candle. Cup is integral to small flower bowl elevated on taper above larger flower bowl on three gilt feet. Base is decorated with gold rope and single and double tassels, and (though not marked) is a Doulton Slater Patent. 10.25"h x 9.25"dia. $1500-2000

Fig. 479
Jeweled ornaments inserted into two Christmas trees on fairy-size bisque dome, marked "Reg N.146726, Made in Austria." Dome resting on ribbed shoulder in signed Doulton Burslem handled and tiered Tapestry Ware base with distinctive rope and tassel decorations. Base embossed "Doulton & Slater Patent, US Pat #314002," and "Rd No 99929." "S. Clarke's Patent Trade Mark Fairy" in recessed candle holder. 8.5"h x 8.25"w. $1000-1500

Fig. 480
Acid Burmese fairy-size dome, white on top and bottom with pink swirl on upper portion, decorated in hops pattern. Dome rests on ribbed shoulder in Tapestry Ware bowl with integral lamp cup, marked "S. Clarke Patent Trade Mark Fairy" in black, containing Clarke Trade Mark ribbed candle holder and Clarke's Trade Mark "Pyramid" candle. Bowl is attached to larger matching flower bowl also decorated with gilt rope and single and double tassels. Bottom of base decorated, so no markings appear, but item is nonetheless Doulton Slater Patent. 5.875"h x 7"dia. $1500-2000

Right:
Fig. 481
Acid Burmese fairy-size dome decorated in prunus pattern, resting on shoulder of offset integral lamp cup, marked "S. Clarke's Patent Trade Mark Fairy" in black in candle recess. Cup set on Tapestry Ware base, decorated with gold cording and single and double tassels, marked "Doulton Burslem, US Patent 314002," and in red block "R&M 99932." 5.5"h x 6.5"w. $750-1000

Fig. 482
Cobalt blue Arabesque fairy-size dome resting in integral lamp cup, marked S. Clarke's Patent Trade Mark Fairy, holding Price's Sentinel Night Light candle in ribbed clear candle holder. Lamp cup above heart-shaped Tapestry Ware base, decorated with gold single and double tassels and cord. Base marked "Doulton Burslem, US Patent 314002, #6, Rd No 99929," and impressed with "159." 5.5"h x 7.5"l. $750-1000

Fig. 483
Cream-cased Peach Blow domes; fairy-size (left) and pyramid-size (right); satin finish shading from rose to pink, heavily decorated in Lace pattern, resting on glazed creamware bases with gold highlights, marked "S. Clarke Patent Trade Mark Fairy" and "Fairy Pyramid" in black in lamp cup bases and "Taylor, Tunnicliffe & Co" on bottom. 5"h x 4.25"dia, 3.75"h x 3.125"dia. $350-500 each

Left:

Fig. 484
Glossy Peach Blow, cased pyramid-size dome resting on corrugated shoulder of signed Taylor, Tunnicliffe & Co. creamware base. Base is signed "S. Clarke Patent Trade Mark Fairy Pyramid" in recessed candle holder and marked "1514" on bottom. Base is decorated with heart-shaped leaf vine in gold and holds Price's Sentinel Night Light candle. 4.125"h x 4.25"dia. $350-500

Fig. 485
Acid Burmese pyramid-size dome, decorated in ivy pattern, on creamware base decorated in pink and gray with gold highlights. Base signed "S. Clarke's Patent Trade Mark Fairy Pyramid" in recessed candle holder and "Taylor, Tunnicliffe & Co." and "1516" on bottom. 4"h x 4"dia. $500-750

Fig. 486
Pyramid-size dome embossed and decorated with two Christmas trees, drilled with multi-colored jewels inserted to resemble ornaments. "Reg N. 196726" and "Made in Austria" written inside dome, which sits in rose and foliage decorated creamware base signed "Taylor, Tunnicliffe & Co." and "1513" in script on bottom and "S. Clarke's Trade Mark Fairy Pyramid" in blue in candle recess. 4"h x 4"dia. $500-750

Fig. 487
Large dome with faint reverse swirl, 2.5"dia. top vent, girdled base, in blue milk glass cup, ridged to retain dome and depression to hold candle, embossed basket weave beneath. Lamp cup set on three-footed filigree base embossed with upright seahorse wearing crown. 7.625"h x 5"dia. $350-500

Fig. 488
Fairy-size dome, reverse Nailsea-type with white satin ground and red loopings, resting in pegged Clarke Fairy lamp cup containing ribbed candle holder and Burglar's Horror candle. Peg fits into urn figure on gilt and floral decorated base, signed "Copeland" in green, "D 7358," and has a red shepherd's crook. 7.875"h x 4.625"w. $500-750

Right:

Fig. 489
Pyramid-size dome in blue satin embossed swirl, resting on corrugated shoulder of removable lamp cup signed "Taylor, Tunnicliffe & Co." and marked "Rd #93324" and "1512" in gilt. Cup fits in base signed "Taylor, Tunnicliffe & Co." and "Rd #93324" and marked "1512." Base is attached to ormolu foliage footed frame which also supports three matching flower holders and a menu holder arm. Base and flower holders are blue shading to green with textured finish and gilt spatter. 6"h x 5.875"w. $500-750

Fig. 490
Cranberry ground dome with three rows of clear applied tooled elongated leaves in ascending sizes, girdled bottom rim. Decorated "Taylor, Tunnicliffe & Co." lamp cup is also marked "S. Clarke Patent Trade Mark Fairy Pyramid" in blue and attached to ormolu footed frame with three arms holding matching bud vases. Foot embossed with two cherubs, coach and horses, and shepherd with sheep. 9"h x 4.625"w. $500-750

Fig. 491
Acid Burmese pyramid-size dome, decorated in prunus pattern, in creamware lamp cup marked "Taylor, Tunnicliffe & Co., Rd. No. 93323" and "1511" in script and containing Clarke Trade Mark Pyramid candle. Cup is attached to menu holder-style ormolu frame, which has curved arms that act as feet and also hold three matching bud vases. 6.375"h x 5.5"w. $1000-1500

Left:
Fig. 492
Gold Mother-of-Pearl fairy-size dome in peacock pattern, cased, with three air vents in bottom rim. Dome rests in Clarke Patent Trade Mark Fairy lamp cup with smooth rim, smooth top, containing Clarke candle holder and candle. Cup rests in pottery base with applied water lily stems, leaves which help hold lamp cup, and flowers serving as bud vases. Base impressed "1511," marked "1151, Rd. No. 47870, Moon" and "51" in plum color. 5.875"h x 7.25"w. $750-1000

Fig. 493
Blueberry blue pyramid-size dome, overshot, in embossed Berry pattern. Dome rests on ribbed shoulder of creamware lamp cup marked "S. Clarke's Fairy Pyramid" in blue in candle recess, containing ribbed candle holder marked "Field's," "1" with line below. Base marked "Taylor, Tunnicliffe & Co.," "1519" in script, with line and three red dots. 4.25"h x 3.5"dia. $350-500

Fig. 494
Acid Burmese fairy-size dome, decorated in moss rose and butterfly pattern, on ribbed shoulder in creamware base containing Clarke ribbed candle holder and Clarke candle. Tapestry Ware footed base is marked "S. Clarke Patent Trade Mark Fairy" in rounded depression of integral lamp cup and "Taylor, Tunnicliffe & Co., Patent" with large "S" below, and in script "1446." 5.875"h x 4.5"dia. $1000-1500

Fig. 495
Acid Burmese fairy-size dome decorated in prunus pattern, resting on ribbed shoulder in creamware base with integral lamp cup marked "S. Clarke's Trade Mark Fairy" in blue, containing Clarke ribbed candle holder and Burglar's Horror candle. Tapestry Ware bowl-shaped base marked "Patent, Taylor, Tunnicliffe & Co., S," and in script "1449." 5.5"h x 4.75"dia. $1000-1500

Fig. 496
Acid Burmese wee-size dome, decorated in ivy pattern, sitting on ribbed shoulder in upturned acorn cap attached to twig and oak leaf. Base impressed "Rd. No. 113219, S. Clarke's Patent Trade Mark 'Wee Fairy', China Manufactured in France." 3.125"h x 3.625"w. $1500-2000

Right:

Fig. 497
Acid Burmese fairy-size dome, decorated in oak leaf pattern, on ribbed shoulder in creamware lamp cup marked S. Clarke's Trade Mark Fairy in blue, containing Burglar's Horror Trade Mark candle in ridged candle holder. Cup is intrical to Tapestry Ware flower bowl marked "Taylor, Tunnicliffe & Co." and (in script) "1440." 6"h x 7.5"dia. $1000-1500

Fig. 498
Satin Peach Blow pyramid-size dome, cream-cased, decorated in ivy pattern, resting in a signed "Taylor, Tunnicliffe & Co." Tapestry Ware base marked "#1440A." Integral lamp cup signed "S. Clarke's Patent Trade Mark Fairy Pyramid" in candle holder depression containing Price's Sentinel Night Light candle. 4.75"h x 6"dia. $1000-1500

Fig. 499
Satin Peach Blow pyramid-size dome, cased, decorated in Lace pattern in goldwash, in creamware lamp cup marked "S. Clarke Patent Trade Mark Fairy Pyramid" in blue in candle recess. Cup is on short pedestal in integral Tapestry Ware flower bowl, glossy enamel finish with inward ribbon rim. Base marked "Taylor, Tunnicliffe & Co." and in script "1444A." 4.875"h x 5.75"dia. $750-1000

Fig. 500
Acid Burmese fairy-size dome, decorated in woodbine pattern, resting on ribbed shoulder in creamware lamp cup marked "S. Clarke's Patent Trade Mark Fairy" in blue, containing candle in frosted Clarke candle holder. Cup on short standard is integral to flower bowl base with inward ribbon rim decorated in heavy enamels under a glaze. Base marked "Taylor, Tunnicliffe & Co." and in script "1444." 6.375"h x 7.5"dia. $1000-1500

Fig. 501
Acid Burmese fairy-size dome, decorated in prunus pattern, resting on ribbed shoulder in creamware lamp cup marked "S. Clarke's Patent Trade Mark Fairy" in blue, containing ribbed Clarke candle holder and Burglar's Horror candle. Cup on short standard is integral to Tapestry Ware flower bowl base with inward ribbon rim. Base marked "Taylor, Tunnicliffe & Co." and in script "1438." 6.5"h x 7.25"dia. $1000-1500

Fig. 502
Cranberry pyramid-size dome, flashed, impressed cut-velvet type pattern. Dome rests on shoulder of pedestal lamp cup in polychrome floral decorated creamware flower bowl with inward ribbon rim. "S. Clarke's Patent Trade Mark Fairy Pyramid" impressed in blue in recessed candle holder. "Taylor, Tunnicliffe & Co." and "1438A" marked on bottom. 4.5"h x 6.25"dia. $500-750

Fig. 503
Fairy-size dome, reverse Nailsea-type with red looping and white satin ground. Dome rests in creamware base with large flower bowl, light gray interior, ribbon inward rim with seven outward pulls, integral lamp cup, marked "S. Clarke's Patent Trade Mark Fairy" in blue, containing Clarke ribbed candle holder. Base is marked "Taylor, Tunnicliffe & Co." and in script "1442." 6"h x 8.125"dia. $500-750

Fig. 504
Blue pyramid-size shade, flecked with mica and drag-looped with silver threading, in creamware base with "S. Clarke Trade Mark Fairy Pyramid" marked in blue in recess holding Burglar's Horror Pyramid candle. Cup on short pedestal is integral to Tapestry Ware flower bowl with upright ribbon rim. Base marked "Patent, Taylor, Tunnicliffe & Co.," "S" and "1442A." 4.875"h x 6.125"dia. $500-750

Right:
Fig. 505
Pyramid-size dome in blue, white, and opaque swirl Cleveland pattern, with pleated and swirled top rim, slightly scalloped bottom rim. Dome rests in creamware lamp cup marked "Clarke's Patent Trade Mark Fairy Pyramid" in blue in candle recess containing paper-wrapped candle. Lamp cup is on short pedestal and integral flower bowl, decorated with swirl tapestry pattern, with inward ribbon rim. Base marked "Patent, Taylor, Tunnicliffe & Co.," "S," and "1443A." 4.75"h x 6.25"dia. $500-750

Fig. 506
Acid Burmese pyramid-size dome, decorated in forget me not pattern, in lamp cup marked "S. Clarke Trade Mark Fairy Pyramid" in blue, containing Burglar's Horror Pyramid candle in Price's Co. Limited Patent ribbed candle holder. Cup set in creamware base with integral flower bowl. Base marked "Taylor, Tunnicliffe & Co." and in script "1440A." 4.875"h x 5.75"dia. $750-1000

Fig. 507
Acid Burmese pyramid-size dome, decorated in single prunus pattern, resting in Tapestry Ware flower bowl base signed "Taylor, Tunnicliffe & Co.," and also marked "1441A." Rim of flower bowl has six perforations for flowers. Base has integral lamp cup marked "S. Clarke's Trade Mark Fairy Pyramid" in candle holder depression. 4.875"h x 6.125"dia. $750-1000

Left:

Fig. 508
Fairy-size dome with white satin ground, faintly melon-ribbed and decorated with red wavy lines, green-cased. Dome rests in lamp cup marked "S. Clarke's Patent Trade Mark Fairy" in blue and containing ribbed candle holder and Clark's Pyramid Fairy candle. Lamp cup is integral to creamware flower bowl base, greenish gray interior, eight pierced stars on flat rim to hold flowers. Base is marked "Taylor, Tunnicliffe & Co., Patent" and in script "1771." 6.375"h x 7.5"dia. $500-750

Fig. 509
Acid Burmese fairy-size dome, resting on a signed "Taylor, Tunnicliffe & Co." Tapestry Ware flower bowl base with polychrome flowers. Lip of bowl is pierced in starbursts for flower insertions. Integral lamp cup has raised ribbed shoulder and pearled-top dome retainer, "S. Clarke's Patent Trade Mark Fairy" marked inside candle depression and "1439" on bottom of bowl. 6"h x 7.875"dia. $500-750

Fig. 510
Acid Burmese pyramid-size dome, decorated in woodbine pattern. Dome rests on ribbed shoulder in creamware lamp cup, marked "S. Clarke's Patent Trade Mark Fairy Pyramid" in blue and containing "Waxine Nacht Licht 8" candle. Cup on short standard is integral to Tapestry Ware flower bowl base with six star-like openings on horizontal rim to hold inserted flowers. Base marked "Taylor, Tunnicliffe & Co." and in script "1439A." 4.75"h x 5.75"dia. $1000-1500

Fig. 511
Red craquelle fairy-size dome, applied clear daisy-type flowers with blue centers. Bottom rim of dome is quite flat and fits into lamp cup marked "S. Clarke's Patent Trade Mark Fairy" in blue, also containing ribbed candle holder and Clarke's Burglar's Horror candle. Lamp cup is integral to creamware flower bowl base with eight pierced stars on flat rim to hold flowers. Base is marked "Taylor, Tunnicliffe & Co." 7"h x 7.25"dia. $750-1000

Fig. 512
Acid Burmese pyramid-size dome, decorated in prunus pattern, on signed "Taylor, Tunnicliffe & Co." creamware flower bowl base decorated in polychrome flowers. Lip of bowl is pierced in starbursts for flower insertions. Integral lamp cup has ribbed shoulder and pearled-top dome retainer, marked "S. Clarke's Patent Trade Mark Fairy" inside candle depression. Marked "1437A" on bottom. 5"h x 5.875"dia. $750-1000

Right:

Fig. 513
Acid Burmese pyramid-size dome, decorated in forget-me-not and butterfly pattern. Dome rests on ribbed shoulder in creamware lamp cup with rib pattern petticoat rim, "S. Clarke's Patent Trade Mark Fairy Pyramid" in blue inside recessed candle holder. "Taylor, Tunnicliffe & Co." and in script "1518' in red on cup bottom. Ormolu frame supports lamp, three matching Tapestry Ware bud vases with gilt knobs, and finger hold for moving lamp. 4.5"h x 6"w. $1000-1500

Fig. 514
Glossy Burmese pyramid-size dome, resting in "Taylor, Tunnicliffe & Co." Tapestry Ware lamp cup with smooth petticoat rim, "S. Clarke Patent Trade Mark Fairy Pyramid" inside recessed candle holder. Ormolu frame supports lamp, three matching bud vases, and brass fitting to support menu card. 4.75"h x 5.75"w. $750-1000

Fig. 515
Light pink satinized pyramid-size dome in smock pattern, set in decorated creamware lamp cup marked "S. Clarke's Patent Trade Mark Fairy Pyramid" in blue in recess and "Taylor, Tunnicliffe, Co." in script "1519" on bottom. Cup and three matching bud vases all held in rings on ormolu stand with peg for menu holder in rear. 5"h x 5.5"w. $500-750

Left:

Fig. 516
Pyramid-size dome, satin Peach Blow shading from rose to pink, cream-cased, decorated in English robin and foliage design, resting in signed "Taylor, Tunnicliffe & Co." Tapestry Ware base also marked "Rd. No. 93320." Base has integral lamp cup signed "S. Clarke's Patent Trade Mark Fairy Pyramid" in candle holder depression. Three integral bud vases also act as menu holder. 4.75"h x 5"w. $1000-1500

Fig. 517
Acid Burmese pyramid-size dome in 'Aladdin's lamp'-style creamware base signed "Taylor, Tunnicliffe & Co.," "1529" in red with zigzag line beneath, and "Rd #93321." The candle recess is marked "S. Clarke Patent Trade Mark Pyramid." 4.875"h x 4.25"w x 8.25"l. $500-750

Fig. 518
Acid Burmese fairy-size dome decorated in prunus pattern, set in Clarke Fairy lamp cup. Cup inserted in reversible decorated Tapestry Ware base signed "Taylor, Tunnicliffe & Co." and "1450" under crest, and "S. Clarke's Patent Trade Mark Fairy" inside the tubular post. 6.25"h x 7.5"w. $1000-1500

Fig. 519
Fairy-size dome in green Mother-of-Pearl and gold swirl with air trap, inward pinched top rim, resting in creamware lamp cup marked "S. Clarke's Trade Mark Fairy" in black in candle recess which holds Price's Sentinel Night Light candle in ribbed candle holder. Cup rests in footed porcelain base, decorated with foliage that is repeated inside bowl. Bottom of base impressed "Moore" and in script "M C Frier" with a thistle flower or upside-down crown. 5.375"h x 6.875"w. $750-1000

Fig. 520
Porcelain dome resembling a peeled orange with ribbing and coloring. Base resembles peel of orange with orange blossoms around sides and three small attached oranges as bud vases. Recess of integral lamp cup is marked "Rd No 113915, China Manufactured in France, S. Clarke's 'Fairy Pyramid' Patent Trade Mark," and holds clear curved candle holder with Price's Childs' Night Lights candle. 4.75"h x 5.125"w. $2000-3000

Right:
Fig. 521
Fairy-size dome in yellow satin Peloton glass with embossed ribs, cased, in matching ribbed lamp cup with rayed star impressed on exterior. Cup contains Clarke's Pyramid candle with sticker on bottom that reads "Made in England," in ribbed Clarke candle holder. Cup rests in 'Aladdin's lamp'-style pottery base impressed "S. Clarke's Patent Trade Mark Fairy" in cup base and "Doulton Burslem, Rd S3913," and impressed "Doulton & Slater Patent, AS63442" on bottom of base. 6.75"h x 7.75"w. $1500-2000

Fig. 522
Fairy-size dome, opalescent blue with embossed reverse drape pattern, set in Clarke lamp cup holding Burglar's Horror candle in ribbed Clarke candle holder. Cup rests in handled bowl-shaped pottery base decorated in blues and browns. Base marked "S. Clarke's Patent Trade Mark Fairy," impressed "Doulton Burslem" and "3276." 7.125"h x 6.5"w. $750-1000

Fig. 523
Fairy-size dome, opalescent and light sea green swirl, in matching lamp cup with tight upturned piecrust rim. Cup inserted in pedestal bowl with flared foot, marked on bottom "Doulton Slater Patent," "g," "g" in reverse, "u" with "t" coming off bottom corner, Doulton Burslem seal, "Clarke's Patent Trade Mark Fairy." 13.375"h x 5"w. $1000-1500

Fig. 524
Bisque floral dome, twenty petals in glossy pink shading white applied to bottom band. Dome rests in green and brown base footed with brown twigs, leaves forming upper rim. 4.625"h x 5.875"w. $500-750

Fig. 525
Frosted fairy-size dome, embossed ribs, marked "Clarke Trade Mark Pyramid" on forest green handled pottery base with integral candle holder and radiating ribs to lamp cup rim. Base embossed "Hampshire Pottery." 4.75"h x 4.75"w. $150-200

Fig. 526
Glazed porcelain decorated candle holder with child's head forming handle. There is no dome associated with this lamp. 2.5"h x 3.375"w x 5"l. $200-350

Fig. 527
Glazed porcelain decorated candle holder with angel's head and wings. Head forms handle. No dome associated with this lamp. 2.5"h x 3.375"w x 5"l. $200-350

GROUP 11

THREE-PIECE LAMPS, SKIRTS DOWN

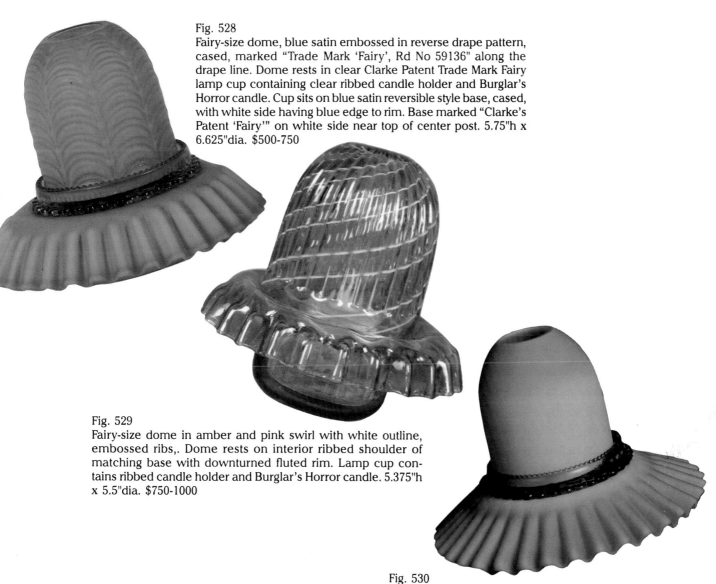

Fig. 528
Fairy-size dome, blue satin embossed in reverse drape pattern, cased, marked "Trade Mark 'Fairy', Rd No 59136" along the drape line. Dome rests in clear Clarke Patent Trade Mark Fairy lamp cup containing clear ribbed candle holder and Burglar's Horror candle. Cup sits on blue satin reversible style base, cased, with white side having blue edge to rim. Base marked "Clarke's Patent 'Fairy'" on white side near top of center post. 5.75"h x 6.625"dia. $500-750

Fig. 529
Fairy-size dome in amber and pink swirl with white outline, embossed ribs,. Dome rests on interior ribbed shoulder of matching base with downturned fluted rim. Lamp cup contains ribbed candle holder and Burglar's Horror candle. 5.375"h x 5.5"dia. $750-1000

Fig. 530
Acid Burmese fairy-size dome in straight-sided S. Clarke Trade Mark Fairy lamp cup containing clear ribbed candle holder and Clarke Pyramid candle. Cup rests on Burmese reversible base with ruffled rim. 5.5"h x 7.125"dia. $500-750

Left:

Fig. 531
Acid Burmese fairy-size dome in Clarke Patent Trade Mark Fairy lamp cup, bars on shoulder, slight depression for candle holder, and five dimple feet. Cup rests on rim of reversible base, decorated in larch pattern on petticoat rim. 5.25"h x 7"dia. $750-1000

Fig. 532
Acid Burmese pyramid-size dome decorated in prunus pattern, set in Burmese lamp cup marked "Clarke Trade Mark Fairy Pyramid" and containing Clarke's Pyramid ribbed candle holder marked "S. Clarke" in reverse on bottom. Cup rests on rim of matching reversible base with petticoat fluted rim. 4"h x 5"dia. $1500-2000

Fig. 533
Acid Burmese fairy-size dome decorated in woodbine pattern. Dome rests in S. Clarke Trade Mark Fairy Burmese lamp cup, containing S. Clarke Fairy ribbed candle holder and Clarke's Burglar's Horror candle. Cup rests in center post of matching reversible base with petticoat rim. Base signed "Thos. Webb & Sons Queen's Patent Burmese Ware" in reverse image and "Clarke's Patent Trade Mark Fairy" on opposite sides in interior of center post. 5.375"h x 6.75"dia. $2000-3000

Fig. 534
Acid Burmese pyramid-size dome, decorated in fuchsia pattern, in S. Clarke Fairy Pyramid lamp cup containing Clarke Trade Mark Fairy Pyramid candle holder and Burglar's Horror candle. Cup rests in center post of Burmese reversible base with petticoat rim decorated in a foliage pattern. 4.5"h x 4.75"dia. $750-1000

Fig. 535
Fairy-size dome with red satin ground, two-color Cameo design. Dome rests in clear Clarke Patent Fairy lamp cup, smooth-edged rim and top, containing slightly tapered ribbed Fairy candle holder and Clarke candle. Cup rests on rim of matching footed base, 2.625"dia. foot, flared petticoat rim similarly decorated with butterfly on back. 5.625"h x 5"dia. $3000-5000

Right:

Fig. 536
Fairy-size dome in three-layer Cameo design, white and pink on frosted ground, depicting cherry branch in flower. Dome rests in S. Clarke's Patent Trade Mark Fairy lamp cup containing ribbed Clarke candle holder and double wick candle incised "Saml Clarke's New Patent, Fairy." Cup rests on matching low footed bowl with petticoat skirt depicting mature cherry fruit on branch and dragonfly on back. Base signed "Thos. Webb & Sons, Cameo." Paper label still attached reading "Bailey, Banks & Biddle." This lamp was acquired with original box of remaining candles and an 1887 hand written note to the bride. 5.5"h x 5.5"w. $5000-7500

Fig. 537
Fairy-size dome in Herringbone pattern, cased, with four air vents in bottom rim. Dome rests on smooth shoulder in matching lamp cup containing Clarke candle holder. Cup rests on pink Mother-of-Pearl base in reverse drape pattern with air traps, cased base, marked "Clarke's Patent Fairy" in interior, downturned petticoat rim. 5"h x 6.125"dia. $500-750

Fig. 538
Nailsea-type pyramid-size dome with blue ground, sitting in clear lamp cup with crenelated ribbed top rim. Cup rests in bulbous bowl with a nearly horizontal 2.625"-wide rim in Northwood pull-up pattern. 4.625"h x 7.75"dia. $500-750

Fig. 539
Fairy-size dome, satin pink shading lighter in a reverse drape pattern, cased, marked "Rd 59136," "Trade Mark," and "'Fairy'" around exterior of bottom rim. Dome in Clarke Cricklite lamp cup containing double wick Clarke candle. Cup rests on downturned, embossed reverse drape rim of glossy cased base. 5.625"h x 7.25"dia. $500-750

Fig. 540
Fairy-size cased dome, yellow satin decorated with English robin and multi-colored foliage. Dome rests in double-shouldered S. Clarke's Patent Trade Mark Fairy lamp cup, smooth rim and upper edge, holding ribbed candle holder marked "US Patent 352296, Nov. 9, 1886," and Burglar's Horror Trade Mark Pyramid candle. Cup resting on downward fluted rim of matching yellow bowl with 2.25"dia. frosted foot. 6.5"h x 5.25"dia. $500-750

Fig. 541
Blue satin fairy-size dome, cased, resting in Clarke Patent Trade Mark Fairy lamp cup, which is ribbed and straight-sided. Lamp cup rests on petticoat rim of matching base with frosted round foot. Inside base marked "Clarke Patent Fairy." 6.5"h x 5.75"dia. $350-500

Fig. 542
Lightly cased fairy-size dome in a reverse drape pattern, resting in Clarke Patent Trade Mark Fairy lamp cup containing ribbed Clarke candle holder and Burglar's Horror candle. Cup rests in cased pink satin base marked "Clarke's Patent 'Fairy'," with downward petticoat rim, and 2.375"dia. frosted foot. 6.375"h x 5.5"dia. $500-750

Fig. 543
Acid Burmese fairy-size dome, decorated in prunus pattern, with paper label on interior reading "Queen's Burmese Ware Patented Thos. Webb & Son." Dome rests in Burmese lamp cup marked "S. Clarke Patent Trade Mark Fairy," containing ribbed Clarke candle holder and Burglar's Horror candle. Cup rests on top of petticoat rim of matching base with 2.375"dia. unrefired foot. 5.875"h x 5.25"dia. $2000-3000

Right:

Fig. 544
Red satin Mother-of-Pearl dome in acorn and flower pattern with air traps, cased, slightly egg-shaped with crimped and twisted top rim, in Clarke Patent Fairy lamp cup containing ribbed Clarke candle holder and Price's Sentinel candle. Cup sits on DQMOP cased base with 2.5"dia. frosted foot and downward petticoat rim. 6.5"h x 5.375"dia. $500-750

Fig. 545
DQMOP fairy-size dome, cased, slightly balloon-shaped, resting in Clarke Fairy lamp cup containing S. Clarke Trade Mark candle holder and Clarke's Patent Pyramid candle. Dome rests on edge of matching bowl with downturned fluted rim and 2.5"dia. frosted foot. Bowl marked "Clarke's Patent 'Fairy'." (#43, Appendix I) 6.25"h x 5.625"dia. $750-1000

Fig. 546
Fairy-size dome in pink, opaque, and white striped Cleveland pattern, sitting in frosted Clarke lamp cup containing Clarke ribbed candle holder and Burglar's Horror candle. Cup rests in matching base with 2.5"dia. frosted foot and downturned petticoat rim. (#37, Appendix I) 5.75"h x 5.25"dia. $500-750

157

Left:

Fig. 547
Fairy-size dome, pink DQMOP with embossed reverse swirl, cased. Dome sits in matching ribbed lamp cup, which rests on petticoat rim of matching base with 2.375"dia. opaque foot. 6"h x 5.875"dia. $750-1000

Fig. 548
Fairy-size dome in blue, white, and opaque Cleveland swirl pattern, in clear double-shouldered Clarke lamp cup containing clear candle holder. Cup rests on petticoat rim of matching color base with opaque 2.5"dia. foot. (Dome #4, Appendix I) 6"h x 5.5"dia. $750-1000

Fig. 549
Fairy-size dome in pastel rainbow DQMOP, cased, marked "Clarke's Patent Fairy" around exterior of bottom rim. Dome sits in Clarke Trade Mark Fairy lamp cup, which rests on petticoat rim of triangular matching base, marked "Patent," with berry prunt and three clear tooled feet. 6.75"h x 6"w. $3000-5000

Fig. 550
Acid Burmese fairy-size dome in straight-sided ribbed lamp cup marked "S. Clarke Patent Trade Mark Fairy," containing ribbed candle holder and Clarke candle. Cup rests on petticoat rim, sharply downturned, on matching triangular base with three unrefired applied feet. 6.875"h x 6"w. $750-1000

Fig. 551
Blue satinized fairy-size dome with translucent diamonds. Diamonds are thinner glass than opaque cross lines. Dome sits in blue diamond smooth-rimmed lamp cup, which rests on petticoat rim of matching reversible base. Down-turned petticoat rim loses the diamond pattern. 5.125"h x 5.375"dia. $500-750

GROUP 12

THREE-PIECE LAMPS, SKIRTS UP

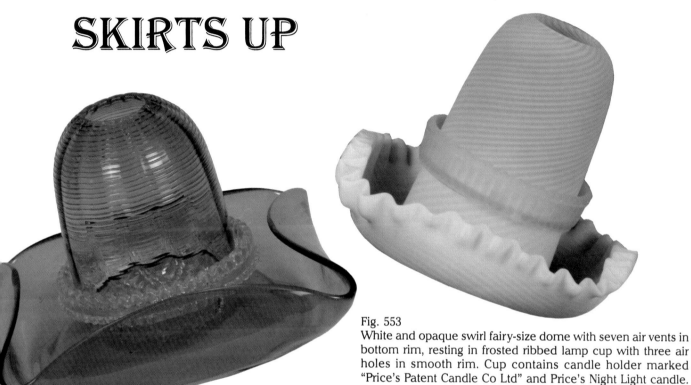

Fig. 552
Cranberry threaded fairy-size dome, lightly paneled, resting in Clarke lamp cup. Cup sits in cranberry quadrafold base with raised center to support cup. 4.875"h x 6.75"sq. $500-750

Fig. 553
White and opaque swirl fairy-size dome with seven air vents in bottom rim, resting in frosted ribbed lamp cup with three air holes in smooth rim. Cup contains candle holder marked "Price's Patent Candle Co Ltd" and Price's Night Light candle. Cup rests in center post of matching base with squared upright piecrust rim. 5.5"h x 6.375"sq. $750-1000

Fig. 554
Fairy-size dome in a two-tone aqua swirl, with six vents in bottom rim. Dome rests in matching lamp cup with upright piecrust rim, which sits in center post of matching square base with upright fluted rim. Lighter stripes have heavier texture. 6.25"h x 5.875"sq. $750-1000

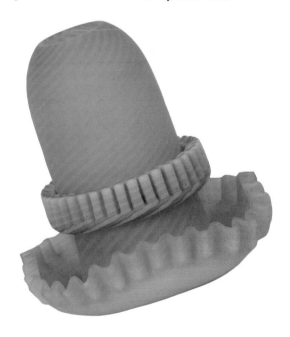

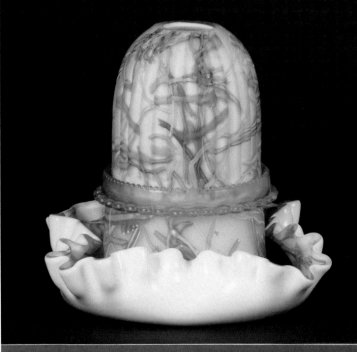

Left:

Fig. 555
Peloton glass fairy-size dome with embossed ribs, cased, marked "US Patent Nov 9, 1886." Dome rests in opaque lamp cup marked "S. Clarke's Fairy Patent" with "Trade Mark" across center, containing ribbed candle holder marked "352296" holding single-wick Clarke candle. Cup sits on center post of matching Peloton base with squared upright ruffled rim. 6"h x 6.5"sq. $750-1000

Fig. 556
Fairy-size dome in blue, white and opaque Cleveland swirl pattern with embossed ribs, in Clarke Fairy lamp cup containing Clarke ribbed candle holder and Clarke candle. Cup rests in matching swirled base with upright fluted rim. 4.875"h x 6"dia. $750-1000

Fig. 557
Fairy-size dome in cranberry waffle pattern with embossed ribs, resting in cranberry lamp cup in reverse swirl pattern. Cup sits in center post of matching waffle base with upright fluted rim. 5.5"h x 7.75"dia. $500-750

Fig. 558
Nailsea-type pyramid-size dome with citron ground, in S. Clarke Trade Mark Fairy Pyramid lamp cup containing Clarke candle holder and paper-wrapped, plaster-base candle. Cup rests in flared center post of matching base with upright ribbon rim. 4.25"h x 5.75"dia. $500-750

Fig. 559
Nailsea-type pyramid-size dome with red ground, in clear Clarke lamp cup resting on rim of center post of matching base. (#92, Appendix I) 5"h x 6.75"dia. $500-750

Right:

Fig. 560
Fairy-size dome, cranberry cut to clear in a four-in-one diamond pattern, with cut ribbed top rim. Dome rests in double-shoul-dered Clarke Patent Trade Mark Fairy lamp cup, ribbed crystal with smooth top and chrysanthemum-cut bottom, containing ribbed candle holder and Clarke candle. Cup sits in cranberry center post and bottom of base. Cut pattern repeats on upright sides of base. 5.375"h x 6.675"dia. $750-1000

Fig. 561
Fairy-size dome, opalescent white to green, diamond pattern. Dome sits in Clarke Trade Mark Fairy lamp cup resting on cen-tral post of opalescent base with upright green ribbon-edged rim. 5"h x 6.75"dia. $500-750

Fig. 562
Fairy-size dome in frosted yellow, white, and opaque swirled Cleveland pattern, resting in lamp cup marked "George Davidson, Est 1867, England." Cup rests in central post of match-ing base with upright piecrust edge. 5.75"h x 7.75"dia. $500-750

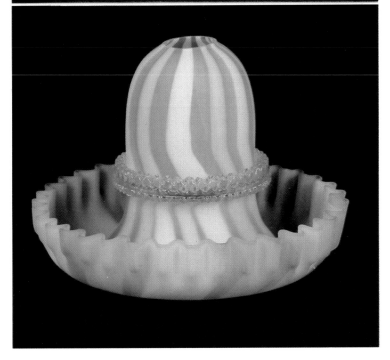

Left:

Fig. 563
Cranberry satin fairy-size dome in Clarke lamp cup containing Price's Sentinel candle. Cup rests in center post of matching base with upright fluted rim. 6"h x 7.5"dia. $500-750

Fig. 564
Fairy-size dome with opalescent diamond pattern over clear ground (forming thousand-eye type of design), in S. Clarke Patent Trade Mark Fairy lamp cup with smooth rim and smooth top. Cup contains ribbed clear candle holder, and rests in opalescent base shading to yellow with upright ribbon rim with clear crest. 5.25"h x 6.5"dia. $500-750

Fig. 565
China columnar dome, waisted with flared piecrust top rim, resting in clear lamp cup in center post of matching base with upright fluted rim. Dome and base decorated with blue flowers, brown leaves and gilt around rims. 7"h x 8"dia. $350-500

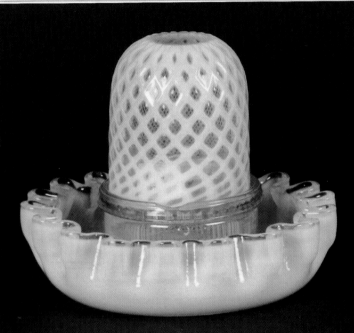

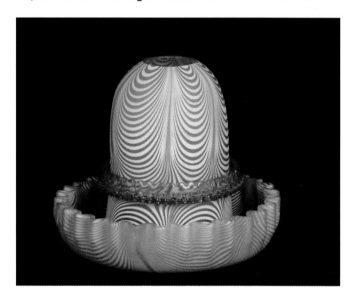

Fig. 566
Nailsea type fairy-size dome with blue ground, in clear Clarke lamp cup resting in center post of matching base with upright fluted rim. (#90, Appendix I) 5.25"h x 6"dia. $500-750

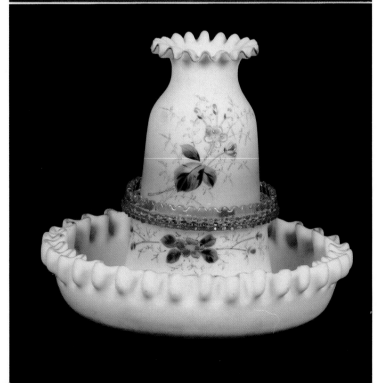

Fig. 567
Satin Peach Blow fairy-size dome, deep rose shading to light pink decorated with foliage, cream-cased. Dome rests over center post of matching base on a ring of exterior applied frosted rigaree. Post holds crossed metal straps that support Clarke ribbed candle holder and Clarke candle. Base has smooth upright rim. 5.5"h x 5.5"dia. $750-1000

Right:

Fig. 568
Fairy-size dome, yellow shading lighter, DQMOP, cased. Dome rests on upper row of yellow applied rigaree on central post of matching base with upward fluted rim. Post contains clear candle cup supported by crossed metal straps crimped over rim. 5.5"h x 6.625"w. $1500-2000

Fig. 569
Dome removed on Fig. 568 showing clear candle cup supported by crossed metal straps crimped over rim of central post.

Fig. 570
Cranberry fairy-size dome, lightly paneled and threaded, resting in Clarke lamp cup. Cup sits in center post of cranberry base with upward ruffled and fluted rim with threading below. 5.75"h x 8.5"dia. $500-750

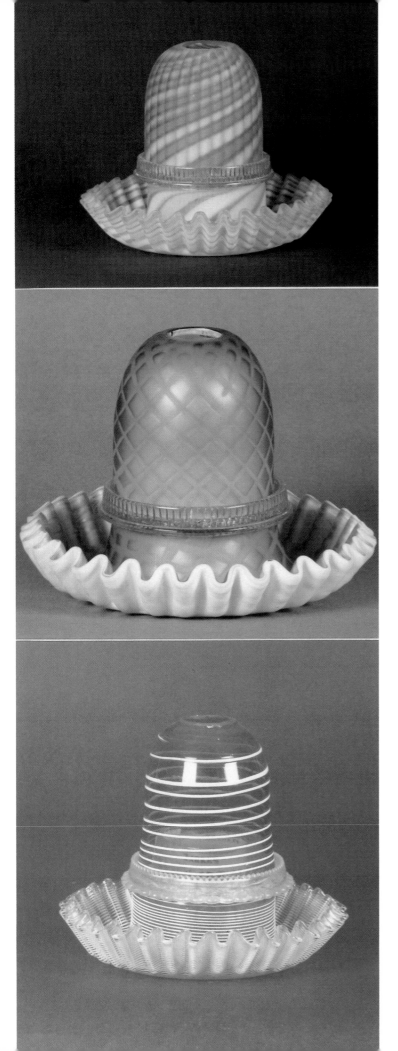

Left:

Fig. 571
Fairy-size dome in pink, white and opaque Cleveland swirl with embossed ribs, marked "'Rd' 50725, Trade Mark 'Fairy'" up the ribs. Dome rests on S. Clarke Patent Trade Mark Fairy lamp cup, double-shouldered with smooth-edged rim and upper edge, containing Clarke ribbed candle holder and Burglar's Horror candle. Cup rests on center post of matching base with upward fluted rim. (#55, Appendix I) 5.125"h x 7.5"dia. $750-1000

Fig. 572
Fairy-size dome, blue DQMOP, cased, resting in Clarke Fairy lamp cup with smooth-edged rim and top, containing Clarke Fairy candle holder with beaded top rim and Price's Sentinel 8 hr. candle. Cup rests on flared center post of matching base with upward flared piecrust rim. 5"h x 7"dia. $750-1000

Fig. 573
Cranberry fairy-size dome with applied white thread in spiral and narrowing pattern. Dome rests in Clarke's Fairy lamp cup containing ribbed Clarke candle holder and Clarke's Pyramid Trade Mark candle. Cup rests in center post of matching threaded base with upward flared ribbon rim. 5.5"h x 6.5"dia. $750-1000

Fig. 574
Acid Burmese fairy-size dome decorated in prunus pattern, resting in Burmese lamp cup embossed "S. Clarke Patent Trade Mark Fairy." Cup resting on rim of center post of Burmese reversible base decorated in prunus on the side with upward rim. 5.75"h x 5.25"dia. $2000-3000

Fig. 575
Nailsea-type fairy-size dome with red ground. Dome sits in S. Clarke Trade Mark Fairy lamp cup, which rests on rim of center post of matching base with upward flaring fluted rim. 6"h x 9.25"dia. $750-1000

Right:

Fig. 576
Fairy-size dome with embossed ribs, shading from deep to light raspberry, cased, marked "Rd 50725" and "Trade Mark 'Fairy'" on vertical front ribs. Dome sits in clear Clarke lamp cup, which rests on center post of matching reversible base. (#61, Appendix I) 4.75"h x 6.625"dia. $500-750

Fig. 577
Fairy-size dome with blue reverse drape, cased, etched on exterior of base "Rd No 59136" and "Trade Mark 'Fairy'." Dome sits in clear Clarke Fairy lamp cup, which rests in center post of matching reversible base with petticoat rim. 5"h x 6.5"dia. $500-750

Fig. 578
Fairy-size dome, blue satin shading lighter and decorated in enamel and Coralene in floral pattern, cased, with a crimped top rim, signed "WEBB" along exterior bottom rim in blue. Dome sits in satin cased base with integral lamp cup and upward flared and fluted rim signed "WEBB." Cup holds Clarke candle holder and Price's Sentinel Night Light candle. 5.375"h x 6.75"dia. $750-1000

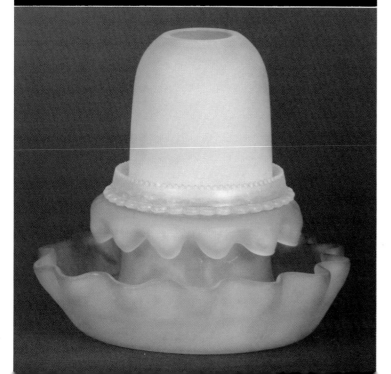

Left:

Fig. 579
Acid Burmese pyramid-size dome in S. Clarke Trade Mark Fairy Pyramid lamp cup containing Burglar's Horror Trade Mark Pyramid candle. Cup sits in center post of matching reversible base with upward flared piecrust rim. Base in this position has ormolu handled ring attached to center post in a .0625" deep x .375"w notch in Burmese. Frame marked "Menu Holder" on shaft going down center post, and "Clarke's Patent" on arm terminating in handle which is modeled as an embossed double-handled basket of flowers. 4.25"h x 5.625"w including handle. $500-750

Fig. 580
Acid Burmese fairy-size dome. Dome rests in opaque Clarke Patent Trade Mark Fairy lamp cup, double-shouldered with smooth rim, containing Clarke's Pyramid candle. Cup rests in matching reversible base signed "Thos Webb & Sons Queen's Burmese Ware" in reverse. 6.25"h x 7.125"dia. $500-750

Fig. 581
Fairy-size satin dome, shading from moss green to light green, in Clarke Trade Mark Fairy lamp cup. Cup rests on downturned ribbon top rim of tubular center post. Integral flower bowl has matching upright ribbon rim. 6"h x 6.75"dia. $500-750

Fig. 582
Cased fairy-size dome in medium blue shading to light blue satin, with impressed stars. Dome sits in Clarke Fairy lamp cup containing ribbed candle holder and Clarke Pyramid Trade Mark candle. Cup rests in short center post of cased, blue shaded base with upward fluted rim. 4.625"h x 6.5"dia. $500-750

Fig. 583
Cased fairy-size dome, deep pink satin shading lighter, impressed on two sides with angel head, stars, and new moon. Dome rests in Clarke's Patent Trade Mark Fairy opalescent lamp cup holding clear ribbed candle holder and "Saml Clarke Patent Fairy Trade Mark" candle. Cup rests in center post of matching base with upward flared fluted rim. 5.25"h x 6.5"dia. $750-1000

Fig. 584
End of Day fairy-size dome with crystal overlay, embossed reverse swirl, cased. Dome rests in clear lamp cup with heavy serrated rim. Cup, marked "Geo. Davidson, England, Est. 1867," holds clear candle holder and Clarke's Burglar's Horror Pyramid candle. Cup rests on lightly fluted, inward-crimped points of the matching base's flared rim, which is in the shape of an eight-pointed star. 5.75"h x 5.125"dia. $500-750

Fig. 585
Nailsea-type fairy-size dome with citron ground and very unusual *twisted* white looping. Dome sits in clear Clarke lamp cup resting in central post of matching base with upward fluted and ruffled rim. 5.5"h x 8.5"dia. $750-1000

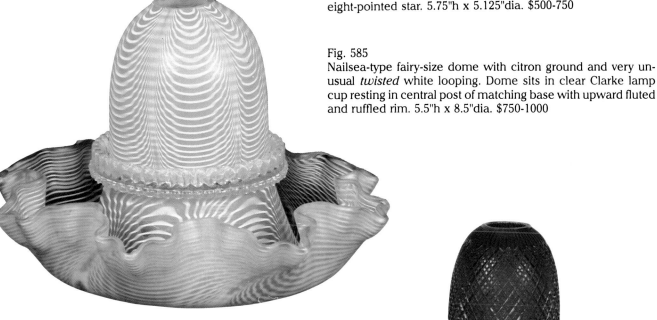

Fig. 586
Deep blue fairy-size dome, pressed glass in four-in-one diamond pattern with ribbing at both rims, in Clarke lamp cup. Cup rests on ruffled rim of center post of unmarked Doulton Burslem-type pottery base with upward floral decorated ribbon rim. 5.75"h x 8.5"dia. $350-500

Fig. 587
Nailsea-type fairy-size dome with red ground. Dome sits in Clarke Fairy lamp cup resting on center post of matching base with upright ribbon rim. Dome and base have strong red interiors. (#93, Appendix I) 5.75"h x 8.25"w. $500-750

Left:
Fig. 588
Pastel rainbow DQMOP dome, cased, elongated, with pinched upper rim. Clear lamp cup, marked "Patent Trade Mark S. Clarke Fairy," contains clear ribbed candle holder with Burglar's Horror candle. Matching base has a flared ribbon rim, and a center post shaped like a six-pointed star. Cup sits on the crimped top rim of the center post. 7.5"h x 7.75"dia. $5000-7500

Fig. 589
Nailsea-type fairy-size dome with green ground, on smooth shoulder of frosted lamp cup with tapered inward tight piecrust rim containing clear Clarke candle holder and Price's Sentinel candle. Cup sits on low matching bulbous base with horizontal fluted rim. 4.375"h x 5.625"dia. $750-1000

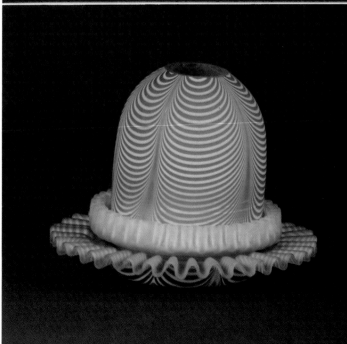

Fig. 590
Satin Fireglow pyramid-size dome, decorated in enamels, in Clarke Fairy Pyramid lamp cup holding Price's Palmitine ribbed candle holder. Cup inserted into matching low bowl base with 3.625" dia. foot. 4.75"h x 4.5"dia. $500-750

Fig. 591
Faintly reverse swirl fairy-size "Acorn" dome, shading from opaque to rose. Dome rests in Christmas-candy swirled ribbed lamp cup with inward piecrust rim. Cup rests on center post of matching base with upright piecrust rim. Colors in swirl are pink, yellow, pink, and blue repeated. Dome is not original to lamp. 5.75"h x 8"dia. $500-750

Right:

Fig. 592
Fairy-size dome in pink, white, and opaque swirled Cleveland pattern. Dome sits in Clarke lamp cup resting on rim of matching deep basket base with slightly fluted, ribbon rim. 6"h x 7.25"w. $350-500

Fig. 593
Fairy-size dome in yellow/green, embossed ribs with pulled spatter appearance. Dome sits in ribbed S. Clarke's Patent Trade Mark Fairy lamp cup, smooth-edged rim and top, containing holder and Clarke candle. Cup sits on rim of matching base with upright fluted rim. 5.375"h x 4"dia. $500-750

Fig. 594
Fairy-size dome with embossed ribs, pulled blue and white spatter appearance. Dome rests in ribbed S. Clarke's Patent Trade Mark Fairy lamp cup with beaded rim, containing holder and Clarke candle. Cup sits in matching base with upright fluted rim. 4.5"h x 5.5"dia. $500-750

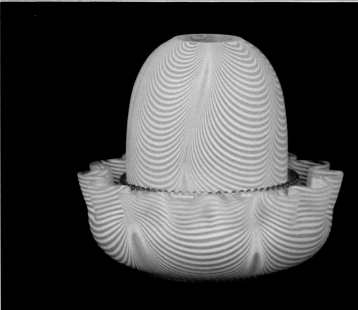

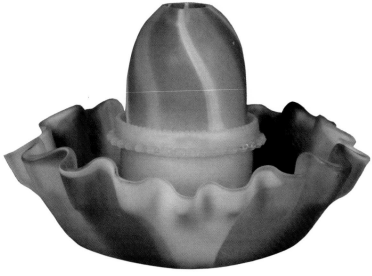

Left:

Fig. 595
Fairy-size dome in aqua satin Peach Blow, cream-cased, crimped top rim. Dome sits on clear Clarke lamp cup resting in matching upright curved bowl with six outward-drawn loops. 5.75"h x 6"w. $500-750

Fig. 596
Nailsea-type fairy-size dome with clear frosted ground, resting in Clarke Patent Trade Mark Fairy lamp cup containing ribbed Clarke candle holder. Lamp cup recessed in matching low bowl base with upright ribbon rim. 4.5"h x 5.375"dia. $750-1000

Fig. 597
French rainbow reverse swirl fairy-size dome, in frosted Clarke lamp cup. Cup is marked "S. Clarke Patent Trade Mark Fairy," and contains ribbed Clarke candle holder and Burglar's Horror candle. Cup rests in center post of large matching bowl with upward flared ribbon rim. 6"h x 10"dia. $1000-1500

Fig. 598
Fairy-size dome in pink, white, and opaque Northwood pull-up pattern. Dome sits in Clarke Patent Fairy lamp cup containing clear candle holder and Price's Sentinel Night Light candle. Cup rests on center post of matching base with outward flared ribbon rim. Base signed "Clarke's Patent 'Fairy'" on exterior of center post near top. 5.5"h x 6.875"dia. $500-750

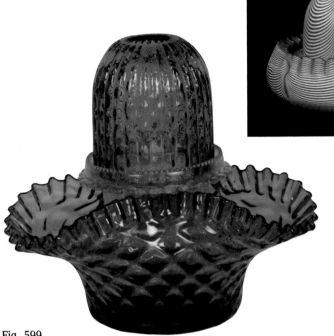

Fig. 600
Three Nailsea-type fairy-size domes, with (left to right) red, citron, and blue grounds. All sit in clear Clarke lamp cups in matching rounded bases with inward crimped rims. Diameter opening of end bases are 4.125". Opening of center base is 3.875" diameter. Red is 4.125"h, citron is 5.25"h, and blue is 4.375"h. All are 6"dia. $500-750 each

Fig. 599
Fairy-size dome in cranberry diamond-quilted, embossed rib pattern. Dome sits in Trade Mark Fairy lamp cup containing Clarke candle holder and double wick candle. Cup rests on three places of pulled, ruffled, fluted rim of the basket-shaped base, which is cranberry diamond-quilted. 7.5"h x 8"w. $500-750

Fig. 601
Satin Peach Blow fairy-size dome, deep rose shading to light pink, waisted, fluted and deeply ruffled top rim with opaque edge, four air vents in bottom rim. Dome rests in satin lamp cup with upright and slightly inturned heavy piecrust rim holding ribbed candle holder and Burglar's Horror candle. Cup rests on rim of Peach Blow bowl, which has six loops and is cream-cased. 6.5"h x 5.625"dia. $500-750

Fig. 602
Acid Burmese fairy-size dome decorated in forget-me-not pattern. Dome sits in Burmese lamp cup marked "Clarke's Patent Trade Mark Fairy," which rests on rim of gilt-edged triangular Burmese bowl, also decorated in forget-me-not pattern. 6.25"h x 5.25"w. $2000-3000

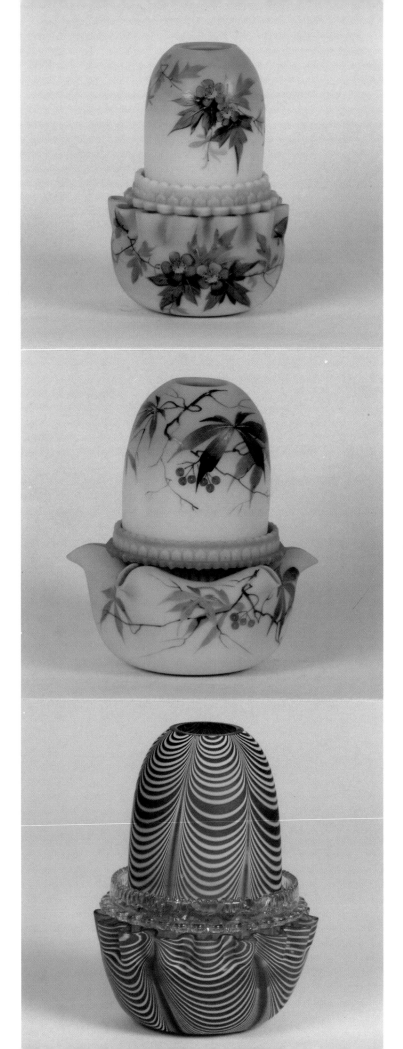

Fig. 603
Acid Burmese pyramid-size dome decorated in prunus pattern. Dome sits in Burmese lamp cup marked "Clarke's Fairy Pyramid Trade Mark," containing Burglar's Horror candle, resting on upright ribbon rim of small matching bowl. 5.125"h x 3.5"dia. $2000-3000

Fig. 604
Acid Burmese fairy-size dome decorated in woodbine pattern. Dome sits in Burmese lamp cup marked "S. Clarke Patent Trade Mark Fairy," containing clear candle holder. Cup rests on rim of matching bowl with rim pulled inward and down with five pulled-out spouts. Base signed "Thos. Webb & Sons, Rd. No. 67648, Queen's Burmese Ware." 6.375"h x 5.25"w. $2000-3000

Fig. 605
Nailsea-type fairy-size dome with dark blue ground and white loopings, in clear Clarke lamp cup resting on fluted rim of matching close-fitting bowl. 5.5"h x 4.5"w. $500-750

Fig. 606
Nailsea type pyramid-size dome with red ground. Dome sits in S. Clarke Fairy Pyramid lamp cup, which rests on inverted ribbon rim of ball-shaped matching base. 5.625"h x 4.75"dia. $500-750

Fig. 607
Satin Peach Blow fairy-size dome, cream-cased, decorated with Wild Rose pattern in dark green. Dome sits in clear Clarke lamp cup, containing a Radiant Night Light 8Hr candle. Cup rests on upright square-fluted rim of matching bowl. 5.75"h x 4.25"dia. $500-750

Right:
Fig. 608
Fairy-size dome in pink Mother-of-Pearl ribbon satin swirl, with pinched-in top rim. Dome rests in double-shouldered Clarke Fairy lamp cup with smooth top and rim, containing ribbed candle holder and "Saml Clarke's Patent Pyramid" candle. Cup rests on pinched-in rim of matching bowl. (#98 Appendix I) 6.125"h x 5.25"dia. $750-1000

Fig. 609
Satin fairy-size dome, shaded brown to pale gold, cream-cased, with crimped upper rim. Dome sits in US Patent Trade Mark Fairy lamp cup, which contains clear ribbed candle holder. Cup rests on six rounded scallops on upright crimped rim of matching bowl base. 5.625"h x 5.125"w. $500-750

Fig. 610
Citron Nailsea-type fairy-size dome in clear Clarke Patent Trade Mark Fairy lamp cup, which contains ribbed Clarke candle holder and Clarke Burglar's Horror candle. Cup rests on scalloped and fluted rim of matching oval-topped base with four pulled-out sections. 6.675"h x 7.875"w. $750-1000

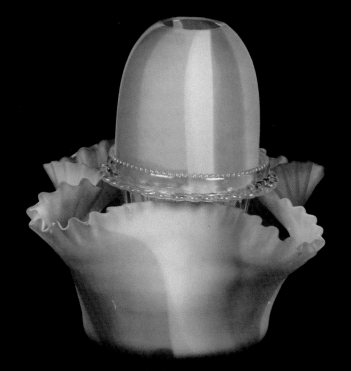

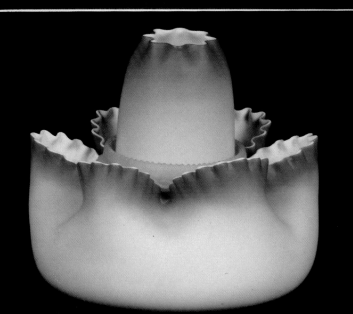

Left:

Fig. 611
Fairy-size dome in brilliantly colored satin finish Rainbow glass, sitting in clear Clarke Trade Mark Fairy lamp cup. Cup rests on crimped upright rim of a large rainbow glass bowl, which has four pulled-out sections. 7.25"h x 8.5"w. $1500-2000

Fig. 612
Satin Peach Blow fairy-size dome, shading from rose to light pink, cream-cased, with crimped top rim. Large matching bowl has a crimped five star formed rim to support the frosted Clarke Fairy lamp cup. 6.25"h x 7.5"dia. $750-1000

Right:

Fig. 613
Nailsea-type fairy-size dome, frosted deep pink ground with heavy wide white loops. Dome rests on clear Clarke lamp cup inserted in base's lamp cup cover on center post. Base has light pink ground and a lower bowl with upright piecrust edge. 6"h x 6"dia. $500-750

Fig. 614
Nailsea-type fairy-size dome with red ground, resting in pedestal lamp cup with clear ground and red Northwood pull-up pattern. Lamp cup is integral to the square base with upward fluted rim. Lamp cup has a base opening through the hollow pedestal. 6"h x 7.25"w. $500-750

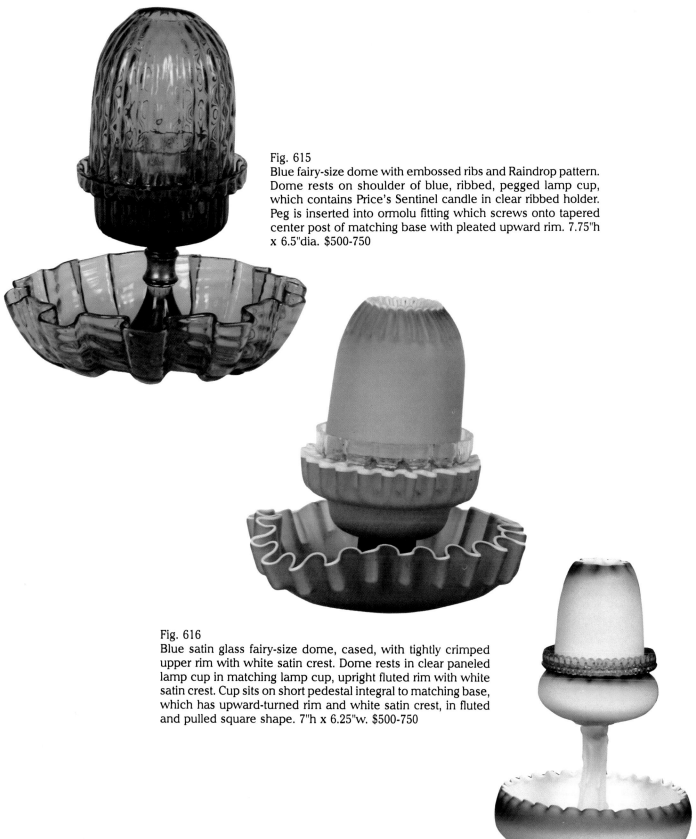

Fig. 615
Blue fairy-size dome with embossed ribs and Raindrop pattern. Dome rests on shoulder of blue, ribbed, pegged lamp cup, which contains Price's Sentinel candle in clear ribbed holder. Peg is inserted into ormolu fitting which screws onto tapered center post of matching base with pleated upward rim. 7.75"h x 6.5"dia. $500-750

Fig. 616
Blue satin glass fairy-size dome, cased, with tightly crimped upper rim with white satin crest. Dome rests in clear paneled lamp cup in matching lamp cup, upright fluted rim with with white satin crest. Cup sits on short pedestal integral to matching base, which has upward-turned rim and white satin crest, in fluted and pulled square shape. 7"h x 6.25"w. $500-750

Fig. 617
Butterscotch Peach Blow fairy-size dome, cream-cased, with inward fluted top rim. Dome sits in Clarke lamp cup containing Clarke ribbed candle holder and Burglar's Horror candle. Cup rests on inward fluted rim of cup, which is supported by frosted footed pedestal with tree-like roughness. Pedestal is applied to center of matching flower bowl base marked "BW" and underlined with Arabic script, with evidence of another illegible mark. This is part of Rustic Series. 9.5"h x 7"dia. $750-1000

GROUP 13

THREE-PIECE LAMPS WITH FEET

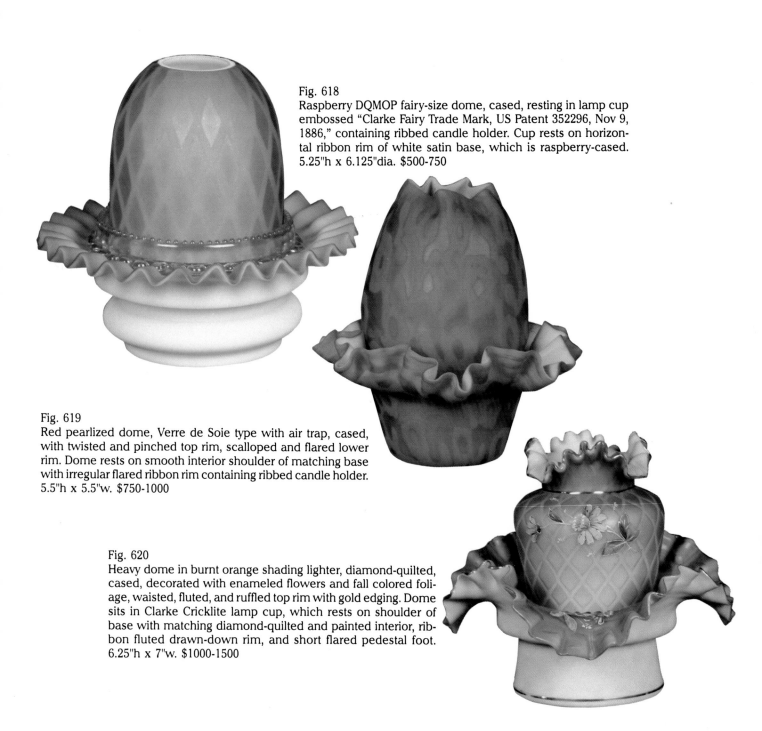

Fig. 618
Raspberry DQMOP fairy-size dome, cased, resting in lamp cup embossed "Clarke Fairy Trade Mark, US Patent 352296, Nov 9, 1886," containing ribbed candle holder. Cup rests on horizontal ribbon rim of white satin base, which is raspberry-cased. 5.25"h x 6.125"dia. $500-750

Fig. 619
Red pearlized dome, Verre de Soie type with air trap, cased, with twisted and pinched top rim, scalloped and flared lower rim. Dome rests on smooth interior shoulder of matching base with irregular flared ribbon rim containing ribbed candle holder. 5.5"h x 5.5"w. $750-1000

Fig. 620
Heavy dome in burnt orange shading lighter, diamond-quilted, cased, decorated with enameled flowers and fall colored foliage, waisted, fluted, and ruffled top rim with gold edging. Dome sits in Clarke Cricklite lamp cup, which rests on shoulder of base with matching diamond-quilted and painted interior, ribbon fluted drawn-down rim, and short flared pedestal foot. 6.25"h x 7"w. $1000-1500

Fig. 624
Satinized cranberry fairy-size dome, with Florentine decoration on all sides and three air vents in bottom rim. Dome rests in matching lamp cup with double stripe of Florentine, containing ribbed lamp cup and Clarke candle. Cup rests on waisted shoulder in bulbous bowl with 2.5"dia. footed base and outward flared fluted rim. 6.5"h x 5.25"dia. $350-500

Fig. 623
White satinized fairy-size dome, pink-cased, decorated with white and gold enameled flowers and green chevrons. Dome sits in Clarke Cricklite lamp cup, which rests on glossy petaled and slightly tooled rim of cased base. 7.75"h x 6.5"dia. $500-750

Fig. 622
Peach Blow fairy-size dome shading from blue to white, decorated with fall foliage outlined in gold enamel, waisted, horizontal piecrust rim edged in gilt. Dome sits in Clarke Cricklite lamp cup containing Clarke Pyramid candle. Cup rests in matching bulbous base with horizontal fluted rim. 6.5"h x 5.375"dia. $750-1000

Fig. 621
Cranberry fairy-size dome in diamond waffle pattern, with waisted, flared piecrust top rim shading to opaque, and seven air vents in bottom rim. Dome rests in Clarke lamp cup containing Clarke candle holder. Matching bulbous base also has outward flared piecrust rim. 7"h x 5.75"dia. $350-500

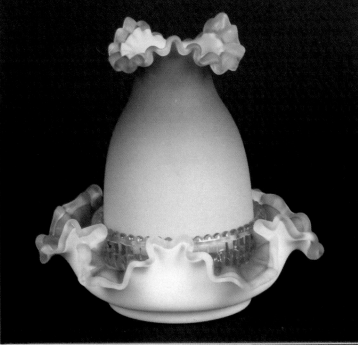

Fig. 625
Conical satin fairy-size dome, shading from deep burgundy to lavender, cased in pale blue, widely flared, ruffled and fluted rim with opaque glass edge. Dome in S. Clarke Trade Mark Fairy lamp cup resting in footed satin base, cased interior shading darker near fluted and ruffled rim with opaque glass trim. 6"h x 5.875"w. $350-500

Fig. 626
Lemon yellow DQMOP fairy-size dome, cased. Dome rests in Clarke's Patent Fairy lamp cup with smooth-edged rim and top, containing ribbed candle cup and "Saml Clarke's Patent Pyramid" candle. Cup sits in yellow matching base with horizontal fluted rim. 4.5"h x 6"dia. $500-750

Fig. 627
Cylindrical dome, marblized yellow with clear overlay, waisted, flared piecrust top rim with gilt edge, heavy gilt decorations on dome, two air vents in bottom rim. Dome sits in Clarke lamp cup, which rests on horizontal piecrust rim of matching low bulbous base. 5.875"h x 5.5"dia. $500-750

Fig. 628
Slightly rounded dome, opalescent green flared piecrust top rim shading to clear. Inverted opalescent thumb prints are formed from thicker glass. Dome sits in clear Clarke lamp cup, which rests on horizontal piecrust rim of bulbous footed opalescent green base. 5.5"h x 5.5"dia. $500-750

Fig. 629
Blue DQMOP fairy-size dome, with waisted and flared piecrust top rim, four vents in bottom rim. Dome rests in matching bulbous base on shoulder formed by waisted and heavily ruffled outward rim. 5"h x 5.5"w. $500-750

Fig. 630
Acid Burmese fairy-size dome in clear Clarke cup, resting within a matching bowl with flaring upward piecrust rim and 2.375"dia foot. 5.5"h x 5.5"dia. $500-750

Fig. 631
Pyramid-size dome, white satin milk glass decorated in small floral designs, three air vents in bottom rim. Dome sits in Eden Light lamp cup, which rests in recess of tri-color floral French Cameo quadrafold base. 3.675"h x 4.75"sq. $500-750

Fig. 632
Light orange DQMOP fairy-size dome with impressed drape pattern, cased, with four air vents in bottom rim. Dome rests in clear lamp cup holding Price's Improved Export Night Light candle. Cup rests in matching cased base, orange color shading lighter in recess, with a step or ridge on flared fluted rim with white crest. 4.75"h x 6.125"dia. $500-750

Fig. 633
Alexandrite fairy-size dome, shading from brownish blue to rose to pale citron yellow, by Thos. Webb & Sons, in Clarke's Fairy double-shouldered lamp cup containing Clarke's Patent Pyramid candle. Cup sits in matching bowl-shape base with an upright, twisted, fluted rim. 4.75"h x 5"dia. $2000-3000

Fig. 634
Two fairy-size satinized domes in blue and green, faintly swirled and textured, in clear lamp cups which have three small feet and center hole. Cups contain three-footed candle holders, and rest in hobnail bases that shade from near opaque at rim to dome color. These lamps resemble acorns. Made by Hobbs, Brocunier & Co., Wheeling, West Virginia. 5.5"h x 4.75"dia. $350-500 each

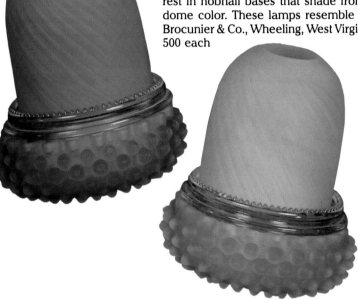

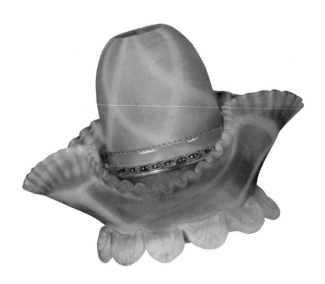

Fig. 635
Pyramid-size dome in stretch Millefiori, cased. Dome sits in matching lamp cup with short pedestal and 2.375"dia. foot. Colors terminate in a blob in center of foot, the remainder of which is clear. 4.625"h x 2.875"dia. $200-350

Fig. 636
Tartan pattern fairy-size dome, impressed "Tartan, Rd 46498" near the upper rim. Dome sits in clear S. Clarke Fairy lamp cup, which holds ribbed candle holder and Burglar's Horror candle. Cup rests on crimped rim of matching base pulled to form three loops. Base is supported on ring of tooled and applied frosted leaves. 5.5"h x 7.625"w. $1500-2000

Fig. 637
Arabesque fairy-size dome with cranberry ground, resting in Clarke Fairy lamp cup holding Burglar's Horror candle. Cup sits on ribbon rim of six pull-ins from the matching base, which has four frosted feet. 7"h x 6"w. $350-500

Fig. 639
Teal blue fairy-size dome, alternating diamond and four-in-one diamond pressed pattern, ribbed and scalloped bottom rim, marked "Rd No 92571" on interior just below top vent. Dome sits on smooth shoulder in matching chrysanthemum-impressed lamp cup, ribbed and scalloped rim marked "Rd No 92571." Cup sits in center post of matching embossed flower bowl base, which has upward flared ribbon rim, six applied tooled feet, and is marked "Rd No 92571" on interior. This lamp is known as the Floral Bijou Illuminator. 5.25"h x 4.625"dia. $350-500

Fig. 638
Cased pyramid-size dome in peppermint swirl pattern with embossed ribs, resting in matching lamp cup. Cup rests on crimped eight-pointed rim of matching base, which has four applied clear tooled feet. 5.625"h x 4.125"w. $350-500

Fig. 640
Blue and white spatter dome with clear overlay, embossed with half-round balls, with waisted and tooled top rim flared to form an eight-pointed star. Dome rests in matching base with tooled flared rim and applied clear icicle feet. Base holds Price's Export Night Light candle. 7.25"h x 6.5"w. $350-500

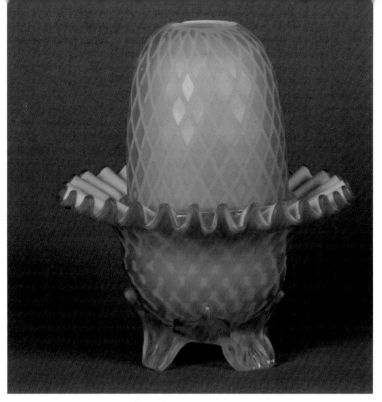

Fig. 641
Pink DQMOP fairy-size dome, cased, marked "Patent 'Fairy'" along exterior bottom rim. Dome rests on heavy serrated shoulder in Clarke's Fairy lamp cup, which has a smooth rim and contains a ribbed candle holder and Night Light candle. Cup rests on edge of outward fluted rim of matching base. Bottom has four frosted applied tooled feet and berry prunt. Inside bottom of base is marked "Clarke's Patent 'Fairy'." (#34, Appendix I) 6.25"h x 5.5"dia. $1000-1500

Fig. 643
Acid Burmese fairy-size dome, resting in lamp cup that is embossed "S. Clarke Patent Trade Mark Fairy," with straight ribbed side and pearled rim. Cup rests on waisted, flared, and scalloped rim of matching bowl base with three unrefired Burmese applied feet. 6.5"h x 4.875"dia. $750-1000

Fig. 642
Cranberry dome, etched "Clarke Patent Fairy" at bottom rim, resting in smooth-rimmed Clarke Patent Trade Mark Fairy lamp cup that contains clear ribbed candle holder. Tall cranberry base has petticoat piecrust rim with clear, tooled and applied petals that flare upward to hold lamp cup. Base also has clear, tooled and applied petal feet. 8.25"h x 6"dia. $750-1000

Fig. 644
Nailsea-type fairy-size dome with blue ground, sitting in clear Clarke lamp cup. Cup rests on inward flared ribbon edge rim of matching bowl base with three applied frosted wishbone feet. 7.5"h x 5.5"dia. $750-1000

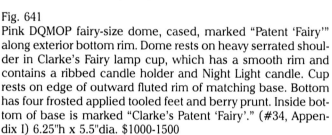

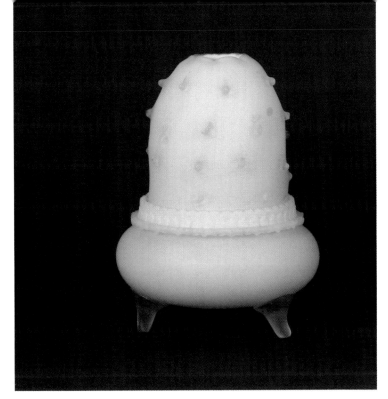

Fig. 645
Fairy-size dome with reverse swirl Cleveland pattern in blue, opaque and white. Dome rests in Clarke Patent Trade Mark Fairy lamp cup with smooth rim and top, containing ribbed candle holder and Burglar's Horror candle. Cup sits in base with wide shoulder, upright ribbon rim, and four frosted, tooled and applied wishbone feet. 5.75"h x 6.125"dia. $500-750

Fig. 647
Pale yellow satin fairy-size dome, cased, with pulled satin yellow thorns and slightly ruffled top rim. Dome rests in unrefired Burmese lamp cup embossed "Clarke Patent Trade Mark Fairy." Cup contains ribbed Clarke candle holder and Price's Sentinel Night Light candle. Cup rests on rim of matching satin bulbous base with three frosted applied feet. 6.125"h x 4.75"dia. $500-750

Fig. 646
Satin Peach Blow fairy-size dome, rose shading to light pink, cased, waisted and flared piecrust top rim with frosted crest, four air vents in bottom rim. Dome rests on smooth shoulder of glossy lamp cup, which has waisted base and clear crest on fluted rim. Waisted cup base inserts in center post of matching bowl with upward flared piecrust rim and eight applied pulled clear feet. 8"h x 7.75"dia. $1000-1500

Fig. 648
Nailsea-type fairy-size dome in shiny, transparent blue glass. Dome rests in Trade Mark Fairy lamp cup holding ribbed Clarke candle holder and Burglar's Horror candle. Cup sits on fluted rim of matching base which is pulled in at three places. Base has three tooled and applied blue feet. 7.5"h x 7.375"w. $1000-1500

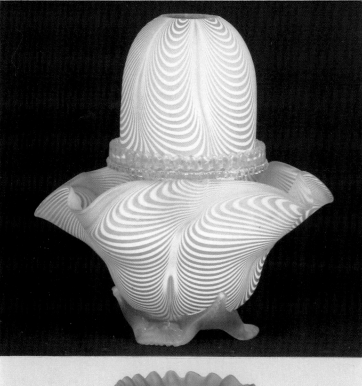

Left:

Fig. 649
Nailsea-type fairy-size dome with blue ground, sitting in clear Clarke Cricklite lamp cup. Cup rests on crimped six-pointed star rim of deep matching base, which has with three wide blue applied and tooled feet. (#46, Appendix I) 7"h x 5.875"w. $750-1000

Fig. 650
Nailsea-type fairy-size dome with blue ground, sitting in clear Clarke lamp cup. Cup rests on the matching base's rim, which is pulled inward to basic rectangular form. Base has applied blue tooled feet. 7.75"h x 7.75"w. $750-1000

Fig. 651
Blue satin fairy-size dome in Coin Spot pattern, waisted, flared and fluted top rim, four vents in bottom rim. Dome sits on shoulder in matching squat base with waisted, flared and fluted rim. 4.5"h x 5.125"dia. $500-750

Fig. 652
Two-color Cameo fairy-size dome with red satin ground, decorated with stylized flowers and two butterflies, lightly crimped top rim accented by Cameo scallops. Dome rests in Clarke lamp cup containing candle. Cup sits on rim of matching trifold base with white Cameo border with impressed chevrons. 4.875"h x 5.75"w. $2000-3000

Fig. 653
French Cameo dome decorated with vining, foliage and mush-rooms, cylindrical with slight bulge below ruffled and flared upper rim, flare near girdled bottom rim containing three vents. Dome rests in recess of low matching saucer with short green 3.5"dia. foot. Base contains Price's Sentinel candle in clear candle holder. Possibly Val St. Lambert. 6.625"h x 5.875"dia. $1500-2000

Right:

Fig. 654
Fairy-size dome in Northwood pull-up design with light blue ground, resting in S. Clarke Patent Trade Mark Fairy opalescent lamp cup with Clarke candle holder. Cup rests on three pulled-up portions of matching base's flared ribbon rim. Paneled base has embossed swirl and 4"dia. frosted blue foot. 6.75"h x 7.25"w. $750-1000

Fig. 655
Nailsea-type fairy-size dome with citron ground and very un-usual *twisted* white looping, in clear Clarke Trade Mark Fairy lamp cup. Cup rests on three pulled-in areas of matching base's upturned fluted and ruffled rim. Base has 3.625"dia. clear frosted foot. 6.5"h x 7"w. $1000-1500

Fig. 656
Nailsea-type fairy-size dome with blue ground and white loopings, in clear Clarke lamp cup. Cup is inserted into match-ing bowl with upright ribbon rim and 3.5"dia. blue foot. 5"h x 5.5"dia. $500-750

Fig. 657
Nailsea-type fairy-size dome with blue ground, in Clarke Cricklite lamp cup. Cup rests on fluted upright rim of matching base, which has four drawn-out spout-like ruffles and an opaque round foot. 6.5"h x 8.75"w. $500-750

Fig. 658
Two-color Cameo fairy-size dome, with light gold satin ground and white flowers and foliage. Dome rests in Trade Mark Fairy lamp cup holding ribbed candle holder and candle. Cup rests on quadrafold matching base with Cameo on each fold and 2.875"dia. foot. 5.625"h x 5.625"sq. $3000-5000

Fig. 659
Red satin fairy-size dome in reverse drape pattern, cased, resting in Clarke Fairy lamp cup with smooth rim and top. Cup holds ribbed candle holder and Clarke candle, and rests on rim of matching quadrafold base with opaque 3"dia. foot. (#150 Appendix I) 6.125"h x 5.5"sq. $500-750

Fig. 660
Acid Burmese fairy-size dome, decorated in ivy pattern highlighted lightly in silver. Dome sits in Burmese lamp cup containing clear ribbed candle holder and Clarke Pyramid candle. Cup rests on quadrafold Burmese base decorated in ivy pattern. 5.75"h x 5.75"sq. $2000-3000

Fig. 661
Acid Burmese fairy-size dome decorated in woodbine pattern, in Burmese lamp cup marked "S. Clarke Patent Trade Mark Fairy," containing ribbed candle holder and Saml Clarke candle. Cup sits on rim of matching quadrafold base with 3"dia. unrefired foot. 5.625"h x 5.5"sq. $2000-3000

Right:

Fig. 662
Acid Burmese fairy-size dome decorated in forget-me-not pattern, in Burmese lamp cup marked "S. Clarke Patent Trade Mark Fairy," containing Clarke ribbed candle holder. Cup sits on rim of matching quadrafold base with 3"dia. foot. Base signed "Clarke's Patent Trade Mark Fairy." 5.875"h x 5.75"sq. $2000-3000

Fig. 663
Acid Burmese fairy-size dome decorated in prunus pattern, in Burmese lamp cup marked "S. Clarke Patent Trade Mark Fairy." Cup contains candle holder with tightly ribbed and pearled top rim, marked "S. Clarke Trade Mark Fairy," and Clarke candle. Cup rests on rim of matching quadrafold base with 3"dia. unrefired foot. Base signed "Thos. Webb Queen's Burmese Ware." 5.75"h x 5.75"sq. $2000-3000

Fig. 664
Acid Burmese fairy-size dome decorated in larch pattern, in Burmese lamp cup marked "S. Clarke Patent Trade Mark Fairy." Cup contains ribbed Clarke candle holder and Clarke candle, and rests on rim of matching quadrafold base with 3"dia. unrefired foot. 5.875"h x 5.625"sq. $2000-3000

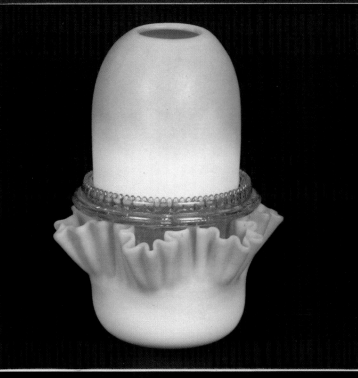

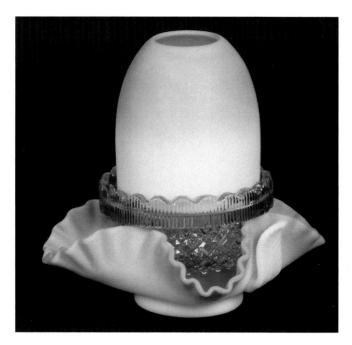

Fig. 665
Acid Burmese fairy-size dome, decorated in ivy pattern, in Burmese lamp cup marked S. Clarke Patent Trade Mark Fairy containing Clarke Pyramid ribbed candle holder and S. Clarke Pyramid candle. Cup rests on all pink Burmese quadrafold matching base with 2.75"dia foot marked "Thos. Webb & Sons, Queen's Burmese Ware." 6"h x 5.75"sq. $2000-3000

Fig. 666
Acid Burmese pyramid-size dome in clear lamp cup with embossed Fairy figure on the interior and "S. Clarke Trade Mark Fairy Pyramid" on exterior. Cup supported on crimped six-pointed star rim, which has deep piecrust edge. 5"h x 4"w. $500-750

Fig. 667
Acid Burmese fairy-size dome in Clarke Patent Trade Mark Fairy lamp cup. Cup rests in Burmese bowl-shaped base with 2.375"dia. foot. (#193 in Appendix I) 6"h x 4.25"dia. $500-750

Fig. 668
Acid Burmese pyramid-size dome in lamp cup with clear ribbed and scalloped rim, impressed multi-petaled chrysanthemum in bottom. Cup rests on four upright edges of matching base's crimped and ruffled rim. Base has 1.75"dia. unrefired foot and applied tooled unrefired leaf to hold menu card. 4.5"h x 3.75"w. $500-750

Fig. 669
Acid Burmese wee-size dome decorated in woodbine pattern, in clear lamp cup marked "Clarke Wee Fairy" and containing ridged clear candle holder and Clarke Wee Fairy candle. Cup sits in depression of squared Burmese base with upright scalloped rim and applied unrefired tooled leaf to hold menu card. Base has 2.125"dia. unrefired foot. 3.5"h x 4"w. $1000-1500

Right:

Fig. 670
Nailsea-type pyramid-size dome with blue ground, in S. Clarke's Trade Mark Fairy Pyramid girdled base lamp cup with Burglar's Horror candle. Matching base alternates three upright portions of ribbon rim with three flared-out portions, and has ring of frosted leaves below with one additional leaf going up to hold menu card. Base has paper label reading "Clarke's Patent" (in center), "Trade Mark Fairy" (across the top), "Class 13, 15, 16, and 47." Bottom of base etched "S. Clarke Patent 'Fairy'." 5.5"h x 5.125"dia. $500-750

Fig. 671
Acid Burmese pyramid-size dome in clear Clarke Fairy Pyramid lamp cup. Cup rests on piecrust crimped six-pointed star rim of matching base, which has an applied unrefired tooled leaf to support a menu card. Base signed "Thos Webb & Sons Queen's Burmese Ware" and "Patented Clarke Trade Mark Fairy." 5.5"h x 4.25"w. $500-750

Fig. 672
Acid Burmese pyramid-size dome in Fairy Pyramid lamp cup, which rests on petticoat rim of matching base with 2.125"dia. foot. One point of rim raised above base exposes an applied tooled feather to hold menu card. Base signed on each side of feather, "S. Clarke Patent Trade Mark" on left, and "Thos. Webb & Sons, Queen's Burmese Ware Patented" on right. 4.75"h x 4.75"w. $500-750

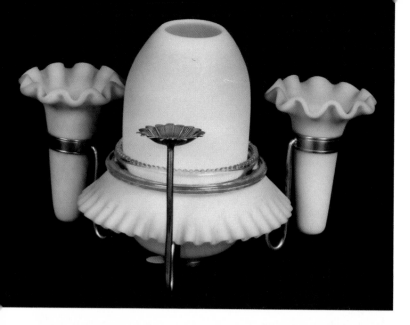

Fig. 673
Acid Burmese pyramid-size dome in Fairy Pyramid lamp cup containing ribbed candle holder. Cup rests on petticoat skirt of matching base, which is attached to an ormolu frame marked "*.. Clarke's Patent Fairy Lamps ..*" on disc at point of attachment. Frame also holds two bud vases with flared fluted rims. The raised petaled flower in front acts as menu card holder. 4"h x 5.25"w. $500-750

Fig. 674
Acid Burmese pyramid-size dome, surrounded by thin undulating horizontal accessory skirt. Dome rests on inner series of eight connected ribbed posts that comprise the lamp cup, marked "Clarke's Patent Pyramid, Rd 158336." The top quarter-inch of each ribbed post is stepped to permit the accessory skirt to rest on cup rim. 4"h x 4.25"dia. $500-750

Fig. 675
Acid Burmese pyramid-size dome shown in Figure 674, in lamp cup embossed "Clarke's Patent Pyramid, Rd 158336." Accessory skirt has been removed.

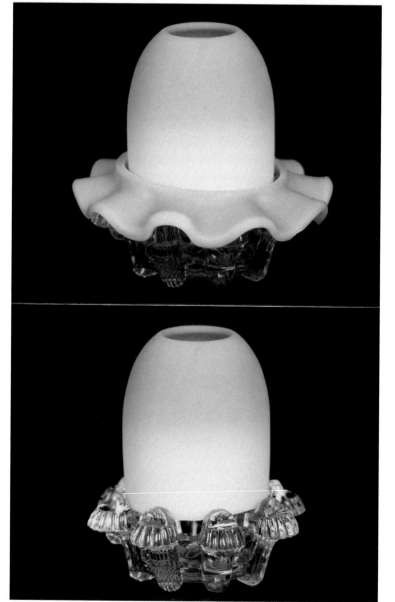

Fig. 676
Acid Burmese accessory skirt from Figure 674. 4.25"dia.

Fig. 677
Clarke's Patent Pyramid Rd 158336 lamp cup from Figure 674.

Fig. 678
Acid Burmese fairy-size dome, decorated with heavy gold in woodbine pattern, signed on interior "Thos. Webb & Sons Queen's Burmese Ware Patent" and "S. Clarke Patent Trade Mark Fairy." Dome sits in Burmese lamp cup marked "S. Clarke Trade Mark Fairy," which contains clear Clarke candle holder and Clarke candle. Cup rests on inward scalloped rim of matching base, attached by wafer to Burmese foot with outward piecrust rim. Base also marked "Thos. Webb & Sons Queen's Burmese Ware" and "S. Clarke Patent Trade Mark Fairy." 7"h x 4"dia. $2000-3000

Right:

Fig. 679
Acid Burmese fairy-size dome decorated in prunus pattern. Dome sits in Burmese lamp cup marked "S. Clarke Patent Trade Mark Fairy," which contains clear Clarke candle holder and Burglar's Horror candle. Cup rests on inward rolled rim with five outward spouts on matching bowl base, which has three applied unrefired Burmese feet. 7.125"h x 4.875"w. $2000-3000

Fig. 680
Acid Burmese fairy-size dome decorated in prunus pattern, resting in Burmese lamp cup embossed "S. Clarke Patent Trade Mark Fairy." Burmese lamp cup containing ribbed Clarke candle holder and Clarke's Burglar's Horror Pyramid candle. Cup rests on three inward curved sides of rim of base, which consists of a round matching Burmese bowl with three outward pulled corners, and three unrefired, applied Burmese looped legs. 7.25"h x 4.375"dia. $2000-3000

GROUP 14

FAIRY LAMPS ON STANDARDS OR EPERGNES

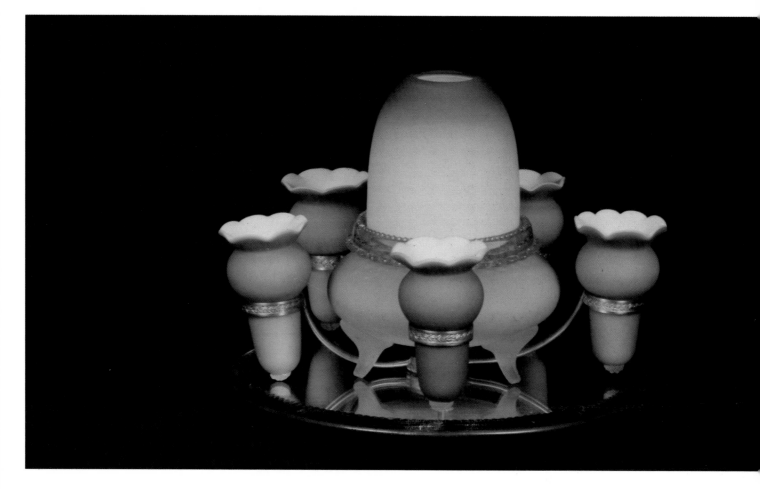

Fig. 681
Chocolate satin Peach Blow fairy-size dome, cream-cased, in clear Clarke Fairy lamp cup holding clear Clarke Fairy candle holder. Cup rests on inward turned rim of matching bowl with three applied opaque feet. Bowl straddles ormolu frame attached to round, notched mirror plateau with beveled edge. Frame is comprised of five arms each attached to decorated ring holding matching bulbous bud vase with flared scalloped top rim and applied opaque berry prunt. 6.5"h x 10.25"w. $2000-3000

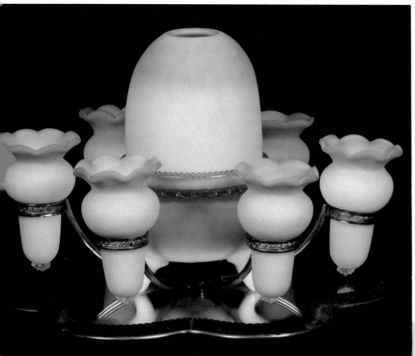

Fig. 682
Acid Burmese fairy-size dome in clear Clarke Fairy lamp cup. Cup rests on the inward turned rim of matching bowl with three unrefired applied feet. Bowl straddles ormolu frame marked "S. Clarke's Patent Trade Mark Fairy" in red on center attachment to a notched mirrored plateau with beveled edge and six scallops. Base of Burmese bowl signed identically around pontil mark. Frame is comprised of six arms, each attached to decorated ring holding matching Burmese bulbous bud vase with flared scalloped top rim and applied opaque berry prunt. 6"h x 10.25"w. $2000-3000

Fig. 683
Fairy-size dome in light blue satin shading lighter, cream-cased. Dome sits in frosted Patent Trade Mark Fairy lamp cup, which rests on upright ribbon rim of matching cream-cased base with four frosted applied feet. Lamp straddles the ormolu frame which is attached to a notched mirror plateau with six scallops and beveled edge. Frame supports six ornate embossed rings, each holding matching bulbous bud vases with flared scalloped top rims and applied opaque berry prunts. 6.75"h x 10.25"w. $2000-3000

Fig. 684
Acid Burmese pyramid-size dome in Clarke Fairy Pyramid lamp cup. Cup rests in center ring of cast brass frame with eight arms – four forming legs and feet, alternating with four holding rings for Burmese bud vases with Burmese retaining rings and berry prunts. Burmese is all decorated in prunus pattern. 4.25"h x 7.5"w. $1000-1500

Fig. 685
Three acid Burmese pyramid-size domes in Clarke Fairy Pyramid lamp cups resting in footed ormolu frame. Frame also supports three small bud vases with fluted and flared upper rims and berry prunts. Raised center rod with Burmese trim holds larger vase with petticoat rim. All vases have unrefired retaining rings. 8.25"h x 7"w. $1000-1500

Left:

Fig. 686
Epergne comprised of two acid Burmese fairy-size domes, signed "S. Clarke Patent Trade Mark Fairy" and "Queen's Burmese Ware" in red. Domes sit in clear Clarke lamp cups resting in footed cup rings, signed "....... S. Clarke's Patent Trade Mark Fairy .." on ormolu frame. Frame also holds two bud vases with flared ruffled rims and berry prunts, as well as a Burmese sleeve on central brass rod holding larger central bud vase with ruffled petticoat rim and Burmese knob on bottom. All vases are Burmese and have unrefired retaining rings. 10"h x 10"w. $750-1000

Fig. 687
Four acid Burmese fairy-size domes in Clarke Cricklite lamp cups containing Clarke Pyramid candles. Cups supported in rings on ormolu frame rising from a mirrored plateau. Three ormolu leaves attach to the frame between the three lower rings and arch downward toward the mirror. 9.675"h x 10.75"w. $1000-1500

Fig. 688
Ormolu metal frame with heart-shaped top in which sits clear frosted bird, below which are two small and two larger frosted tooled leaves with marked green veins. Ten additional leaves (three around each lamp, two on either side in center) decorate four-footed heavy brass rod stand. All glass attached with calyx-type fittings from which wire tendrils arise. Rings hold two pyramid-size domes, each green spangled, drag-looped, threaded in clear green glass. Domes rest in Clarke Fairy Pyramid lamp cups containing clear candle holders. 13.375"h x 10"w x 11.625"l. $1000-1500

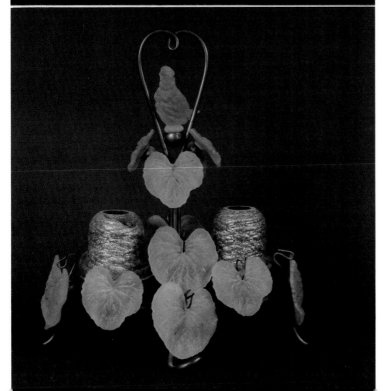

Fig. 689
Three fairy-size domes with embossed ribs, in pink, white, and narrow opaque striped Cleveland pattern, each marked "Rd 50725," "Trade Mark," and "'Fairy'" up vertical ribs. Domes sit in S. Clarke Trade Mark Fairy straight-sided lamp cups. Cups are supported by cup rings on ormolu frame, which also has smaller rings for three matching bud vases with horizontal piecrust rims, frosted retaining rings, and knobs. Ornate central post arises from round mirrored footed plateau, and holds ball-shaped bowl above frame. 10.25"h x 10"w. $1000-1500

Fig. 690
Epergne comprised of three acid Burmese pyramid-size domes in clear Clarke lamp cups. Each cup rests on six-pointed star crimped rim of a Burmese base. Bases are supported by crystal arms attached to holder in center of round mirrored plateau. Central crystal rod supports another Burmese base, which has a six-pointed star crimped rim that holds a fairy-size Burmese dome and Clarke lamp cup. Threaded wide brass base on central rod, when assembled, holds other rods in place. 13.5"h x 11"w. $1500-2000

Right:

Fig. 691
Three light blue Nailsea-type fairy-size domes in clear Clarke Cricklite lamp cups, supported on ormolu frame with tiered arms terminating in ringed cup holders. The frame is mounted in the center of oval mirrored plateau. 9.5"h x 6"w x 12"l. $750-1000

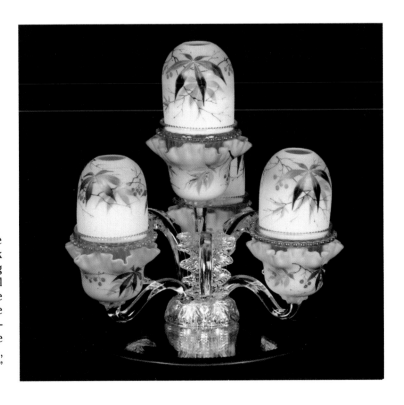

Fig. 692
Four acid Burmese fairy-size domes decorated in woodbine pattern, in clear lamp cups marked "Clarke Patent Trade Mark Fairy." Round mirrored plateau has attached holder supporting three tooled recurved crystal fronds and three curved crystal arms. Each arm is attached to woodbine decorated Burmese bowl with crimped star-formed rim to support the cup. Wide brass base of central crystal rod is attached to the fourth Burmese cup, and when assembled holds the other pieces to the plateau. Burmese cups are all signed "Thos. Webb & Sons, Queen's Burmese Ware" and "Clarke Patent Trade Mark Fairy." 13.75"h x 13"w. $3000-5000

Fig. 693
Three acid Burmese fairy-size domes decorated in ivy pattern. Each dome sits in Burmese lamp cup marked "S. Clarke Patent Trade Mark Fairy," containing Clarke ribbed candle holder and Clarke Burglar's Horror candle. Each cup rests in petticoat rimmed matching bowl signed "Thos. Webb & Sons Queen's Burmese Ware, Patent" on exterior and "S. Clarke's Patent Trade Mark Fairy" on interior near bottom. Base held under skirt by oversize ormolu ring with arm, one marked "Clarke's Patent Trade Mark 'Fairy'" with five dots before and three dots after, attached to central fitting. Matching elevated bud vase, with ivy decorated petticoat rim and throat, is inserted into decorated miniature rose bowl, which is attached to central ormolu fitting. This fitting sits atop trumpet-shaped standard and base, also in ivy pattern. 10.5"h x 13.5"w. $7500-10,000

Fig. 694
Epergne comprised of three acid Burmese fairy-size domes in Clarke lamp cups and three Burmese bud vases with fluted flaring rims, retaining rings, and berry prunts. These elements are fitted into rings on a six-armed ormolu frame arising from a miniature Burmese rose bowl. Bowl is supported by ormolu fitting on tubular center post of large Burmese flower bowl with upward turned piecrust rim and four unrefired Burmese ball feet. (#194, Appendix I) 13"h x 11.25"w. $2000-3000

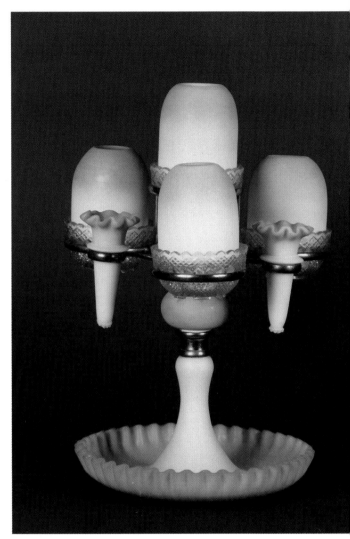

Fig. 695
Four acid Burmese pyramid-size domes in Clarke Fairy Pyramid lamp cups, and four flower vases with outward fluted upper rims, unrefired retaining rings, and berry prunts. These elements are all held in rings on ormolu frame with attached arms. Arms terminate in Burmese miniature rose bowl attached by ormolu fitting to wide flaring pedestal base with upright piecrust rim. 11.625"h x 7.75"w. $2000-3000

Fig. 696
Two pyramid-size acid Burmese domes, decorated in prunus pattern with single flower on each dome, in unrefired Burmese lamp cups. Cups are marked "S. Clarke Fairy Pyramid Trade Mark" and contain Burglar's Horror candles. Cups rest in rings on ormolu frame, which also has rings for two matching flower vases with applied unrefired retaining rings, berry prunts, and flared rims. The longer top vase resting in elevated ormolu ring has decorated downturned petticoat rim, berry prunt, and retaining ring. Frame terminates in decorated miniature rose bowl above ormolu spacer. Below ormolu spacer is Burmese trumpet-shaped pedestal and a low bowl-shaped base with upward flared fluted rim. Base is signed "Thos. Webb & Sons Queen's Burmese Ware" and "S. Clarke's Patent Trade Mark Fairy" on interior of trumpet. 9.75"h x 8.5"w. $3000-5000

Fig. 697
Four acid Burmese pyramid-size domes decorated in prunus pattern, in Clarke Fairy Pyramid lamp cups containing candle holders and candles. Cups sit in retaining rings on ormolu frame which elevates one lamp. Frame has small rings for three matching bud vases with flared ruffled rims, unrefired retaining rings, and berry prunts. Arms of frame gather in matching miniature rose bowl above ormolu fitting, which is attached to standard that terminates into matching upward flared base with piecrust rim. All Burmese pieces are decorated. 11.625"h x 7.75"w. $3000-5000

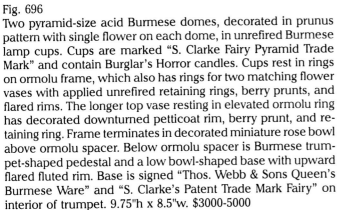

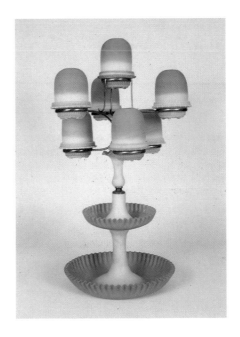

Fig. 698
Acid Burmese epergne with seven matching fairy-size domes in seven marked Clarke Burmese lamp cups, each containing Clarke signed candle holders and Clarke candles. Lamp cups are set in ormolu frame marked "Clarke's Cricklite" on cup rings. The single top cup ring is 21.5"h, the second tier of three rings is 18"h and the lower tier of three rings is 14"h. Epergne has bottom flower bowl with center post surmounted by bulbous brass fitting, which supports smaller upper flower bowl with center post. Upward threaded rod passes through hollow posts and brass fitting, to center the upper bowl and to hold the deep-throated ribbon-rimmed Burmese floret centered on rod with cast brass washer embossed "S. Clarke Patent Trade Mark Fairy." Cup frame attaches to center rod. 25.25"h x 24"w. $7500-10,000

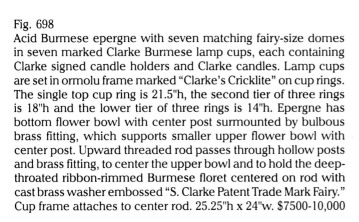

Fig. 699
From left to right: 1. Glossy puffy Poppy dome, stylized decoration, on matching hollow glass stand. 7.875"h x 4.25"w. 2. Glossy puffy undecorated Lilac and Butterfly dome on hollow glass stand. 8"h x 4.125"w. 3. Frosted puffy Lilac and Butterfly dome, naturalistic decoration, on mahogany stand. 10"h x 4.125"w. 4. Frosted puffy Poppy dome, naturalistic decoration, on mahogany stand. 10"h x 4.5"w. 5. Same, 7.625"h x 4.25"w. 6. Frosted puffy Chrysanthemum dome, naturalistic decoration, on metal stand with perforated air vents and integral candle holder. Stand inscribed "Pairpoint." 7.25"h x 4.5"w. All domes have waisted bottom rims signed "Pairpoint." $1000-1500 each

Fig. 700
Side views of lamps shown in Figure 699.

Fig. 701
Clear satin dome, decorated in blue cornflowers and green Coralene leaves on exterior and blue spatter on interior, giving decor an added dimension. Dome is signed "Pairpoint" and rests on smooth shoulder of matching lamp cup. Cup is supported by footed hollow pedestal base with interior spatter and ring of Coralene. 7.875"h x 4.25"dia. $3000-5000

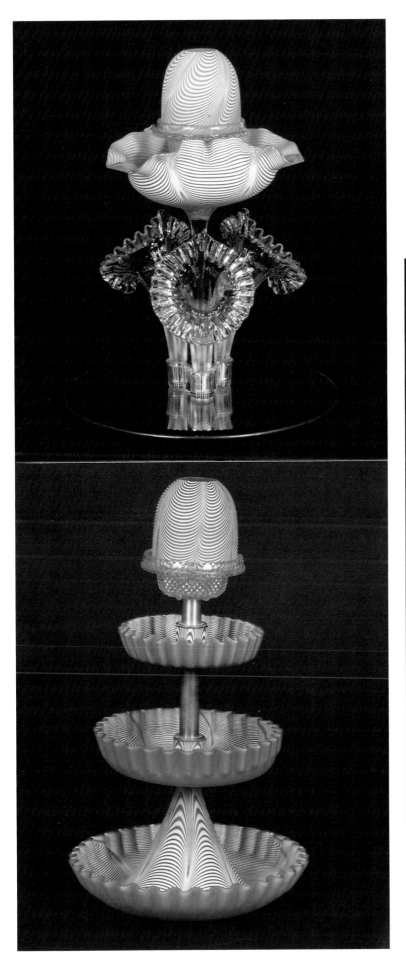

Fig. 702
Nailsea-type fairy-size dome with light blue ground, in clear Clarke Fairy lamp cup. Round mirrored epergne has attached holder supporting three clear trumpet-shaped flower holders and central crystal rod. Crystal rod holds matching Nailsea-type ruffled bowl, which supports the lamp cup on an upright rim pulled out in three places. Threaded wide brass base on central rod, when assembled, hold trumpets securely in place. 15"h x 12"dia. $750-1000

Fig. 703
Nailsea-type fairy-size dome with red ground and white loopings, resting on pegged clear Clarke Cricklite lamp cup. Cup sits atop three tiers of successively larger matching flower bowls. (#96, Appendix I) 16.25"h x 10"dia. $1000-1500

Fig. 704
Parian dome with four different embossed cherubs and ormolu bands on top and bottom rims, resting on porcelain lamp cup containing Price's Sentinel Night Light candle. Cup sits on integral footed standard with young peasant girl in patched dress holding sheath of wheat by column. Basket match holder at her feet. Base marked "SGDG, Registered, Germany." 13"h x 5.75"dia. $350-500

Left:

Fig. 705
Clear ribbed dome resting on smooth shoulder of painted glazed porcelain lamp cup. Cup sits on decorated standard behind Victorian woman dressed in high fashion, holding closed fan in left hand. Round base marked illegibly. 9.25"h x 3.25"dia. $200-350

Fig. 706
Rose DQMOP pyramid-size dome, cased. Dome rests in lamp cup atop bisque tree-like standard behind two figures — cavalier, and lady with bun hairdo and fruit in left hand. Figures stand on oval footed base marked on bottom "DEP," "17991" with "56" below and "Germany." 10.74"h x 4"w x 4.5"l. $350-500

Fig. 707
Pair of porcelain rose-shaped domes with applied petals, green bands and applied calyxes. Domes rest in lamp cups on footed standards, behind bisque cherubs which hold garlands of flowers. Bases marked "SGDG." Each is 11.5"h x 4"w. $350-500 each

Fig. 708
Clear ribbed dome with bottom vents, resting on smooth shoulder in lamp cup. Painted bisque girl holding cup and wearing yellow underskirt, blue dress, pink hat, and black shoes. She stands by square footed embossed pedestal painted in various shades of green, which supports an applied lamp cup embossed with pink and green flower swags. Bottom of pedestal embossed "DRGM" and "Registered" (in block letters). 10.75"h x 3.125"dia. $200-350

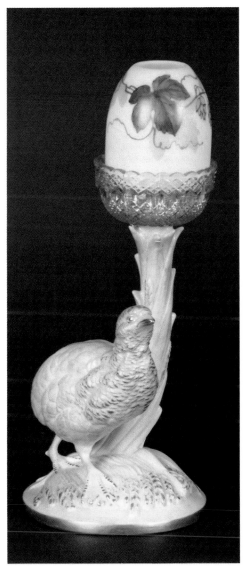

Fig. 709
White acid Burmese pyramid-size dome, decorated in hops pattern, in pegged Clarke Fairy Pyramid lamp cup holding clear candle holder. Peg is inserted in foliage stalk on base depicting young turkey with sheath of wheat under his feet. Base marked "Royal Worcester, England," nine dots, "(1900)," and "G 9 85, Grainger Factory, 1897." 10.375"h x 4.5"w. $750-1000

Fig. 710
Pyramid-size dome, pale gold DQMOP, cased, resting in pegged Clarke Fairy Pyramid lamp cup. Cup sits in standard of footed pottery base marked "Royal Worcester, England, Rd 41797, 1131" in plum color and impressed "40" and "25." "Hadley" is marked on side of statue. 13.75"h x 4.25"w. $750-1000

Fig. 711
Spun glass dome in the shape of devil with horns, goatee, and hair emerging from ears, in Christmas candle cup with flared and scalloped top rim. Cup rests on clear footed pedestal base that used to be gilt decorated. Fabric leaves are attached with tape. 9"h x 2.25"w. $500-750

Fig. 712
Eight pink tooled glass petals attached to green metal base, decorated with calyx, on metal stem with two tooled light green leaves arising from metal base. 10"h x 4.25"w. $150-200

Fig. 713
Embossed artichoke-shaped dome in overshot orange flashed glass, with waisted bottom rim. Dome sits on pedestal frame marked "Goldsmiths and Silversmiths Co Ltd., 112 Regent St, W" (London). Top of pedestal is intertwined branches attached to circular platform holding dome and Burglar's Horror Trade Mark Pyramid candle. 11.125"h x 5.5"w. $500-750

Fig. 714
Blue satin Peach Blow dome, cased, decorated with English robin and foliage, resting in pegged Cricklite lamp cup. Lamp cup is inserted in S-shaped ormolu stand with applied metal leaves. Cup contains clear candle holder and Burglar's Horror Pyramid candle. Stand has rings, marked "Trade Mark Cricklite," for two crystal bud vases with retaining rings and bottom knobs. Stand is supported on rayed crystal foot. 16"h x 8.875"w. $750-1000

Left:

Fig. 715
Pair of crystal domes with brass rings embossed "Cricklite" in Clarke Cricklite lamp cups. Cups are supported in cup rings signed "Clarke's Trade Mark Cricklite" on ormolu frame. Miniature Cairo water carrier and standard in glazed Parian is made in Royal Worcester Ware, and base is signed "Trade Mark Cricklite, Rd No 84463, #1890, Royal Worcester, England" with twelve dots (indicating manufacture in 1903). Base impressed "P11" and "10." 19"h x 15.5"w. $1000-1500

Fig. 716
Pair of clear Cricklite domes on clear Cricklite lamp cups, with white silk replacement shades on original frames (originally seen with deep red, beaded shades). Cups rest in rings signed "Clarke Cricklite," supported by arms of ormolu frame attached to Ming tree standard. Base also contains female figure, decorated in heavy gilt, holding lyre. Base marked "Trade Mark 'Cricklite', Royal Worcester, Made in England," "143" over "H," and ....*.... (1924). 25.25"h x 17.5"w. $1000-1500

Fig. 717
Pair of clear Cricklite domes with brass rings embossed "Cricklite" in clear Cricklite lamp cups. Domes have second ridge to hold silver shades lined in pink silk with strings of glass beads attached. Double arm ormolu frame, marked "Clarke Trade Mark Cricklite" inside cup rings, is on swirled crystal standard with swirl pattern footed base. Standard also holds an ormolu frame with two crystal bud vases in Clarke Cricklite signed rings. 19.25"h x 16.5"w. $500-750

Fig. 718
Pair of crystal domes with brass rings embossed "Cricklite," in Cricklite lamp cups resting in rings signed "Clarke's Trade Mark Cricklite." Rings supported on two arms of bright ormolu frame, attached to decorated, mottled alabaster Corinthian column. Column sits on square, stepped alabaster base. 26.5"h x 15"w. $1000-1500

Fig. 719
End of Day fairy-size domes with embossed ribs, cased, in clear Clarke lamp cups. Cups are held in "Clarke Trade Mark Cricklite" cup rings on ormolu frame attached to classic weighted brass Corinthian column. 18"h x 15"w. $500-750

Fig. 720
Pink porcelain rose-shaped domes, inner band with applied series of petals, marked "Rd 46391." Domes rest in Clarke Trade Mark Patent Fairy lamp cups in ormolu frame marked "Clarke Cricklite" in rings. Frame attached to sharply cut footed standard. 17"h x 15"w. $1500-2000

Fig. 721
Pair of crystal domes with brass rings embossed "Cricklite" in Cricklite lamp cups. Cups rest in signed "Clarke's Trade Mark Cricklite" rings on two arms of ormolu frame, which is attached to pressed glass footed standard in swirl pattern. 20.5"h x 15"w. $500-750

Fig. 722
Three yellow DQMOP fairy-size domes in matching lamp cups with corrugated shoulders and applied crystal knobs. Cups are marked "Clarke Patent Fairy" on exterior below rim. Three matching bud vases with applied clear retaining rings and knobs are also supported in this cast brass frame. Frame is attached to footed crystal pedestal in swirled, ribbed pattern. Pedestal is surmounted by matching onion-shaped finial. 14.75"h x 9.75"w. $2000-3000

Fig. 723
Three crystal domes, each with four cut stylized stars, in Clarke Cricklite lamp cups. Cups are resting in rings marked "Clarke's Trade Mark Cricklite" on silver frame attached to crystal standard and footed base, cut in diamond pattern. Ring at junction of cup frame and standard is marked "Clarke's Trade Mark Cricklite." Three crystal bud vases with diamond-cut tops are held in silver rings, marked "Trade Mark Cricklite," attached by second frame below ball on standard. 19.875"h x 13.25"w. $750-1000

Left:

Fig. 724
Three Nailsea-type fairy-size domes with red ground, resting in Clarke Cricklite lamp cups held by rings signed "Clarke Cricklite." Rings supported by silver pegged frame in silver Corinthian candle stick. 15.75"h x 13"w. $750-1000

Fig. 725
Three Nailsea-type fairy-size domes with red ground, resting in clear Clarke Cricklite lamp cups containing Clarke Cricklite candle holders. Cups are supported by cup rings, marked "Clarke's Trade Mark Cricklite," at the end of three arms of ormolu frame. Frame supported by frosted glass standard depicting three seahorses bordered by feathered wings on ribbed base. 14.25"h x 12.5"w. $1000-1500

Fig. 726
Three clear Cricklite domes with second ridge to hold matching pierced silver shades signed "Gorham & Co." Domes rest in Clarke Cricklite lamp cups held by rings on silver-plated frame. Frame is mounted on cut crystal standard embossed on base "US Pat 696275, 18th Aug 1908, English Pat 28495, Dec 1907." 22"h x 18.75"w. $750-1000

Fig. 727
Four clear domes with brass bands embossed "Cricklite," in Clarke Cricklite lamp cups resting in rings on pewter frame. Frame is supported by pewter standard arising from footed mirror plateau. 15"h x 13.25"w. $350-500

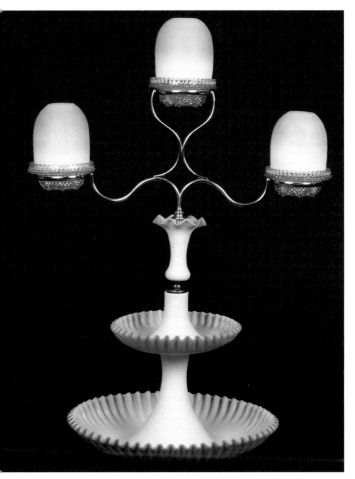

Fig. 728
Three acid Burmese fairy-size domes in Clarke Cricklite lamp
cups in rings on ormolu frame. Epergne has bottom flower bowl
with central post surmounted by bulbous brass fitting which
supports upper smaller flower bowl with central post. Threaded
rod passes through hollow posts and brass fitting to center both
the upper bowl and the deep-throated ribbon-rimmed Burmese
floret, with cast brass washer embossed "S. Clarke Patent Trade
Mark Fairy." Cup frame attaches to center rod. 26"h x 17.75"w.
$1500-2000

Right:

Fig. 729
Three acid Burmese fairy-size domes in Burmese lamp cups
embossed "Clarke Patent Trade Mark Fairy," containing clear
Clarke Cricklite candle holders. Cups rest in rings signed
"Clarke's Trade Mark Cricklite," on ormolu frame. Frame rests
on candlestick pedestal with ribbon drape pattern, four-leaf
clover shape, 11"w. Flower bowl base is decorated in orange,
flesh, and seagreen with gilt highlights. Base marked "Designed
and Made for Clarke's Cricklite Specially. Royal Worcester, England," with seven dots (indicating 1898), "Rd No 323188," beneath is mold mark "2019" and written "B 71." 18"h x 13.5"w.
$2000-3000

Fig. 730
See front jacket and page 2.

Fig. 731
Seven Nailsea-type fairy-size domes with red ground, resting in
Clarke Cricklite lamp cups in retaining rings, signed "Clarke's
Trade Mark Cricklite." Rings are supported by bright ormolu
frame inserted into cut crystal trumpet. The trumpet sits above
signed ormolu fittings, which are atop tapered, faceted crystal
column. The base of the column is bell-shaped cut crystal, supported by a four-footed ormolu base with a cloven hoof design.
A second scrolled frame holds four matching crystal bud vases
with scalloped flared rims, cut bulbous portion, and stems terminating in knobs. (See center lamp, Appendix G) 31"h x 21"w.
$5000-7500

Left:

Fig. 732
Pair of acid Burmese fairy-size domes decorated in forget-me-not pattern, in pegged Clarke Cricklite lamp cups containing Clarke Burglar's Horror Pyramid candles. Cups are inserted into ormolu fitting atop the vessels (decorated with Greek Key design) carried by the barefooted Grecian water carrier figurines, each of which carries a double-handled jug along left side. Bases are marked "Trade Mark 'Cricklite', Royal Worcester, England, .*..," (completed in 1919) and "2" over "125" in plum or purple marking. One is also embossed with "M" (clay mark for 1912). 16.875"h x 4"w. $3000-5000 pair

Fig. 733
Gothic arches embossed in frosted dome with slightly flared base. Dome rests on four bars on shoulder of lamp cup atop frosted standard. Lamp cup impressed "Desmarias" and "Robitille Limitee." Cup holds tulip-form white opalescent candle holder embossed "Pat Sept 1930." 9.5"h x 5"dia. $150 each

Fig. 734
Four clear Cricklite domes with brass bands embossed "Cricklite." Domes rest in clear Cricklite lamp cups supported on pair of double-armed frames terminating in cup rings signed "Clarke's Trade Mark Cricklite." Frames attached to pair of cut glass standards on scalloped bases. 17.75"h x 18.5"w. $2000-3000/pair

Fig. 735
Four crystal domes with brass bands embossed "Cricklite," in Cricklite lamp cups containing clear candle holders. Cups rest in signed "Clarke Trade Mark Cricklite" rings on silver plated frames, which are supported by pair of brilliant cut glass footed standards. 18.75"h x 14.75"w. $2000-3000/pair

Right:

Fig. 736
Chimney-style clear dome engraved with American eagle, resting in lamp cup on square-footed pedestal of hobstar pressed glass. 11.5"h x 3.5"sq. $50-100

Fig. 737
Dome with tooled, petaled top rim, with converging ribs shading from pink opalescent to clear lavender. Dome rests in lamp cup on a clear crystal footed standard with a pressed pattern. 9.5"h x 4.5"dia. $150-200

Fig. 738
Elongated fairy-size dome with opaque and blue swirl, scalloped bottom rim, resting in cut glass lamp cup on cut crystal standard with six embossed feet in "chicken-feet" design. 16.125"h x 5.625"w. $350-500

Fig. 739
Floral pyramid-size dome with blue ground and three rows of applied upturned tooled clear petals, marked "Trade Mark Fairy Made Abroad" in script. Dome rests in diamond point lamp cup on scalloped footed standard. 9.25"h x 4"w. $350-500

Fig. 740
Yellow satin pyramid-size dome, cased, decorated with foliage and English robin, resting in lamp cup of pressed glass on heavy pedestal footed base. Cup contains Clarke's Pyramid candle. 11"h x 4"sq. $350-500

Fig. 741
Crystal cylinder with slightly flared bottom rim, in honeycomb pressed lamp cup on standard. Standard has alternating smooth and beaded swirl pattern, atop honeycomb impressed base with scalloped rim. Price's Sentinel Night Light candle in lamp cup. 11.25"h x 4"w. $150-200

Right:
Fig. 742
Nailsea-type fairy-size dome with blue ground, in pegged Clarke lamp cup inserted in pressed crystal candle stick. 11.5"h x 4"dia. $350-500

Fig. 743
Fairy-size dome with white ground and blue cut-velvet pattern, in pegged Clarke lamp cup containing Burglar's Horror candle. Cup inserted in crystal candle stick. 13.75"h x 4.75"w. $350-500

Fig. 744
Clear double-stepped chimney dome in ten-sided rim, paneled, pegged lamp cup in squatty rayed candlestick. (advertised in the Fostoria catalog on November 11, 1909). 7"h x 5"w. $150-200

Fig. 745
Fairy-size dome in satin Peach Blow, dusty pink to light pink, cream-cased, decorated with English robin and foliage. Dome rests in pegged Clarke Fairy lamp cup containing clear ribbed candle holder and Clarke Pyramid candle. Cup pegged into ormolu candlestick, marble standard, and four-footed base of marble framed in brass. 11"h x 4"w. $500-750

Fig. 746
Fairy-size dome in Peach Blow type glass, rose shading to white, cased in pale blue, with waisted, flared, and scalloped rim. Dome rests in pegged Cricklite lamp cup inserted into crystal candlestick with rows of stalactites and petaled foot. 14.5"h x 4.375"w. $350-500

Fig. 747
Nailsea-type fairy-size dome with light blue loopings on darker blue ground, in Clarke lamp cup. Cup is attached by ormolu screw fitting, marked "Clarke Trade Mark Fairy," to diamond pattern standard attached to beveled mirror plateau. Base on three half-ball feet. 15.75"h x 7.875"dia. $350-500

Right:
Fig. 748
Fairy-size dome in frosted white Peloton glass, resting in Clarke Cricklite lamp cup containing Clarke Burglar's Horror Pyramid candle. Cup is attached to diamond-cut pedestal with rayed footed base by a brass ferrule. 9.5"h x 4"dia. $500-750

Fig. 749
Cased fairy-size dome, blue with embossed reverse drape pattern, marked "Rd 62029" on bottom exterior. Dome rests in pegged Cricklite lamp cup inserted into gold fitting atop cut glass standard. Standard ends in controlled bubble ball supported on rayed round foot. 16.875"h x 4.375"dia. $350-500

Left:

Fig. 750
Fairy-size dome, diamond-cut, cranberry to clear, resting in clear pegged lamp cup containing Clarke Fairy ribbed candle holder and Burglar's Horror candle. Cup inserted into brass fittings on cut glass standard. Square glass base has diamond cut pattern underneath. 13.25"h x 3.75"dia. $750-1000

Fig. 751
Clear dome with brass band marked "Cricklite," in pegged Clarke Cricklite lamp cup. Cup is inserted in brass and cut glass standard marked "Clarke's Trade Mark Cricklite" in brass, on top of square platform. 14.25"h x 4.25"sq. $500-750

Fig. 752
Light blue DQMOP fairy-size dome, cased, marked "Clarke's Patent 'Fairy'" around exterior bottom of rim. Dome sits in matching lamp cup holding Clarke's Pyramid Trade Mark candle in ribbed candle holder. Cup has applied frosted clear rigaree over the rim and is marked "Clarke's Patent 'Fairy'." Cup has ormolu fitting, onion-shaped matching standard, and ring of applied frosted clear rigaree, above flaring trumpet base terminating in ring of frosted rigaree. Interior of trumpet also marked "Clarke's Patent 'Fairy'." (#70, Appendix I) 11.75"h x 12.875"dia. $2000-3000

Fig. 753
Cased Emeralite-type fairy-size dome in Clarke Cricklite pegged lamp cup. Cup sits in brass fitting above crystal swirl and green threaded pedestal above stepped brass footed base. 13"h x 4"sq. $350-500

Right:

Fig. 754
Cased Emeralite-type fairy-size dome in Clarke Cricklite pegged lamp cup. Cup is on top of telescoping brass candlestick marked "Clarke's Patent Trade Mark Cricklite," on square platform above square pedestal. 14"h x 4"sq. $350-500

Fig. 755
The 4" telescoping nickel shaft extended, a feature of the lamp shown in Figure 754. 18"h x 4"sq.

Left:

Fig. 756
Elongated ruby dome, paneled on interior, in matching pegged lamp cup embossed "Blue Cross Candle Lamp." Base of cup and peg are clear glass, integral candle holder and ridging to rim for air. Peg sits in two-piece mold candle stick. 11"h x 3.875"dia. $150-200

Fig. 757
Fairy-size dome in ruby cut-velvet type pattern, resting in pegged Clarke's Trade Mark Cricklite lamp cup. Cup sits in brass fitting above cut glass stem attached to square stepped brass base, which is stamped "Trade Mark Cricklite" on two sides under lip. 13.75"h x 4"sq. $350-500

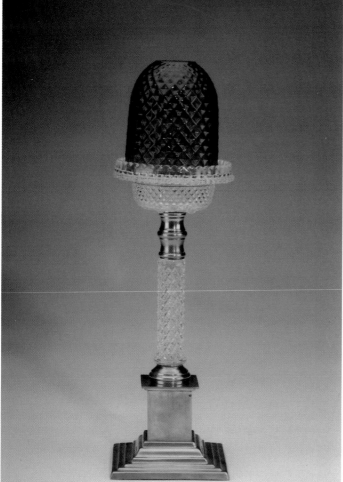

Fig. 758
Elongated fairy-size dome, opalescent blue satin shading lighter, with embossed swirl originating at bottom rim and fading near top. Dome sits on blue and white marbleized glass base with retaining ring, from which radiate upward slanted arms terminating in vertical bars, which allow for a variety of dome sizes. Lamp cup is attached to ormolu fitting and heavy cast brass cone-shaped base, decorated, with "Price's Patent Candle Company Limited" impressed around exterior bottom rim. 9"h x 4"dia. $750-1000

216

Fig. 759
Red and white spatter glass dome, tapered, with double-waisted flared top rim and girdled bottom rim, in bulbous base with stepped standard and round footed base. Fired-on gold and black decorations are continuous across both pieces. The clear pegged candle holder, 2"dia. at top x 3"h, with 1"-long finished peg, inserts into hole in standard's narrow neck. 10.875"h x 4.25"dia. $200-350

Right:

Fig. 760
Satinized cobalt blue dome decorated in white enamel, with waisted top rim and girdled bottom rim. Dome is inserted in white lined rim of matching pedestal and footed base. 10.25"h x 4.125"dia. $200-350

Fig. 761
Pink satinized dome with impressed vertical grooves, flared crenelated top rim, gilt trim and remnants of elaborate painting, in Clarke Cricklite lamp cup. Cup rests on rim of white satinized bowl, which is atop pink satinized footed standard with remnants of elaborate gilt painting. Pedestal wrapped with opaque snake with gilt eyes. 14.25"h x 5.5"dia. $200-350

Left:

Fig. 762
Nailsea-type fairy-size dome with blue ground, resting in Clarke Cricklite lamp cup in matching base. Attached frosted thorn stem sits on tooled feet. Rustic pattern. 7.75"h x 4"dia. $750-1000

Fig. 763
Melon-shaped blue satin dome with blown-out ribs, threaded and cased. Dome rests in matching tall footed standard, shading from light to dark, with same blown-out ribbing and threading plus two pearled rings. 8.25"h x 4.125"dia. $500-750

Fig. 764
Fairy-size dome in yellow, white, and opaque striped Cleveland pattern, in matching lamp cup containing clear stepped candle holder and candle. Cup rests on petticoat rim of bulbous standard base with flared, fluted, inverted bowl-shaped foot. Standard decorated with frosted rigaree at top and bottom. 10.5"h x 5.875"dia. $1500-2000

Fig. 765
Acid Burmese fairy-size dome decorated in woodbine pattern, in signed Clarke Burmese lamp cup. Cup rests on matching decorated bowl with piecrust petticoat rim attached with brass collar to matching decorated footed standard. 10.5"h x 5.75"dia. $3000-5000

Right:

Fig. 766
Fairy-size dome with embossed reverse swirl ribbing, with swirls of white and opaque green, two ground air vents in bottom rim, resting in matching ribbed lamp cup. Cup sits in matching flared base with applied pink petals, on tall pedestal with four applied tooled pink feet in the shape of petals. Another four petals are folded back over standard. 13"h x 5.75"dia. $500-750

Fig. 767
Blue overshot pyramid-size dome with embossed reverse swirl ribbing, with two ground air vents in bottom rim. Dome sits in blue reverse swirl lamp cup, which rests on rim of blue over-shot shell-pattern base. Base is supported by overshot pedestal with applied clear tooled feet. 9"h x 4.5"w. $350-500

Left:
Fig. 768
Pyramid-size dome, blue and white spatter with clear overlay, embossed petal pattern, and two ground air vents in bottom rim. Dome sits in matching ribbed lamp cup, which rests in matching base. Base has petal pattern with downward row of six heavy tooled and applied clear leaves above the standard, which is footed with row of six leaves. 8.5"h x 4.625"w. $350-500

Fig. 770
Pyramid-size dome with embossed reverse swirl ribbing, swirls of white and opaque green, and two ground air vents in bottom rim. Dome rests in matching lamp cup with embossed ribs, supported by matching base on tall pedestal with applied tooled pink feet. 9"h x 3.875"w. $500-750

Fig. 771
Light blue satinized dome with embossed square grid pattern, waisted and scalloped top rim, and multiple small air vents in bottom rim. Dome rests in lamp cup on standard in matching footed base. 5.5"h x 4"dia. $150-200

Fig. 769
Yellow satin pyramid-size dome with embossed swirl and two ground air vents in bottom rim, sitting on shoulder of reverse swirl lamp cup. Cup rests on rim of yellow satin bulbous bowl on footed standard with six applied opaque tooled leaf feet. 9.25"h x 4.25"w. $350-500

GROUP 15

HANGING & WALL-
MOUNTED LAMPS

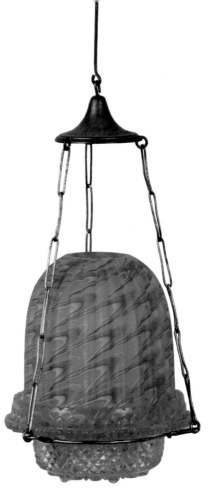

Fig. 772
Smoke bell embossed "Clarke's Patent London, Trade Mark Fairy," supporting long oval links that hold ring, on which rests Clarke lamp cup. Cup contains ribbed opaque fairy-size dome in Northwood pull-up pattern in coral and citron. 13"h x 4.375"w. $350-500

Fig. 773
(Left) Nailsea-type fairy-size dome with citron ground, resting in Clarke lamp cup. Cup is supported by hanging cup ring marked "Clarke's Patent Fairy," suspended by ormolu chain. Metal smoke bell is marked "Clarke's Patent London, Trade Mark Fairy." Overall length from hook is 13" x 4.5"w. Length of chain from smoke bell to ring is 6". (Right) Pyramid-size dome with same markings on hanger. Overall length from hook is 13" x 3.5"w. Length of chain from smoke bell to ring is 6.75". $350-500 each

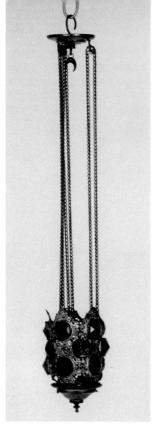

Fig. 774
Jeweled ormolu dome resting on base which contains ribbed Pyramid candle holder. Dome can be raised on chain and pulleys by pulling on the base finial, allowing the candle to be lit or replaced. Note crescent moon hanging between pulleys. 19.25"h inc. chain x 4"w. $200-350

Fig. 775
Pair of Nailsea-type fairy-size domes with citron ground, resting in Cricklite lamp cups. Short chain is attached to handle of fruit basket, and double arms arise from sides of basket bottom to support cup rings. 11"h. including chain x 11.5"w. $500-750

Fig. 776
Citron Nailsea-type pyramid-size dome in lamp cup marked "Eden Light Cup." Cup rests on ruffled ribbon rim of matching hanging base with clear frosted point at bottom. 15.75"h from top of chain to bottom point x 5.5"dia. Lamp itself 6.25"h. $750-1000

Fig. 777
Nailsea-type fairy-size dome with blue ground, in Clarke Fairy lamp cup resting inside rim of matching hanging base with bottom ball and blue frosted point. Rim of base is ribbon petticoat. 14"h from top of chain to bottom point x 7.5"dia. Lamp itself 7.5"h. $750-1000

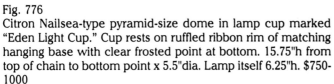

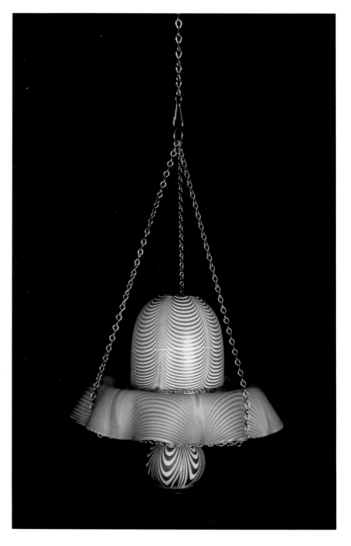

Fig. 778
Nailsea-type fairy-size dome with citron ground, in Clarke Cricklite lamp cup resting on tricorn ribbon rim of matching hanging base with camphor point. 15.5"h including chain x 8"w. Lamp itself 8"h. $750-1000

Fig. 779
Nailsea-type fairy-size dome with red ground, in embossed "Clarke Patent Trade Mark Fairy" lamp cup. Cup rests in matching bowl-shaped hanging base with upward fluted rim, Nailsea ball and clear frosted point. 23.5"h including chain x 6"w. Lamp itself 7.75"h. $750-1000

Fig. 780
Pyramid-size glossy Burmese dome in creamware cup, resting in glossy Burmese base with glossy unrefired Burmese scalloped retaining ring and flared ribbon rim. Ormolu cup ring passes through notched oval mirror. 11.5"h x 7"w. $750-1000

Fig. 781
Blue etched fairy-size dome, French, with Greek Key design around bottom rim. Alternating black and white designs depict maid with water bucket on head (black design), woman looking stern (white design), maid with broken bucket (black design), angry face on woman (white design), maid feeding the chickens (black design), very angry face on woman (white design). Dome rests in lamp cup marked "S. Clarke Patent Trade Mark Fairy" with smooth rim and top in removable ring marked "S. Clarke's Patent Fairy." The number "87" is cast into bracket passing through beveled mirror frame. 8"h x 5"w. $500-750

Fig. 782
Blue pyramid-size dome flecked with mica and drag-looped silver glass threading. Dome rests in Clarke Patent lamp cup in hinged ormolu ring with arm through plush frame, to which a beveled and scalloped mirror is attached. 8"h x 4.75"w. $500-750

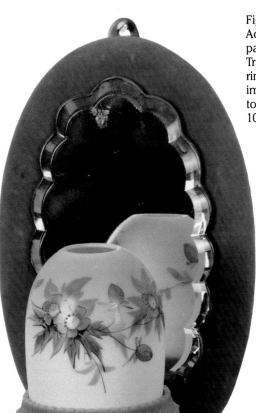

Fig. 783
Acid Burmese fairy-size dome decorated in prunus pattern, in Burmese lamp cup marked "Clarke Patent Trade Mark Fairy." Lamp cup sits in removable cast brass ring marked "Clarke Patent Fairy." Ring inserts in bracket impressed with "19" or "61" going through plush frame, to which a beveled and scalloped mirror is attached. 10.625"h x 6.75"w. $1000-1500

Fig. 784
Pair of green pyramid-size domes, heavily flecked with mica with drag loop of clear green glass threading, in waisted lamp cups marked "S. Clarke Trade Mark Fairy Pyramid." Cups are supported on ormolu hanger bolted through rectangular beveled and notched mirrored plush wall plaque. 8.25"h x 5.375"w. $750-1000

Fig. 785
Two blue Peach Blow pyramid-size domes, cased, decorated in foliage pattern. Domes rest in lamp cups marked "Clarke Trade Mark Fairy Pyramid," which are held in ormolu rings with arm going through wall mirror. Mirror is 6"w, beveled, cut from behind with crosshatch frame and convex circles. 9"h x 7.125"w. $750-1000

Fig. 786
Two pyramid-size domes, red spangled, drag-looped, and threaded with gold glass. Domes rest in lamp cups marked "Clarke Trade Mark Fairy Pyramid." Cups sit in ormolu rings of removable frame, with another lower ring holding 3.75"h clear vase, which hands 1.5" below plush. The vase is impressed with diamond crossnatching and with scalloped top. Rings are attached to bracket going through plush and beveled mirror frame. Mirror painted with foliage on left side. 12"h x 8"w. $750-1000

Fig. 787
Nailsea-type fairy-size dome with blue ground, in S. Clarke's Patent Fairy lamp cup containing S. Clarke Trade Mark Fairy ribbed candle holder. Cup rests on upright fluted rim of matching base, which has a bulbous bottom and blue satin point. The base rests in ormolu cup ring marked "Clark's Patent Fairy," supported by a hanging chain. Ring above smoke bell, marked "Clarke's Patent London Trade Mark Fairy," is suspended from embossed leaf hanger bolted through mirrored oval wall plaque with green velvet plush. Beneath lamp is matching flower bowl with applied crystal supporting arm, which is inserted into brass fitting attached through mirror. Rear of flower bowl ribbon rim is pulled inward for mirror clearance. Flower bowl has blue frosted point on bottom. 16"h x 8"w x 7.25" deep. $1000-1500

Fig. 788
Hanging impressed ormolu rod cover passes through Nailsea-type ball with red ground and tulip top rim, and then attaches to frame depicting three dolphins each with a cup ring coming out of its mouth. Cup rings hold three matching Nailsea-type fairy-size domes with red grounds in Cricklite candle cups. Frame is finished off with crystal faceted ball suspended below center of frame. 27"h x 11.5"w. $2000-3000

225

Left:

Fig. 789
Four acid Burmese fairy-size domes in Clarke lamp cups on ormolu hanging frame. Burmese smoke bell is supported by brass ring and finial from which chains begin. Ormolu frame attaches to Burmese bowl with petticoat rim, then to a brass spacer, an inverted miniature rose bowl, and a finishing brass finial, seen under front lamp cup. 24"h from top casting to bottom fitting x 14.5"w. $1500-2000

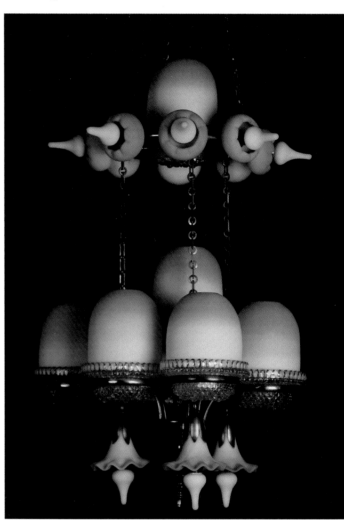

Fig. 790
Cast bronze fitting with attached Burmese smoke bell from which hangs pointed finial in center and three ormolu chains (with alternating circles and oval links). Chains hold ormolu frame with rings for five lamp cups, one elevated, terminating in Burmese bowl with downward petticoat rim, ormolu spacer and inverted Burmese miniature rose bowl from which hangs matching ormolu finial. Five acid Burmese fairy-size domes in Burmese lamp cups with upward scalloped rims and round knobs on bottom are signed "Thos. Webb & Sons, Queen's Burmese Ware" and "Clarke Patent Trade Mark Fairy." All Burmese pieces are decorated in prunus pattern. 32.75"h from top casting to bottom fitting x 11"w. Over $10,000

Fig. 791
Heavy cast brass ring with a scalloped bell below, from which originate three chains (with alternating square and round flat links) which descend to a double ormolu ring. Center ring holds acid Burmese fairy-size dome in clear Cricklite lamp cup. Outer ring holds eight Burmese miniature rose bowls on edge, each containing an unrefired pistil resembling flowers. From this outer circular frame, three chains descend to another frame. This second frame has six arms, each ending in a ring and holding a Burmese fairy-size dome in a clear Cricklite lamp cup. Three curved rods attach to these alternating arms, and support an elevated eighth ring holding a fairy-size Burmese dome in Cricklite lamp cup. Each remaining arm has an additional open curved prong beneath onto which a metal ring slides to suspend three Burmese fuschias. The fuschias consist of an ormolu ring attached to a metal calyx, holding the Burmese trumpet from which descends a metal spacer holding the unrefired pistil of the flower. The frame drops to a circular surface, from which an ormolu fitting continues down to the lowest level. 36"h from ring to bottom of fuschias x 12.5"w. Over $10,000

Fig. 792
See Fig. 791. Close-up of top frame.

Fig. 793
See Fig. 791. Close-up of fuschias. 5.25"l.
This outstanding fairy lamp chandelier and others are on display as part of the Gustave Collection at the Tulare Historical Museum, Tulare, California.

227

GROUP 16

CONTEMPORARY LAMPS

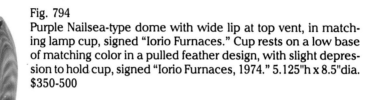

Fig. 794
Purple Nailsea-type dome with wide lip at top vent, in matching lamp cup, signed "Iorio Furnaces." Cup rests on a low base of matching color in a pulled feather design, with slight depression to hold cup, signed "Iorio Furnaces, 1974." 5.125"h x 8.5"dia. $350-500

Fig. 795
Porcelain Bunnykins dome, depicting Mother Rabbit giving cod oil to bunny, signed "Barbara Vernon." Dome rests on matching base with running rabbits border and bunny eating in the center. Marked "13, Royal Doulton, Bone China, Made in England." 3.75"h x 5.125"dia. $350-500

Fig. 796
Gunderson Burmese tapered dome with pinched upper rim and two air vents in bottom rim. Dome rests in lamp cup with flared scalloped rim integral to bulbous base with applied, unrefired, tooled petal feet. 8"h x 5"dia. $350-500

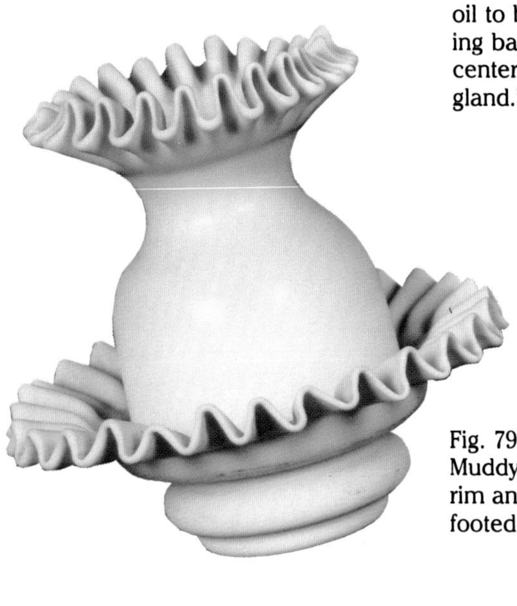

Fig. 797
Muddy Burmese dome with waisted, widely flaring piecrust top rim and two air vents in bottom rim. Domes rests in matching footed base. 5"h x 5.625"dia. $200-350

Fig. 798
Pear-shaped dome in basketweave pattern with handpainted shamrocks. Dome rests in short, matching pedestal base marked "Belleek, Ireland" in gold/brown on base. 6.25"h x 4"dia. $150-200

Fig. 799
Cobalt cone-shaped dome with scalloped upper rim surrounded by gold band, featuring three Coca Cola advertisements with bottle and glass. Dome rests in matching base with wide, gold-trimmed, bowl-shaped rim. 4.5"h x 6.25"dia. $350-500

Fig. 800
Light green, embossed floral dome in clear lamp cup marked "Fenton." Cup rests on short petticoat rim of matching round footed base, marked "Fenton." 6.5"h x 5"dia. $50-100

Fig. 801
Embossed two-faced owl in red frosted glass, with glossy eyes and beaks. Dome rests in oversize Clarke pyramid lamp cup. (Dome shown in *Westmoreland Glass, Volume II,* page 42, listed as "Owl Candlelite, 110-1, in Ruby Mist.") 4.5"h x 4.25"dia. Less than $50

Fig. 802
Acid Burmese pyramid-size dome decorated in Dogwood pattern, signed "Ters. M." Dome sits in clear lamp cup with embossed clover design, on quadrafold rim of footed Burmese base. Fenton. 6.5"h x 5.25"sq. Courtesy of Jody Goyette. $50-100

APPENDICES

APPENDIX A
BRITISH REGISTRY NUMBERS

Rd No. 1	1884	Rd No. 291241	1897
Rd No. 19754	1885	Rd No. 311658	1898
Rd No. 40480	1886	Rd No. 331707	1899
Rd No. 64520	1887	Rd No. 351202	1900
Rd No. 90483	1888	Rd No. 368154	1901
Rd No. 116648	1889	Rd No. 385500*	1902
Rd No. 141273	1890	Rd No. 402500*	1903
Rd No. 163767	1891	Rd No. 420000*	1904
Rd No. 185713	1892	Rd No. 447000*	1905
Rd No. 205240	1893	Rd No. 471000*	1906
Rd No. 224720	1894	Rd No. 494000*	1907
Rd No. 246975	1895	Rd No. 519500*	1908
Rd No. 268392	1896	Rd No. 550000*	1909

* Approximate numbers only

APPENDIX B
FOOD WARMERS

Samuel Clarke's food warmers were comprised of the following components: a covered handled porcelain pannikin, where the food to be kept hot was placed; a separate handled soldered metal vessel where water was placed in sufficient quantity to surround the inserted portion of the pannikin; and a vented, soldered, riveted and handled metal frame which held the water vessel and the candle heating apparatus. Clarke's "Improved Pannikin," in addition to having a controlled pouring spout to prevent spilling when filling a baby bottle, had a handle set perpendicular to the pouring spout. It also had an extended passage from the spout down to near the bottom, so that liquid would be poured from the bottom (rather than from the surface, where grease or scum floated). The dome resting in the depression in the bottom of the frame is usually illustrated as being clear and ribbed, but has been seen in opal or frosted glass and possibly was made in ruby. The dome is shown in a pierced metal lamp cup with handle and can be slipped into the base between the legs. The purpose of the dome was to concentrate the heat on the base of the water vessel and perhaps to give light to the room.

Clarke's "Improved Food Warmer" came in four sizes: No. 1 held 1/2 pint, No. 2 held 3/4 pint, No. 3 held 1 pint, and No. 4 (not pictured) held 1 1/2 pints. In 1880 they were priced in US dollars as follows: #1 - $.84, #2 - $1.20, #3 - $1.44, #4 - $1.73, based on pound/dollar exchange at that time.

The larger warmer on the left has *one pint* capacity, as printed on the pannikin cover. Also printed on the cover is

> Saml Clarke's Pyramid Food Warmer, NOTICE It is important that milk should be boiled as soon as it is received from the dairy as it is liable to turn sour. The pannikin should also be well cleansed prior to use, and CAUTION Paraffin lamps are very dangerous and should on no account be burnt in this food warmer.

Inside the cover is the notice "Pyramid Trade Mark 'Fairy', Reg in U.S. Pat. Off."

On the pannikin itself is impressed "1 pt" on the side, and "Rd #91241" in the spout. Straddling the spout is printed "Clarke's Patent Pyramid Light Night, 9 hrs are only lights suitable for these lamps." On the other side of handle is printed "When nights are dark Then think of Clarke Who's hit the mark precisely: For his Night-Lights Create Light-Nights In which you see quite nicely." On either side of printed crest showing a lion and unicorn over banner marked "dieu et mon droit" are printed "Rd No 91241." The water pot or vessel is stamped "Trade Mark Pyramid, Trade Mark Fairy" and "Cricklite."

The frame just below the upper rim has an applied plate stamped "Clarke's Pyramid Food Warmer" and around the depression for the lamp cup is embossed "Clarke's Pyramid Food Warmer" twice.

The dome is embossed "S. Clarke's Trade Mark Pyramid' in reverse inside the dome just below the vent. The brass pierced lamp cup has a riveted handle embossed "For Burning the Pyramid Night Lights, Saml Clarke Patentee." (Little doubt who gets credit for this device). 12"h x 6.75"w across handle.

The fourth warmer has a missing cover (the Clarke cover does not fit), and has a metal-clad ceramic pannikin marked "Pyramid Food Warmer" on the brass plate on the frame. The handles are much thinner and the frame has legs which are straight, so the dome must be inserted from above. The Clarke name does not appear anywhere, so perhaps this was made by one of the imitators that Clarke warned about. 8.75"h 5.25"w. *Courtesy of Authors.*

APPENDIX C

CANDLES AND CANDLE HOLDERS

From left to right, top to bottom:

1. "Will O' The Wisp
    Patent Jan 5th 1897
    Will & Baumer Co
    New York   Syracuse"

On side is picture of eagle with "Trade Mark" below. Candle is paper-wrapped and has flat plaster bottom.

2. "The 'Burglar's Horror'
    Trade Mark
    "Pyramid"
    N.B. No Water Required"

Vertically on two sides is printed "Clarke's 'Pyramid'," and "Registered in US Patent Office" is printed on rear. Candle is paper-wrapped with flat plaster bottom. This candle was widely touted; customers were told that the Burglar's Horror "Pyramid" Night Light should be lighted in a front and back room of every house as soon as it was dark. House-breakers, they were told, have the greatest dread of a light.

3. "Radiant Night 8Hrs Light
    Place in saucer with water to cover
    the thin line."

Printed on back: "Important Keep out of draught, Do not pull the wick. Candle is paper-wrapped with recessed cardboard base."

4. This is a contemporary candle made by Price's Patent Candle Company Limited and labeled on box "Sentinel Night Light."

5. This is a contemporary votive candle.

6. "Price's
    Childs'
    Night Light
    Place in a saucer with water to cover the line.

Left side: An oval with "Ship Brand" and picture of sailing ship.
Right side: "8 Hours." Both sides are vertically marked "Improved."
Paper-wrapped candle with flat cardboard bottom.

7. "Price's
    'Sentinel'
    Night Light
    Made in England
    Burn Upright in Open Saucer Without Water

Left side: "Keep Away from Draughts and Inflammable Materials."
Right side: "Designed to Burn for 8 Hours."
Paper-wrapped candle with .125" raised cardboard base.

8. "Clarke's
    'Pyramid'
    Trade Mark
    No Water Required"

Paper-wrapped candle with flat plaster bottom. Plaster holds sticker reading "Made in England."

9. "Gleamlight Brand
    Night [Figure of eagle with
        'Trade Mark' below] Light
    The Will & Baumer Company Co.
    New York   Syracuse, NY   Chicago"

Paper-wrapped candle with flat plaster bottom.

10. Candle holder embossed "Price's Palmitine Star" around burst on base exterior with three edge nubbins. Small circular interior depression with three nubbins in center. 1.375"h x 2"w.

11. Candle holder embossed "Fairy Pyramid" around small star in interior base. 1.5"h x 1.875"w.

12. Candle holder embossed "S Clarke Trade Mark Fairy" with "Patent" on bar in center. Words are on base exterior to be read through interior. 1.625"h x 2.5"w.

13. Double rush wick candle with small amount of plaster on base to hold the wick. Candle impressed: "Saml Clarke's New Patent Fairy–Trade Mark." This candle fits in #12 holder.
    Unmarked rounded candle holder with exterior bottom ring. This is a Clarke Cricklite candle holder. 1.625"h x 2.625"w.

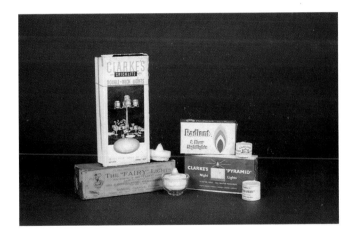

From left to right, top to bottom:

1. "Clarke's
    Cricklite
    Double-Wick Lights
    [picture]
    Price's Patent Candle Co. Ltd,
    Battersea   London, SW 11"

Both ends of bottom of box read:
"Clarke's Patent
Cricklite
Double-Wick Light"
In boxes containing
"12 light to burn 5 hrs each."

2. "Radiant
    8 Hour
    Nightlights"

End of box reads: "Pybus Bros. Limited, Woodsend Works, Flixton, Nr. Manchester." There are eight candles to the box.

3. "By Her Majesty's Royal Letter Patent
    The 'Fairy' Lights
    For Burning in the 'Fairy' Lamps
    Semi-Incandescent–For Lighting
    Ball & Drawing-Rooms, Conservatories & C.
    Will Burn 10 Hours
    Samuel Clarke, Patentee
    "'Pyramid'" and "'Fairy' Light Works,
    Cricklewood London, N.W."

Diagonally across box is stamped in red "Clarke's 'Pyramid' & 'Fairy' Light Company, Limited, Works–Cricklewood, London, NW." There is a fairy figure on the left front with the word "Fairy" beneath. Both ends of box bottom read: "Trade Mark 'Fairy'." There are six double wick candles to the box.

4. "Clarke's 'Pyramid'
    Night Lights
    Plaster Base–No Water Required
    Price's Patent Candle Company Limited
    London"

One end of box reads "Directions, Raise wick before lighting. Avoid draughts. For satisfactory relighting burn for at least one hour. Do not use in vaporisers." The other end reads "8 Clarke's 'Pyramid' Night Lights. Each night light will burn for 9 hours."

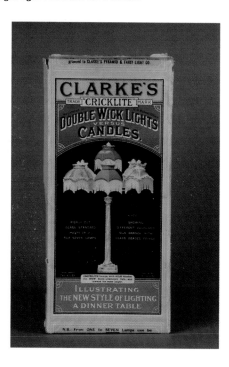

One of Clarke's earlier double wick Cricklite boxes showing his use of color to sell product. On left of lamp: "Richly Cut Glass Standard (Height 18 in.) for seven lamps." On right: "Showing different coloured silk shades with glass beaded fringe."

APPENDIX D
FAIRY-SIZE LAMP CUPS

Lamp cups are constructed to hold a variety of dome diameters. Although the flange may be wide enough to accommodate domes of diameters differing by more than .5", domes that are .2" smaller than the maximum size will be too loose on the lamp cup and slide excessively from side to side.

A sampling of the numerous types of lamp cups, from top to bottom, left to right:

1. The interior of the cup has a recessed depression for candle holder embossed with fairy figure. "Clarke Patent Trade Mark Fairy" circles the figure. The horizontal corrugated annular flange has a maximum diameter of 3.43".

2. The interior of the cup is embossed with a large figure of the fairy, encircled with "S Clarke Trade Mark Fairy." The horizontal annular flange is made of close sharp corrugations with a maximum diameter of 3.28".

3. The interior of the double shoulder flanged cup is embossed S. Clarke's Patent Trade Mark Fairy. The flange consists of undulating ribs. The wider flange will hold a dome of 3.37" diameter, while the lower flange is for a maximum 3.09" diameter dome.

4. The interior of the lamp cup contains a fairy figure and is embossed "Clarke's Patent Trade Mark Cricklite." The horizontal flange consisting of multiple small sharp corrugations has a maximum diameter of 3.34".

5. The interior of this cup contains the fairy figure, encircled with embossed "Clarke's Patent Trade Mark Cricklite." The top of the vertical annular flange is smooth. The multiple sharp corrugated horizontal flange will hold a dome with the maximum diameter of 3.34".

6. This cup is unmarked except for a ray on the external base. The smooth horizontal flange will hold a maximum 3.37" diameter dome.

7. The interior of this cup is embossed in the center "S. Clarke Patent Trade Mark Fairy," around which is embossed "US Patent, Nov. 9th 1886, No. 352296." This double-shouldered cup with undulating corrugations has maximum interior diameters of 3.40" on upper horizontal flange and 3.12" on lower.

8. This unmarked lamp cup has three nubbins on the external base and a hole drilled through the center. This double-shouldered, smooth cup will hold two diameters of 3.37" and 3.03". This is the Hobbs Brocunier "Acorn" lamp cup.

9. This frosted lamp cup is embossed around the interior of the base "S. Clarke Fairy and Patent Trade Mark" across the center. Cup with undulating double-shouldered horizontal flange will support domes of 3.37" and 3.09" diameters.

10. The lamp cup is embossed "S. Clarke" in outer ring with "Fairy" and "Patent" in inner ring and "Trade Mark" across the center. The deeply recessed double-shouldered horizontal flange of loosely undulating corrugations have maximum dome diameters of 3.37" and 3.09".

11. This lamp cup is embossed "Br. Clarke, SGDG, Portieux" in interior, has slightly twisted ribbed sides on cup, wide petal horizontal flange with dimple impressed in each petal from below. This cup has flange with separated rounded bars holding a dome of 3.37" maximum diameter. It will also hold a 2.87" diameter dome with notched or scalloped bottom rim.

12. This pegged lamp cup is embossed "Clarke's Patent Trade Mark Cricklite." The .5" diameter peg is often found inserted in cork or wood to accommodate candlesticks or other receivers. The sharp corrugated horizontal flange will accommodate a 3.28" diameter dome.

13. This lamp cup is embossed with fairy figure surrounded by "S. Clarke's Trade Mark Fairy." The horizontal flange of low separated bars will hold a dome with maximum 3.37" diameter.

Close-up of two selected lamp cups.

APPENDIX E

CLARKE EXTINGUISHER

Flat mica disk, 1.875" diameter, with original wrapper reading "'Fairy' Extinguisher–Place on Top of Glass Shade." Clarke even invented a fairy lamp snuffer.

APPENDIX F

PEARS' CHRISTMAS ANNUAL ADVERTISEMENT

PEAR'S CHRISTMAS ANNUAL 1899
THE PHARAOHS ARE GONE, BUT THE "PYRAMIDS" REMAIN
AND ARE THE
PREMIER NIGHT LIGHTS OF THE WORLD
USED BY
HER MAJESTY THE QUEEN

DAYLIGHT VERSUS DARKNESS

The Egyptian Pyramids,
  they say,
Were built to show the Stars
  by day;
Clarke's "Pyramid" Lights
  so shine at night
They keep e'en Burglars
  well in sight;
Nights dark and drear—we
  no longer fear,
Clarke's "Pyramid"
  Night Lights burn as
  clear as Daylight.

CLARKE'S PYRAMID NIGHT LIGHTS

When Nights are dark
Then think of Clarke
  Who's hit the mark
    precisely,
For his Night Lights
Create light nights
  In which you see quite
    nicely.

CLARKE'S "PYRAMID" NIGHT LIGHTS
THE "BURGLAR'S HORROR" CLARKE'S "PYRAMID" & "FAIRY" LIGHT CO. LTD
LONDON NW   CLARKE'S PYRAMID LIGHTS
CLARKE'S "PYRAMID" NURSERY LAMP FOOD WARMERS
The Standard Nursery Lamp used during FOUR generations
by Her Majesty The Queen and her humblest subjects.

CLARKE'S PATENT
"Pyramid" LAMP
        DIRECTIONS FOR FIXING

FOOD-WARMER   Place the Clips round
    and   the bed-post, insert the
BED-TRAY   Thumb-screw in the square
                   hole at the end of same and
                   screw as tightly as possible.
                   The clips being of spring steel
                   they will fit any size post. A
                   little cloth or wash leather
                   should be placed round the bed-post
                   to prevent scratching the post.

CLARKE'S
PATENT SAFETY NIGHT LIGHT

CLARKE'S
PATENT
"PYRAMID"

THE SHADED PART
REPRESENTS THE
PLASTER FIRE PROOF CASE

            CAUTION
     TO PREVENT BURGLARIES
    A "Pyramid" Night Light
    Should be lighted in the
    front and back of every
    house as soon as it is
    dark. House-breakers have
    the greatest dread of a
    light. The Police
    recommend a "Pyramid"
    Night Light as the best
    safeguard. Almost all the

burglaries perpetrated might
have been prevented, and
much VALUABLE PROPERTY
SAVED, if this simple and
inexpensive plan has
always been adopted. The
"Pyramid" Night lights are
much larger give Double
The Light of the common
night Lights, and are
therefore particularly
adapted for this purpose.

"Pyramids" burn 9 hours each, box of 8 Lights

For upwards of 40 years the Premier NIGHT LIGHT of the WORLD.

CLARKE'S
IMPROVED
PANNIKIN.
(Registered)

FOR USE WITH
Clarke's "PYRAMID"
NURSERY LAMPS

'Universally" used
for more than
Half-a-Century

By this invention any liquid
drink can be poured out or drunk
without scum of grease passing
through the spout, and prevents
spilling when poured into a
feeding bottle, so objectionable
with other pannikins.

    These Pannikins will fit all the
old "Pyramid" Nursery Lamps, and
can be purchased separately.

NO HOUSE SHOULD BE
WITHOUT ONE.

CLARKE'S PATENT
"PYRAMID" FOOD WARMER

INVALUABLE IN EVERY HOUSE
WORTH WEIGHT IN GOLD
SOLD EVERYWHERE
2/6, 3/6, 5/ and 6/ each

For upwards of 50 years the
Premier NURSERY LAMP of the
World.

INVALUABLE
IN
SICKNESS and in HEALTH

CLARKE'S "PYRAMID" & "FAIRY" LIGHT COMPANY, LTD., CRICKLEWOOD,
LONDON, N.W.
A book of Drawings of Useful Articles for Invalids will be sent on
application. Post Free. Also Pattern Book of "CRICKLITE" Lamps.
CLARKE'S West End Depot for "CRICKLITE" Lamps—132, REGENT STREET,
W.
Sole Agents for "Cricklites" for Glasgow: WYLIE HILL & CO., Ltd.,
20, Buchanan Street

APPENDIX G
CLARKE CRICKLITE ADVERTISEMENT

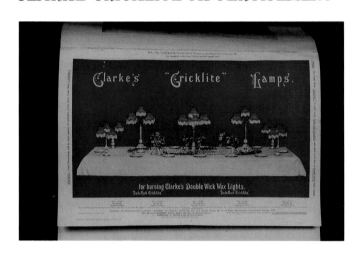

This advertisement appeared in Pears' Christmas 1899 Annual. No 9, Volume 2. *Courtesy of D & N Gole Collection.*

Across the top, it reads "A set of 25 'Cricklite' Lamps, richly cut glass standards, sufficient to light a 16' Dinner Table for 5 Hours for 32 persons at a cost of 25 pence; the lamps always the same height, a perfect light. NB. The "Cricklite" Lamps can be obtained at 132 Regent Street, London W. The standards carry from two to seven lamps each."

On left hand side, up the edge, it reads "Caution. Legal proceedings will be taken against all infringers of the above Trade Mark 'Cricklite'."

Along edge on right side it reads "Notice the Trade Mark 'Cricklite' is upon every lamp and standard and upon every box of Double Wick Wax Lights."

Along the bottom it reads "For burning Clarke's Double Wick Wax Lights. Trade Mark 'Cricklite'. Trade Mark 'Cricklite'."

L to R and under appropriate lamps it reads "No 58231. two lights, 4 Pounds, 12 shillings, 6 pence, Standard 11". No 58231. five lights, 9 Pounds, 15 shillings, 0 pence, Standard 17"."

The middle one reads "No 0356. seven lights, 14 Pounds, 13 shillings, 6 pence, Standard 16". No 58231. five lights, 9 Pounds, 15 shillings, 0 pence, Standard 17"."

One on the right reads "No 58231. two lights, 4 Pounds, 12 shillings, 6 pence, Standard 11"."

Left to right, it reads "The "Cricklite" Lamps are made for burning Clarke's (New Patent) Double Wick Wax Lights, to burn five hours each. Twelve Lights in a box for one shilling. The Standards are made in Royal Worcester Ware, richly-cut Glass, Nickel and Silver Plated, Bronze and Ormolu, and cost from a few shillings each to many pounds, Can be obtained from the Patentees and Manufacturers, CLARKE'S "PYRAMID" & "FAIRY" LIGHT CO., Ltd., 132 Regent Street, W., or at their Manufactory, Cricklewood, London, N.W. Sole Agents for GLASGOW: WYLIE, HILL & CO., Ltd., 20 Buchanan Street. EDINBURGH: C. JENNER & CO., 48 Princes Street."

Far right bottom reads "The prices include the Silk Shades with Bead Fringe."

Far left bottom reads "Catalogues and Price Lists Post Free. Heliochrome. Waterlow & Sons Ltd., Londonwall, London."

To right reads "NB. The patterns were ordered to be made for His Imperial Majesty, The Sultan of Turkey. "

Ad is photographed from Pears' Christmas Annual, #9, Vol 2.

APPENDIX H
CLARKE CRICKLITE ADVERTISEMENT

This advertisement appeared in the *Illustrated London News,* December 1899. *Courtesy of Authors.*

Across the top, it reads "A Dinner Set of Clarke's 'Cricklite' Lamps, consisting of a Centre Mirror Plateau with Three richly-cut Glass Standards to carry NINE 'Cricklite' Lamps, mounted on Ormolu Stand; Four Corner Standards of richly-cut Glass to match, each to carry two 'Cricklite' Lamps, all with handsome Silk Beaded Shades; Two very handsomely-cut Flower Glasses on Ormolu Stand. Sufficient to light a Dinner Table for 18 persons for five hours at a cost of SEVENTEEN PENCE. Total cost of the Set of Lamps. 37 Pounds, 2 shillings, 0 pence.

Along the left and right hand edge, it reads "Trade Mark— 'CRICKLITE'."

Along the bottom under appropriate lamps, L to R, it reads "Four Corner Standards, with Two Lamps, complete as drawn, No. 0375, 12 inches high, 2 pounds, 11 shillings, 6 pence each. the middle reads: Centre Standard, 18 inches high. No. 0364, with Nine Lamps ... ... 26 pounds, 16 shillings, 0 pence."

On the right it reads "Four Corner Standards, with Two Lamps, complete as drawn. No. 0375, 12 inches high, 2 pounds, 11 shillings, 6 pence each."

Below on left it reads "The 'Cricklite' lamp is no trouble to trim and light, is ABSOLUTELY SAFE, the light is always the same height, and sufficiently high to see the guests on the opposite side of the table. A PERFECT LIGHT for a Dinner Table. Clarke's Double Wick Wax Light gives more light than a wax candle, is suitable for ALL CLIMATES, and will keep good for years.

Below on right it reads "The 'Cricklite' Lamps are made for burning Clarke's (New Patent) Double Wick Wax Lights, to burn five hours each. Twelve Lights in a box for One Shilling. The Standards are made in Royal Worcester Ware, richly-cut Glass, Nickel and Silver Plated, Bronze and Ormolu, and cost from a few shillings each to many pounds.

Across the bottom it reads "Can be obtained from the Patentees and Manufacturers, CLARKE'S 'PYRAMID' & 'FAIRY' LIGHT CO., Ltd., 132, Regent Street, W., or at their Manufactory, Cricklewood, London, N.W. Agents for GLASGOW: WYLIE, HILL & CO., Ltd., 20, Buchanan Street. EDINBURGH: C. JENNER & CO., 48, Princess Street. Catalogues and Price Lists Post Free. The prices include the Silk Shades with Bead Fringe."

Ad is photographed from Illustrated London News, Dec., 1899.

APPENDIX I
CLARKE COLORED ADVERTISEMENTS

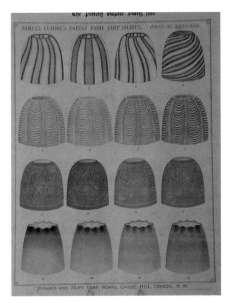

THE POTTERY GAZETTE DIARY, 1888
SAMUEL CLARKE'S PATENT FAIRY LAMP SHADES   Prices on application.

1	2	3	4
5	6	7	8
9	10	11	12
13	14	15	16

PYRAMID AND FAIRY LAMP WORKS, CHILDS' HILL, LONDON, N.W.

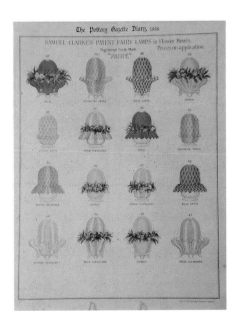

THE POTTERY GAZETTE DIARY, 1888
SAMUEL CLARKE'S PATENT FAIRY LAMPS in Flower Bowls
Registered Trade Mark   Prices on Application
"FAIRY"

32	33	34	35
Blue	Nacre de Perle	Rose Satin	Citron
36	37	38	39
Citron Satin	Rose Cleveland	Blue	Nacre de Perle
40	41	42	43
Nacre de Perle	Citron	Rose Cleveland	Blue Satin
44	45	46	47
Citron Cleveland	Blue Cleveland	Citron	Rose Cleveland

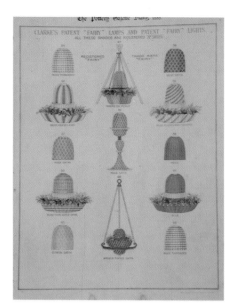

THE POTTERY GAZETTE DIARY, 1888
CLARKE'S PATENT "FAIRY" LAMPS AND PATENT "FAIRY" LIGHTS
All These Shades Are Registered No 50725

	67		
54	Registered	Trade Mark	56
Rose Threaded	"Fairy"	"Fairy"	Blue Satin
52		Nacre de Perle	55
Blue Cleveland		70	Rose Cleveland Twisted
57			59
Rose Satin			Rose
		Rose Satin	
58		69	61
Ruby Threaded Opal			Blue
60			65
Citron Satin		Amber Tinted Satin	Blue Threaded

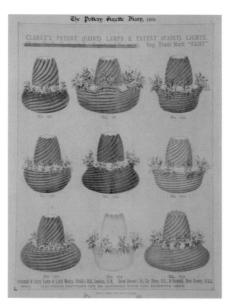

THE POTTERY GAZETTE DIARY, 1888
CLARKE'S PATENT (FAIRY) LAMPS AND PATENT (FAIRY) LIGHTS
ALL THE SHADES CORRUGATED. REGISTERED NO. 50725
Reg. Trade Mark "FAIRY"

No. 98	No. 99	No. 100
No. 101	No. 102	No. 103
No. 104	No. 105	No. 106

Pyramid & Fairy Lamp & Light Works, Child's Hill, London, N.W.
Show Rooms: 31 Ely Place, E.C., & Newark, New Jersey, USA
Scale 1/3 N.B. These Patterns Can Be Obtained From The PATENTEE ONLY

THE POTTERY GAZETTE DIARY, 1888
CLARKE'S PATENT "FAIRY" LAMPS AND PATENT "FAIRY" LIGHTS
Registered Trade Mark "FAIRY." Prices on Application

Top to bottom	Left to Right	
No. 87	No. 88	No. 89
No. 90	No. 91	No. 92
	Rd. 53734	
No. 93		No. 94
No. 95	No. 96	No. 97

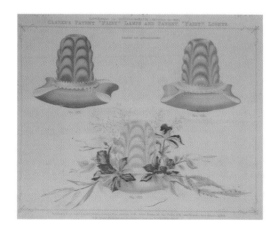

SUPPLEMENT TO "POTTERY GAZETTE". October 1st 1887
CLARKE'S PATENT "FAIRY" LAMPS AND PATENT "FAIRY" LIGHTS
Prices on Application

No. 150		No. 150
	No. 150	

Pyramid & Fairy Lamp & Light Works, Child's Hill, London, N.W.
Show Rooms: 31, Ely Place, E.C., and Newark, New Jersey, USA
NB These Patterns can be obtained from the PATENTEE ONLY

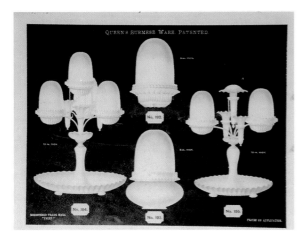

SUPPLEMENT TO "POTTERY GAZETTE" OCTOBER 1ST, 1887
CLARKE'S PATENT "FAIRY" LAMPS & *PATENT* "FAIRY" LIGHTS
QUEEN'S BURMESE WARE. PATENTED

5-in. HIGH
No. 192

16-in. High	6-in. High	12-in. High
No. 194	No. 193	No. 195
Registered Trade Mark		
"FAIRY"		Prices on Application

"Pyramid" and "Fairy" Lamp and Light Works

SUPPLEMENT TO POTTERY GAZETTE OCTOBER 1ST 1887
CLARKE'S PATENT FAIRY LAMPS
combined with
RUSTIC FLOWER STANDS
Registered Trade Mark
"FAIRY"
Prices on Application

196	197	198
199	200	201
202	203	204

Pyramid & Fairy Lamp & Light Works, Child's Hill, London, N.W.
Show Rooms: 31 Ely Place, E.C., & Newark, New Jersey, USA
N.B. These Patterns can be obtained from the PATENTEE ONLY.
G. Simkins & Son, Lith. Newton St. Birmingham

THE POTTERY GAZETTE DIARY, 1888

ROYAL BOTANIC SOCIETY'S	EVENING FETE, 1886
The JUDGES unanimously	awarded to Mr. SAMUEL
CLARKE the Special FIRST	PRIZE, GOLD MEDAL for
his "FAIRY" GARDEN	LAMPS.
CLARKE'S	PATENT
FAIRY No. 8	LAMP
with	Rain Guard.
for out-door	Illuminations.
* to *	* or *
fix in the ground.	hang in trees.
Glasses	various colors.

"Punch"
July 17th, page 34

"Memorable in the Annals of the Royal Botanic Society, - Wednesday night, July 7th, on the occasion of the last Fete of this Season in the Botanical Gardens, was deliciously warm and our enjoyment was not dampened by a single drop, or by any number of drops, of rain. Fancy, a Botanical Fete without a shower! Illuminations perfect. Great success. All Sweetness and Light.

SAML CLARKE
PATENTEE
"Pyramid" and "Fairy" Lamp and Light Works, Child's Hill, London,
NW. Showroom 31 Ely Place E.C.,
"Pyramid" and "Fairy" Lamp and Light Works, Newark, New Jersey, USA

(on back it reads)

No. 8
CLARKE'S
Patent 'FAIRY' Lamp
(weather proof)
for Garden Use
Same as used by the Royal Botanical Society at the Evening Fete, in
the Regents Park, June 30th, 1886.

GLOSSARY

Amberina	shaded glassware formed of homogeneous amber glass, reheated to cause a portion of it to turn ruby red.
applied	decoration attached while in semi-fluid state to external surface of shaped glass body.
Cameo	two or more layers of glass of different colors, carved or acid-etched to produce a raised relief design.
cameo	portrait surrounded by border.
cased	made with a glass layer applied to inner surface, white in color unless otherwise noted.
Coralene	designs with glass beads fused to the glass.
Craquelle	red hot glass plunged into cold water, then reheated and reblown, causing an iced effect on the exterior surface.
DQMOP	abbreviation for "diamond-quilted mother of pearl."
End of Day	multi-colored objects supposedly made from molten glass left over in factory pots at the end of the day.
epergne	ornamental object made to hold items (sweet-meats, flowers, fairy lamps, etc.), usually set on a table, often at dinner.
flashed	covering uncolored glass with a very thin layer of colored glass.
Florentine	transparent colored glass with design, in white or colored enamel, painted on the exterior surface, referred to as "poor man's Cameo."
fluted	an edge design featuring close convolutions.
girdled	pulled in to uniform diameter.
ground	background color.
intaglio	design incised into another layer or layers of glass to form a relief image.
overshot	inflated molten glass rolled into pounded glass to adhere fragments before reheating and shaping.
Peach Blow	heat-sensitive transparent glass, cased or homogeneous, refired to produce a shaded color.
pegged	glass protrusions on the bottom of lamp cup to be inserted into holder.
piecrust	an edge design featuring sharp, close convolutions, as made with a table fork.
pontil mark	roughness on base of an object where rod for handling glass during shaping was removed.
prunt	applied glob of glass, usually tooled or designed.
ribbon	a graceful, rolling edge design.
rigaree	pincered or tooled trails of glass applied and fused to external surface.
ruffled	wavy surface.
shoulder	horizontal and vertical flange of lamp cup that supports and retains the dome.
tooled	glass worked and shaped with implements while still in semi-fluid state.

ENDNOTES

1. Zayn Bilkadi, "The Oil Weapons", *Aramco World* (January/February 1995);20-27.
2. Stanley Wells, *Period Lighting* (Pelham, 1975)
3. W. Klenke, *Candlemaking* (Peoria, Illinois: The Manual Arts Press, 1946).
4. Stanley Wells, *Period Lighting* (Pelham, 1975)
5. *American People's Encyclopedia* (Chicago: Spencer Press, 1957).Vol. 16, 42-43.
6. Loris S. Russell, *A Heritage of Light* (University of Toronto Press, 1968).
6. Dorothy Tibbetts, *Clarke's Fairy Lamps* (Huntington Park, California: Mission Press, 1951).
7. Dorothy Tibbetts, *Clarke's Fairy Lamps*(Huntingdon Park, California: Mission Press, 1951).
8. Geoffrey A. Godden, *Antique Glass and China* (New York: Castle Books, 1966).
9. Harold Newman, *Veilleuses* (Cranbury, NJ: Cornwall Books, 1987).
10. Albert C. Revi, "Samuel Clarke's Designs for Fairy Lamps", *The Spinning Wheel* (March 1973); 28-30 and (March 1974); 22-23
11. *Hobbies* October 1967; 77
12. Amelia MacSwiggen, *Fairy Lamps* (New York: Fountainhead Publishers, 1962).
13. Robert J. Samuelson, "Judgement Calls", *Newsweek* (July 17, 1995); 43
14. *Wall Street Journal* (October 1890).
15. Jack H. Beebe, Sr. VP, Federal Reserve Bank of San Francisco, printed in *Horseless Carriage Gazette* (Vol 57, #5, Sept/Oct 1995); 22
16. Geoffrey A. Godden, *Antique Glass and China* (New York: Castle Books, 1966).
17. Geoffrey A. Godden, *Antique Glass and China* (New York: Castle Books, 1966).
18. Howard Seufer, Fracture Specialist, ret., Fenton Art Glass Co., personal communication.

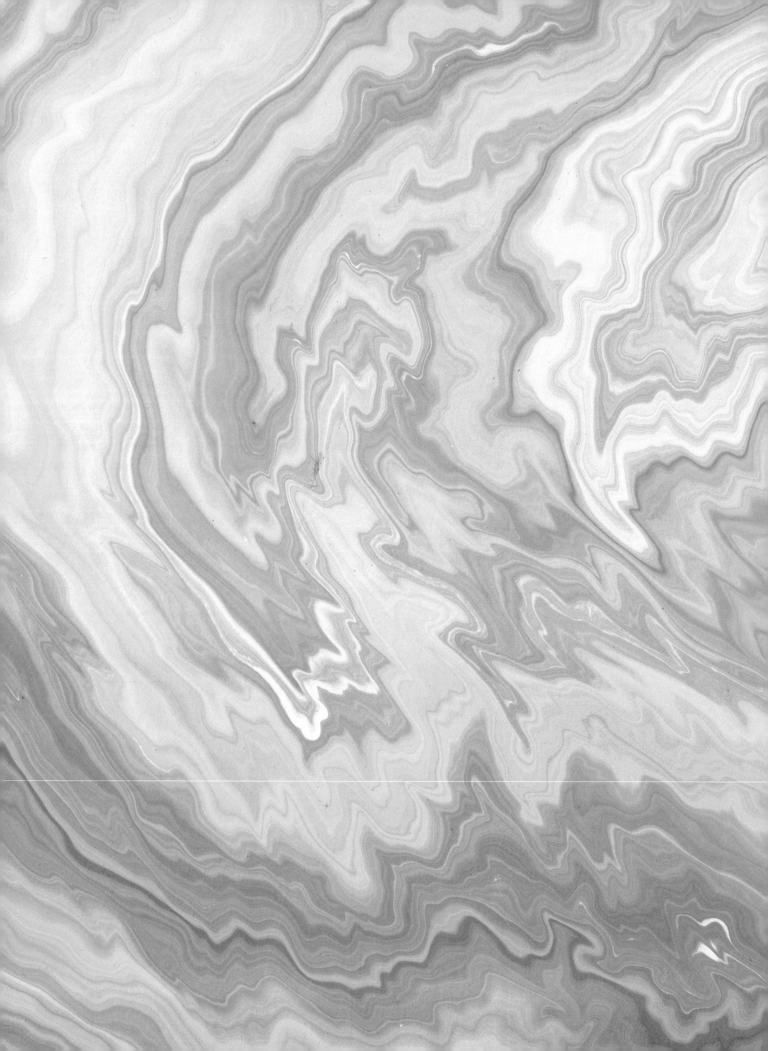